ISBN-13 (pbk): 978-1-4842-1222-6

ISBN-13 (electronic): 978-1-4842-1221-9

Trademarked names, logos, and images may appear in this book. Rather than use a trademark symbol with every occurrence of a trademarked name, logo, or image we use the names, logos, and images only in an editorial fashion and to the benefit of the trademark owner, with no intention of infringement of the trademark.

The use in this publication of trade names, trademarks, service marks, and similar terms, even if they are not identified as such, is not to be taken as an expression of opinion as to whether or not they are subject to proprietary rights.

While the advice and information in this book are believed to be true and accurate at the date of publication, neither the authors nor the editors nor the publisher can accept any legal responsibility for any errors or omissions that may be made. The publisher makes no warranty, express or implied, with respect to the material contained herein.

Managing Director: Welmoed Spahr
Lead Editor: Louise Corrigan
Technical Reviewer: Nikhil Manchanda
Editorial Board: Steve Anglin, Louise Corrigan, Jim DeWolf, Jonathan Gennick, Robert Hutchinson, Michelle Lowman, James Markham, Susan McDermott, Matthew Moodie, Jeffrey Pepper, Douglas Pundick, Ben Renow-Clarke, Gwenan Spearing, Steve Weiss
Coordinating Editor: Mark Powers
Copy Editor: Lori Jacobs
Compositor: SPi Global
Indexer: SPi Global
Artist: SPi Global

Distributed to the book trade worldwide by Springer Science+Business Media New York, 233 Spring Street, 6th Floor, New York, NY 10013. Phone 1-800-SPRINGER, fax (201) 348-4505, e-mail orders-ny@springer-sbm.com, or visit www.springeronline.com. Apress Media, LLC is a California LLC and the sole member (owner) is Springer Science + Business Media Finance Inc (SSBM Finance Inc). SSBM Finance Inc is a Delaware corporation.

For information on translations, please e-mail rights@apress.com, or visit www.apress.com.

Apress and friends of ED books may be purchased in bulk for academic, corporate, or promotional use. eBook versions and licenses are also available for most titles. For more information, reference our Special Bulk Sales–eBook Licensing web page at www.apress.com/bulk-sales.

Any source code or other supplementary material referenced by the author in this text is available to readers at www.apress.com/9781484212226. For additional information about how to locate and download your book's source code, go to www.apress.com/source-code/. Readers can also access source code at **SpringerLink** in the Supplementary Material section for each chapter.

OpenStack Trove

Amrith Kumar
Douglas Shelley

Apress®

I dedicate this book to my dear wife, Kamlu. Without your help, support, and the innumerable lost nights, weekends, and interrupted vacations, this book would never have happened. I've really enjoyed working with Doug on this. I learned a lot in this process, which may be best summarized this way.

कभी-कभी यूँ भी हमने अपने जी को बहलाया है!
जिन बातों को खुद नहीं समझे, औरों को समझाया है!!

... निदा फ़ाज़ली ...

—Amrith Kumar

I dedicate this book to my wife, Debbie, and my daughters, Alexa and Sarah. They have endured many years of listening to me attempt to excite them with descriptions of various technologies – most lately OpenStack and Trove. Their support for my foray into Tesora, Trove, and OpenStack, including the away time with the community, has really made this possible. I have learned a lot working with Amrith on this book and I really hope It is useful to our readers.

—Doug Shelley

Contents at a Glance

Contents

About the Authors

Amrith Kumar is the CTO at Tesora, which he founded, bringing more than two decades of experience delivering industry-leading products for companies specializing in enterprise storage applications, fault-tolerant high-performance systems, and massively parallel databases. He is an active technical contributor to the OpenStack Trove (Database as a Service project), and is a member of the core review team for that project. Before that, he served as vice president of technology and product management at Dataupia, maker of the Satori Data Warehousing platform, and Sepaton's director and general manager where he was responsible for the development of the core virtual tape library product. He is the named inventor in a number of patents on technologies related to high-performance databases and algorithms with wide applicability in distributed computing.

Douglas Shelley is the VP Product Development at Tesora, joining as the first employee and building a team of seasoned enterprise software professionals committed to delivering the Tesora DBaaS platform and actively contributing in the OpenStack community. He has worked in Enterprise IT and software product development for over 20 years, specializing in application delivery, data management, and integration. He is an active technical contributor to the OpenStack Trove project. Prior to Tesora, he spent over 10 years as Director, Product Development at Progress Software where he led various teams tackling challenges related to data synchronization, integration, and transformation.

About the Technical Reviewer

Nikhil Manchanda is a Principal Engineer working at HP Cloud. He has been the Project Technical Lead (PTL) for OpenStack Trove for the Juno, Kilo and Liberty Release Cycles. He designed and wrote significant parts of the OpenStack Trove project, and has been a Trove core contributor since the project's inception. His main areas of expertise lie in Openstack, Python, and databases, but he has also been known to occasionally dabble in C++, and machine learning. He has spent previous lives working on Software Update intelligence, geo-local systems, and mobile applications.

In his spare time you can often find him hunched over his desk either assiduously hacking away on his Raspberry Pi or NAS4Free box, or writing verse and short stories.

Acknowledgments

We would like to thank the entire OpenStack Trove community for their commitment and dedication to the Trove vision, and making the OpenStack Database as a Service a reality. Without the many developers, reviewers, and operators contributing to the project over several years, we wouldn't have had such a rich topic to write about.

A very special thanks to the entire team at Tesora who have supported this book through reviews, answering technical questions and providing ideas for content.

Our thanks to the team at Apress, Mark Powers, Louise Corrigan, Christine Ricketts, and Lori Jacobs; you were great.

We would like to specifically thank Laurel Michaels, who has done so much for improving the documentation of Trove for the community, for painstakingly reviewing each chapter after initial draft, and providing valuable suggestions for improvement.

—Amrith & Doug

■ ■ ■

## CHAPTER 1

An Introduction to Database as a Service

Database as a Service (DBaaS) is not only a relatively new term but also a surprisingly generic one. Various companies, products, and services have claimed to offer a DBaaS, and this has led to a fair amount of confusion.

In reality though, DBaaS is a very specific term and provides very clear and well-defined benefits. In this chapter, we introduce DBaaS and broadly address the following topics:

- What is DBaaS
- The challenge databases pose to IT (information technology) organizations
- Characteristics of DBaaS
- The benefits of DBaaS
- Other similar solutions
- OpenStack Trove
- Trove in the OpenStack ecosystem
- A brief history of Trove

What Is Database as a Service?

As the name implies, DBaaS is a database that is offered to the user *as a service*. But, what does that really mean?

Does it, for example, imply that the DBaaS is involved in the storage and retrieval of data, and the processing of queries? Does the DBaaS perform activities such as data validation, backups, and query optimization and deliver such capabilities as high availability, replication, failover, and automatic scaling?

One way to answer these questions is to decompose a DBaaS into its two constituent parts, namely, the *database* and the *service*.

The Database

There was a time when the term *database* was used synonymously with relational database management system (RDBMS). That is no longer the case. Today the term is used to refer equally to RDBMS and NoSQL database technologies.

A database management system is a piece of technology, sometimes only software, sometimes with customized and specialized hardware, that allows users to store and retrieve data. The Free Online Dictionary of Computing defines a database management system as "A suite of programs which typically manage large structured sets of persistent data, offering ad hoc query facilities to many users."

The Service

Looking now at the other half—*as a Service*—we can see that its very essence is the emphasis on the delivery of the service rather than the service being delivered.

In other words, *Something* as a Service makes it easier for an operator to provide the *Something* for consumption while offering the consumer quick access to, and the benefit of, the "Something" in question.

For example, consider that Email as a Service offerings from a number of vendors including Google's Gmail and Microsoft's Office365 make it easy for end users to consume e-mail services without the challenges of installing and managing servers and e-mail software.

The Service as a Category

The most common use of the term *as a Service* occurs when referring to the broad category of Software as a Service (SaaS). This term is often used to refer to applications as a service, like the Salesforce.com customer relationship management (CRM) software, which is offered as a hosted, online service. It also includes Infrastructure as a Service (IaaS) offerings like AWS and Platform as a Service (PaaS) solutions like Cloud Foundry or Engine Yard.

DBaaS is a specific example of SaaS and inherits some of the attributes of SaaS. These include the fact that DBaaS is typically centrally hosted and made available to its consumers on a subscription basis; users only pay for what they use, and when they use it.

DBaaS Defined

One can therefore broadly define a DBaaS to be a technology that

- Offers these database servers "on demand";

- Provisions database servers;

- Configures those database servers, or groups of database servers, potentially in complex topologies;

- Automates the management of database servers and groups of database servers;

- Scales the provided database capacity automatically in response to system load; and

- Optimizes the utilization of the supporting infrastructure resources dynamically.

Clearly, these are very broad definitions of capabilities and different offerings may provide each of these to a different degree.

Just as Amazon offers EC2 as a compute service on its AWS public cloud, it also offers a number of DBaaS products. In particular, it provides Relational Database Service (RDS) for relational databases like MySQL or Oracle, a data warehouse as a service in Redshift, and a couple of NoSQL options in DynamoDB and SimpleDB.

OpenStack is a software platform that allows cloud operators and businesses alike to deliver cloud services to their users. It includes Nova, a computing service similar to Amazon's EC2, and Swift, an object storage service similar to Amazon's S3, as well as numerous other services. One of these additional services is Trove, OpenStack's DBaaS solution.

Unlike Amazon's DBaaS offerings, which are database specific, Trove allows you to launch a database from a list of popular relational and nonrelational databases. For each of these databases, Trove provides a variety of benefits including simplified management, configuration, and maintenance throughout the life cycle of the database.

The Challenge Databases Pose to IT Organizations

Databases, and the hardware they run on, continue to be a significant part of the cost and burden of operating an IT infrastructure. Database servers are often the most powerful machines in a data center, and they rely on extremely high performance from nearly all of a computer's subsystems.

The interactions with client applications are network intensive, query processing is memory intensive, indexing is compute intensive, retrieving data requires extremely high random disk access rates, and data loads and bulk updates imply that disk writes be processed quickly. Traditional databases also do not tend to scale across machines very well, meaning that all of this horsepower must be centralized into a single computer or redundant pair with massive amounts of resources.

Of course, new database technologies like NoSQL and NewSQL are changing these assumptions, but they also present new challenges. They may scale out across machines more easily, reducing the oversized hardware requirements, but the coordination of distributed processing can tax network resources to an even greater degree.

The proliferation of these new database technologies also presents another challenge. Managing any particular database technology can require a great deal of specialized technical expertise. Because of this, IT organizations have typically only developed expertise in a specific database technology or in some cases a few database technologies. Because of this, they have generally only offered their customers support for a limited number of choices of database technologies. In some cases, this was justified, or rationalized as being a *corporate standard*.

In recent years, however, development teams and end users have realized that not all databases are created equal. There are now databases that are specialized to particular access patterns like key-value lookup, document management, map traversal, or time series indexing. As a result, there is increasing demand for technologies with which IT has limited experience.

Starting in the latter part of the 2000s, there was an explosion in the so-called NoSQL databases. While it was initially possible to resist these technologies, their benefits and popularity made this extremely difficult.

Yet, how is an IT organization supposed to support all the various flavors of NoSQL and SQL databases without having in-depth knowledge of each of them?

Amazon led the way by making computing ubiquitous and easy to consume with a couple of key-clicks and a credit card. It then automated many of the complexities around databases and offered them as a service, forcing IT organizations to respond. It did this, however, by building up staff with expertise in each of these technologies, and still, like the IT staffs of old, offering only a limited number of options.

OpenStack Trove offers IT organizations the ability to operate a complete DBaaS platform within the enterprise. IT organizations can offer a rich variety of databases to their internal customers with the same ease of use that Amazon offered with its AWS cloud and the RDS product. Users of Trove get this benefit without requiring the same scale or large investment in specialized teams of experts in specialized database technologies that Amazon was able to staff internally.

Characteristics of DBaaS

Given how broadly the term *Database as a Service* is used, it is worthwhile trying to understand some characteristics of DBaaS. This characterization helps one quickly assess each candidate solution and organize solutions into meaningful groups.

Some common characteristics are

- **The operating plane:** data plane vs. management/control plane

- **Tenancy:** single tenancy vs. multitenancy

- **Service location:** private cloud vs. public cloud vs. hosted private cloud

- **Delivery model:** service vs. platform

- **Supported database:** single vs. multiple, SQL vs. NoSQL

The Management Plane and the Data Plane

An important characteristic of a DBaaS solution relates to the kind(s) of activities it performs, and we can categorize these activities broadly into two groups.

In the operation of a database, there are a number of activities like provisioning, installing and configuring, backing up and restoring, configuring replication (or mirroring, or clustering), resizing the storage attached with an instance, and other administrative activities. These activities broadly fall into the category of *system management* and are considered part of the *management plane*. For these operations, the actual content of the data being managed is opaque to the user issuing the commands.

There are also entirely independent but equally important activities like inserting, querying, and modifying data; creating tables, namespaces, indices, triggers, and views; and inspecting query plans. All of these activities broadly fall into the category of *data management* and are considered part of the *data plane*. In these cases the content of the data being stored is what the user is actually accessing and manipulating.

A managed database instance provides the operator and administrator a set of interfaces in the management plane while providing the end user and analyst of the database a set of interfaces in the data plane.

Different activities and clients participate in each of these planes, depicted graphically in Figure 1-1.

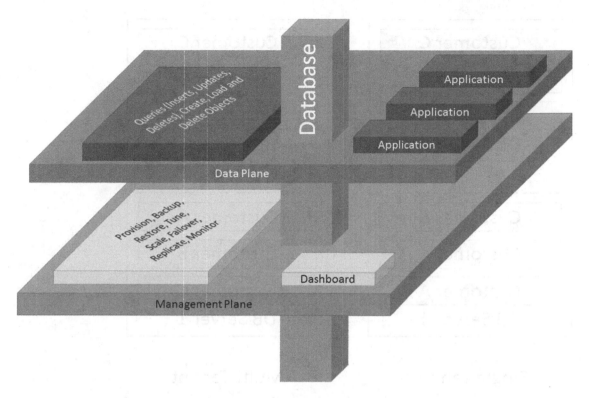

Figure 1-1. *A graphical representation of the data plane and management plane*

The database (depicted by the solid block) operates at two distinct planes—the data plane and the management plane.

OpenStack Trove operates almost exclusively in the management plane. Similarly, Amazon's RDS offering features a database and code developed by Amazon that orchestrates this database. This code that Amazon developed operates almost entirely in the management plane. A similar analogy can be made to SQL Server and Microsoft's Azure SQL Database offering. Other DBaaS offerings (such as DynamoDB from Amazon) operate in the data plane as well.

Trove, therefore, gives applications transparent and complete access to the data API (application programming interface) exposed by the database being offered while automating and simplifying the management aspects. For example, when a user uses Trove to provision MySQL, the database server that is provisioned is a standard, unmodified copy of the MySQL server and the user's subsequent interactions to query and update data on that server are all directly with that underlying server, not with Trove itself.

Tenancy

Tenancy is a very important attribute of a DBaaS solution. There are two commonly understood tenancy models, single tenancy and multitenancy. We examine each in turn.

Figure 1-2 helps describe this concept: single tenancy on the left and multitenancy on the right.

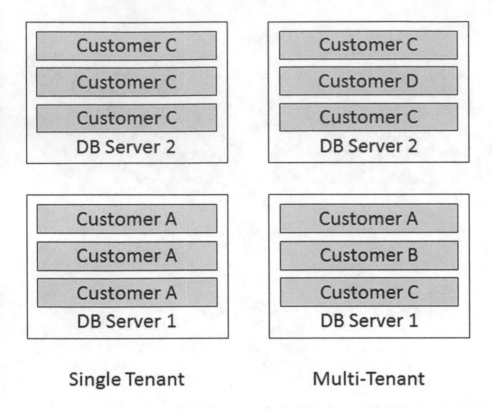

Figure 1-2. *Illustrating single and multitenancy with two database servers*

Single-Tenant Solution

A single-tenant DBaaS solution is a solution where the database provisioned by each tenant (user, consumer) resides on dedicated resources (database, compute, storage, networking, etc.). In some cases, this means that a user who requests two database instances gets two instances, each of which has its own dedicated resources, and in other cases, this this indicates that the two instances may share the same resources but these resources are not shared with any other tenant.

Amazon RDS, Amazon RedShift, and OpenStack Trove are some examples of single-tenant solutions. Each customer request for a database would result in the creation of a single instance (potentially a virtual machine with a database instance on it). While they may be considered multitenant at the compute infrastructure level, at the DBaaS level, they are single-tenant solutions.

The benefit of a single-tenant architecture is that each user's activity is fairly well isolated. Since each user has a dedicated pool of resources on which to run database functions, one user performing many queries or updates at a particular time is unlikely to affect the performance of the system for other users accessing their data. Note, however, that this isolation can be impacted by the lack of isolation at the infrastructure level if that tier is in fact multitenant.

Multitenant Solution

A *multitenant* DBaaS solution is one where databases provisioned by different tenants may share the same resources. The sharing may be on a single physical or virtual machine or across a cluster of machines.

Oracle 12c is an example of a database that when offered as a service would constitute a multitenant DBaaS solution. A single database server instance would host one or more container databases. Each container database would have a *pluggable* database for each customer/tenant/user, and these pluggable databases would house each user's data. Another example would be Amazon's DynamoDB where a user's data is stored alongside the data of other users across a large cluster of underlying shared hardware.

While a multitenant system may result in less isolation and a greater potential for resource conflict among users, it typically provides a more efficient use of resources overall since resources not in use by one user can be more easily consumed by others sharing the same infrastructure.

Service Location

DBaaS solutions can operate in a variety of locations (e.g., a public cloud, a private cloud, or a hosted private cloud).

The Public Cloud

In the public cloud, some third party owns, manages, and operates a computing infrastructure and allows other individuals and companies to purchase and use services on this infrastructure.

Amazon AWS is the most commonly cited example of the public cloud model. Other similar solutions include Microsoft Azure, Google Cloud Platform, and Hewlett Packard's (HP) Helion Public Cloud.

To the average consumer, public clouds provide little by way of service-level agreements (SLAs) and guarantees on response times or the ability to control the service being provided.

One common issue with public clouds is the fact that they are mostly multitenant and therefore they share infrastructure. One consumer's compute instance could, for example, be negatively impacted by the behavior of some other compute instance owned by another tenant that just happens to share the same physical machine. This is often referred to as the *noisy neighbor* effect.

Some public clouds give very little control over the placement of your resources on the infrastructure beyond very coarse controls. In deploying an instance on Amazon, for example, you can choose the Availability Zone (coarse control) but cannot guarantee that two instances in the same Availability Zone aren't on the same physical machine. This could unexpectedly lead to issues with availability. If the machine hosting both of these instances fails, both services will cease operation.

A major driver to the public cloud is that the user only pays for exactly what he or she consumes. This alleviates concerns such as resource utilization and capacity planning and transforms what is a capital expense in the private cloud into a variable, operating expense. In addition to this, it is extremely easy to get up and running on a public cloud. There is no need to set up machines and networks to begin work, and if something goes wrong, the public cloud operator is responsible for fixing it.

The Private Cloud

Many larger enterprises operate their own internal IT infrastructure as a cloud and use tools to provision and manage the various components of this infrastructure.

In many respects, the private cloud is a natural evolution of the corporate data center. These private clouds offer compute, storage, and networking infrastructure as well as corporate identity management.

In addition, some organizations allow end users to provision and consume database services where the data is stored and processed on infrastructure provided by the IT organization within the private cloud.

Private clouds most often provide their customers with SLAs such as guarantees on response times and service characteristics such as outage times and downtime.

Private clouds also often provide users with greater control over the placement and operation of the infrastructure, something that is typically lost in other models like the public cloud.

Typically, considerations such as data privacy, data security, and cost drive the choice of a private cloud solution. Risk aversion and inertia are also significant drivers of the private cloud.

Managed Private Cloud

The managed private cloud is a hybrid of the public and the private cloud whereby the resources are owned and operated by one organization, for another. Often these resources are dedicated to the customer.

Examples of the managed private cloud include companies like RackSpace, BlueBox, Peer1, and Contegix. Many public cloud operators also provide managed private cloud offerings. Amazon's GOV Cloud and HP's Managed Cloud Services are two examples.

As the private cloud is the evolution of the corporate data center, the managed private cloud is the evolution of the outsourced data center.

The customer gets the benefits of the private cloud (SLAs, guarantees, dedicated resources, etc.) while not having to manage the infrastructure themselves. Managed private cloud providers often operate large data centers, and customers get the economies of scale.

In some cases customers have the option of physically isolating their infrastructure (such as in locked cages) for improved security and privacy.

Service vs. Platform

When a user consumes database services from Amazon RDS, it is clear that the user is interacting with a service. The user cannot get access to the software that operates RDS. A service is software that a user can purchase and consume on demand with no care or access to systems that are at work to provide the service.

On the other hand, a company could download and install OpenStack from `openstack.org` and it could install OpenStack Trove, software the company can use to operate on its own infrastructure. That, by itself is not a DBaaS. The user still has to install, configure, and operate it, and do a variety of things (which will be discussed in later chapters), such as building guest images, establishing configuration groups, establishing security groups, and so on. OpenStack Trove therefore represents a platform on which to operate a DBaaS.

Similarly, companies can build and offer platforms that are fully functional *DBaaS in a box* products. These would include all the things one would need to operate a complete DBaaS on one's own infrastructure. Tesora's DBaaS platform is one example of such a platform. This platform is based on OpenStack Trove and offers complete Trove capabilities and several extensions, along with certified guest images for many commonly used databases.

The Benefits of DBaaS

DBaaS solutions attempt to automate many of the complex and error-prone procedures, as well as the mundane and repetitive tasks involved in the operation of a database, while providing application developers and client applications access to a scalable and reliable data management infrastructure.

With DBaaS (as with other as-a-Service offerings), clients have access to the database of their choice without having to concern themselves with the underlying operational complexities.

Ease of Provisioning

An immediate benefit of DBaaS is that provisioning a database instance, something which used to take weeks if not months in the old world of centralized IT, can now be performed in a matter of seconds or minutes.

The user gets to choose the database type, version, and some other basic attributes. The database is then quickly provisioned and connection information is returned.

Consistent Configurations

The complexities involved in provisioning a database frequently lead to hard-to-detect differences between one instance and the next. Unfortunately, this subtle and often innocuous difference can translate into a critical problem in the middle of the night, often involving the loss or corruption of data.

Automating the provisioning mechanism with a DBaaS solution ensures that each database instance provisioned has exactly the same configuration, with no exceptions.

It also means that when a configuration change is required, it can be easily applied to all the database instances, and any deviation is easier to detect.

Automated Operations

During the life of a database, numerous management tasks need to be performed. These include generating a backup, updating a configuration parameter, upgrading to new database versions, rebuilding indices, or reclaiming unused space.

Automation can be set up to perform these tasks either on a specific schedule (time-based, full backup on Friday, incremental backup every day) or on a certain event or threshold (when deleted record space exceeds X%, when free space falls below Y%).

Automating these activities considerably simplifies the role of an IT operations team and also ensures that these operations are performed consistently without fail.

Autoscaling

Databases face variable workloads and provisioning for peak leads to enormous underutilization during non-peak times. Autoscaling is a capability whereby the resources allocated to the database are *right-sized* based on workload.

Scaling a database without downtime is possible with many databases, and a very attractive feature of operating in the cloud. But, it is an exacting process and automation considerably simplifies it.

Autoscaling is an example of an automated operation that can be performed at a threshold like queries per second or levels of resource utilization.

Improvements to Development Agility

While simplified and automated provisioning makes it easier and quicker to make a database instance available, there is more to development agility than just that. In many fields, like data analysis, for example, the thought process of the analyst is iterative. One doesn't always know what the right question is, and often the answer to the first question helps frame and qualify the next one.

While quick provisioning helps one quickly cycle through database instances during iterative discovery, it is important to recognize the value of quickly deprovisioning, or destroying, a database instance when it is no longer needed.

If DBaaS just made it easier to provision a database, it wouldn't help agility if the database came with a long commitment. The benefit of DBaaS is that one can quickly destroy a database when one is done with it, thereby releasing the allocated resources back to the pool.

Better Resource Utilization and Planning

With a DBaaS platform, IT organizations can monitor overall database demands and trends within the organization. You can expand and renew the underlying cloud infrastructure on a regular basis. This could be based on industry trends, which drive such a change. It could also be because of newer architectures and improved price points for selected hardware configurations. Finally, it could also be in response to the changing demands within the organization.

One goal of an IT organization is to maximize resource utilization and deliver the most responsive service while keeping in mind anticipated trends in demand within the organization.

One way to achieve this goal is by operating a pool of resources that can be shared within the organization and allowing users to provision, consume, and only pay for the time(s) when the infrastructure is in use. IT organizations can also resort to the judicious use of overprovisioning in the face of unexpected demand.

This not only improves the bottom line for the organization but also allows the organization to be more responsive to the needs of its customers.

Simplified Role for Provider or Operator

In an enterprise that does not provide DBaaS, the IT organization must be completely knowledgeable in all aspects of the databases that it allows internal customers to use. The customers have some DBA (database administration) knowledge and skills, and for the most part the administration skills are centralized within the IT organization.

In essence, this means that IT organizations can only allow internal customers to use database technologies in which they have considerable expertise. This is often the rationale for restricting the choice of database technology to the so-called *corporate standard.*

With the evolution of on-demand services and DBaaS that embody the best practices, the software automates and simplifies most common workflows and administrative activities. This eases the burden on the IT organization and reduces the requirement that the IT organization have deep expertise in every database technology. This also enables more choice for internal customers to select the right database technology for the problem at hand.

Other DBaaS Offerings

Here are some other DBaaS solutions that offer capabilities similar to OpenStack Trove.

Amazon RDS

Amazon RDS is the umbrella product that provides managed database instances running MySQL, Oracle, PostgreSQL, SQL Server, or Amazon's own MySQL compatible database, Aurora.

All of these are available in the Amazon AWS cloud in a variety of configurations including multi-availability zones. Amazon RDS includes useful features like automatic scaling, instance monitoring and repair, point-in-time recovery, snapshots, self-healing, and data encryption (at rest and in flight).

Amazon RedShift

Amazon RedShift is a fully managed petabyte-scale data warehouse solution that is based on the technology developed by ParAccel (now Actian). It uses standard PostgreSQL front-end connectivity, which makes it easy to deploy RedShift with standard SQL clients and tools that understand PostgreSQL. It features integrations with many other Amazon solutions like S3, DynamoDB and Elastic MapReduce (EMR).

Microsoft Azure SQL Database

Microsoft offers a version of its popular relational database, SQL Server as a Service. This service is offered as part of Microsoft's IaaS offering Microsoft Azure.

Google Cloud SQL

Google Cloud SQL is another MySQL compatible DBaaS offering, similar to Amazon's RDS for MySQL. This offering is delivered as part of Google Cloud Platform, formerly known as Google App Engine.

Amazon DynamoDB

Amazon DynamoDB is a fast, flexible NoSQL database service. It is a fully managed database service and supports both document and key-value data models. DynamoDB is also multitenant by design and transparently scalable and elastic. The user need do nothing in order to get the benefits of scalability with DynamoDB; that is all managed completely by the underlying service.

For this reason, DynamoDB is able to promise applications consistent (single-digit millisecond) latency at any scale.

OpenStack Trove

The stated mission of the OpenStack Trove project is as follows:

> *To provide scalable and reliable Cloud Database as a Service provisioning functionality for both relational and nonrelational database engines, and to continue to improve its fully-featured and extensible open source framework.*

It is important, therefore, to understand that unlike the other DBaaS solutions presented previously, Trove attempts, very consciously, to provide a platform for DBaaS that allows users to consume both relational and nonrelational database engines.

This mission statement is carried forward into the architecture (as discussed in a later chapter). Trove aims to provide a platform that would allow consumers to administer their databases in a technology agnostic way, while at the same time orchestrating a number of very different database technologies.

It is for this reason that Trove operates almost exclusively in the management plane and leaves data access to the application (in the native protocols supported by the selected database technology). Contrast this, for example, with DynamoDB, which provides data APIs.

Trove provides reference implementations for a variety of database technologies, or *datastores*. Trove users are free to modify these datastores and provide additional ones, and to modify the way in which Trove manipulates a specific datastore.

Some users have been able to extend Trove for their own purposes and to provide additional functionality not available in the reference implementations.

A Brief History of Trove

The Trove project came into existence early in 2012 with initial contributions from Rackspace and HP. At the time, the project was called RedDwarf, something that is still seen in many places in the code, such as the redstack tool, or the mysterious rd_ prefix on variables.

Initial code for Trove was available (during incubation) as part of the Grizzly and Havana releases. Trove was formally integrated into OpenStack as part of the Icehouse release.

OpenStack releases come out every six months and are alphabetical.

The initial release of Trove as an integrated project in April 2014 in the Icehouse release of OpenStack featured support for MySQL, MongoDB, Cassandra, Redis, and Couchbase. Each datastore had slightly different capabilities. It also included a basic framework of strategies that enabled extensibility and simplified the addition of capabilities in future releases.

The Juno version of Trove, six months later, debuted two new frameworks; one for replication and the other for clustering. This release included a basic implementation of replication for MySQL and clustering for MongoDB.

The Kilo release extended these frameworks and introduced additional capabilities for MySQL replication. In addition, this release also added support for many new databases, including DB2, CouchDB, and Vertica.

Tenancy in OpenStack Trove

Architecturally, OpenStack Trove is a single-tenant DBaaS platform by default. This means that each request for a new Trove database by a tenant results in the provisioning of one (or in some cases more than one) Nova instance, each with its own dedicated storage and networking resources. These instances are not shared with any other database request from either this user or any other user.

This does not in any way imply that the database instances that are created in response to a tenant's request will have dedicated hardware. Nova is by default intended to be a multitenant system, but an operator could configure policies or plug-ins that effectively ensure that different instances do not share the same hardware. Trove does not control that.

As described previously, Trove is a platform for DBaaS, and as discussed in later chapters, this means that the tenancy model that Trove implements can in fact be changed by a provider or operator.

Trove in the OpenStack Ecosystem

OpenStack is organized into a collection of services. Each OpenStack service exposes a public API and other services can interact with the service using the public API.

Figure 1-3 shows a simplified representation of such a service.

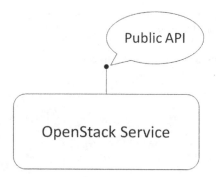

Figure 1-3. *Illustrating a simple OpenStack service*

The OpenStack service depicted has a public API which is RESTful. Trove is one such service, and it provides the functionality of a *Database as a Service*.

In OpenStack, identity is managed by a service called Keystone, networking by Neutron, block storage by Cinder, object storage by Swift, and compute instances by Nova.

Horizon is the dashboard service and presents the web interface. Some other OpenStack services are Heat (orchestration), Ceilometer (event management), and Sahara (Hadoop as a Service).

A simple OpenStack deployment typically consists of at least four services: Keystone, Neutron, Cinder, and Nova. Many deployments also include Swift.

Figure 1-4 shows a typical OpenStack deployment.

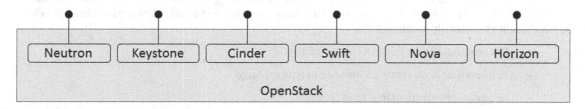

Figure 1-4. *A graphical representation of a simple OpenStack setup*

Client applications and other OpenStack services alike access each of these services using their public APIs.

Trove is a service that is a client of, and consumes the services of, the other core services, and you can add it to this diagram as shown in Figure 1-5. Trove, shown at the top left of Figure 1-5, exposes its own public API. It consumes services from the other OpenStack core services by invoking these on their respective public APIs.

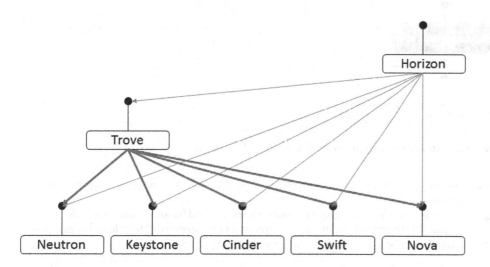

Figure 1-5. *Showing a simple OpenStack setup with Trove as a client of the other services*

One of the important tasks performed by Keystone is identity management—validation of access credentials by users to the public APIs of the various services. But, it serves another very important task and that is as the single directory of all OpenStack services.

All OpenStack services are required to register with Keystone and in so doing, these services then become accessible to users who have access to Keystone.

Trove registers as the database service. Therefore, a user who knew the Keystone end point and had access to Keystone could query Keystone to get the DBaaS end point registered by Trove.

In later chapters, we will also delve into more detail about how Trove works. However, at a high level, when Trove receives a request (e.g., a request for a new database instance with 300 GB of storage attached to it and of flavor type m1.large), Trove will authenticate the client (using Keystone), verify the client's quotas by inspecting its own persistent datastore, and, if the request appears to be valid, then perform the following operations (not necessarily in this order):

- Request that Cinder create a volume of 300 GB

- Request that Nova create an instance of type m1.large

- Request network interfaces from Neutron

And it would do all of these things by interacting with those services on their respective public APIs which it would determine using the directory in Keystone.

Without loss of generality therefore, you can see how each service can operate just fine on its own private machine (hardware); it would just have to register the publicly accessible IP address as the end point in Keystone.

This architecture of OpenStack makes it particularly well suited for large-scale deployments. Consider an example of an enterprise that would like to offer a highly available OpenStack service. This could be configured as shown in Figure 1-6.

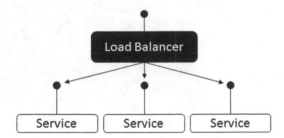

Figure 1-6. *Showing a service configured for redundancy with a load balancer*

Three copies of the service are launched on three different machines, and a load balancer is placed in front of these three machines.

In this configuration, the "Service" will register the public IP of the load balancer machine in the Keystone service catalog, and therefore any client wishing to contact this service will be told to connect with the load balancer, which will then be able to forward the request appropriately.

Summary

We conclude this introductory chapter with the same question we started with: What is Database as a Service?

Broadly speaking, one can define a DBaaS as software that allows a user to simplify and automate administrative and management activities that must be performed when using database technologies. This includes capabilities like provisioning, user management, backup and restore, ensuring high availability and data resiliency, self-healing, autoscaling, patch, and upgrade management.

Some DBaaS solutions do this by abstracting away the database and the management activities and inserting themselves into the data path (data plane). Others do this by providing only an abstraction of the management and administrative actions (the management plane), and staying entirely or almost entirely out of the data path.

Some are database specific (e.g., Microsoft's Azure Cloud Database and Cloudant), others provide database-specific capabilities under the umbrella of a single unified product set (like Amazon RDS), while OpenStack Trove is unique in that it aims to be database agnostic.

Many DBaaS solutions are single tenant by architecture. OpenStack is unique in that it is available as software that a user can deploy in a private cloud and it is also something that a service provider can deploy and offer as a managed private cloud or a public cloud.

While OpenStack Trove architecturally implements a single-tenant model, extensions can allow users to offer multitenant databases. An example of this is Oracle 12c in the Tesora DBaaS offering.

OpenStack Trove is an open source DBaaS platform that is part of the OpenStack project. Thus, OpenStack Trove can form the basis for a DBaaS solution in the private, public, or managed private cloud.

The next chapter dives headlong into Trove, starting with how to download, install, and configure it.

CHAPTER 2

■ ■ ■

Downloading and Installing OpenStack Trove

This chapter provides an overview of how to download and install OpenStack Trove. You will learn two ways to install OpenStack Trove and get a working Trove deployment with a MySQL database image.

- Deploying a single-node development environment

- Deploying a multinode OpenStack environment

Deploying a Single-Node Development Environment

By far the simplest way to get started with Trove is to deploy a single-node development environment. For this, all you need to have is a machine running a supported host operating system. In this book we use the Ubuntu operating system (version 14.04 LTS) from Canonical for most installation and configuration steps.

Set Up the Ubuntu Environment

Begin with a freshly installed Ubuntu 14.04 LTS system, and assume that you have set up this machine with a single-user account named *ubuntu*.

In many situations, Ubuntu is set up as a guest operating system with some virtualization software. If you do this, make sure that you configure your host operating system and your hypervisor to enable the efficient execution of VMs in your guest operating system. This configuration is sometimes referred to as *nested hypervisors*.

OpenStack will require that you launch nested virtual machines. Therefore, ensure that virtualization extensions like Intel VT or AMD-V are enabled in the BIOS. If you are using VMWare, you have to ensure that these are enabled in the settings for the virtual machine (VM) you are launching. Later in this chapter (in the section: "Verify That Virtualization Is Enabled") you will ensure that nested hypervisors can be run effectively.

Figure 2-1 shows a typical development environment. In this case, the Ubuntu VM running within VMWare is the development machine on which the user will install OpenStack and Trove.

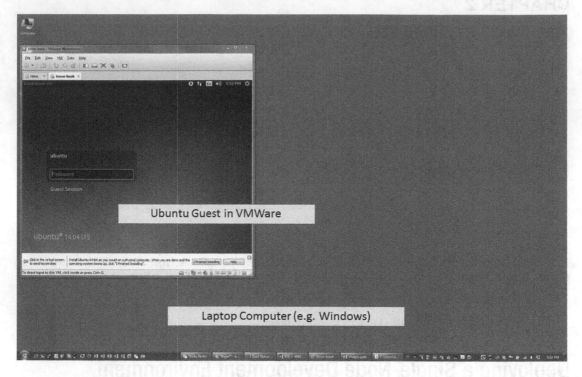

Figure 2-1. *A development environment with Ubuntu in a VM*

■ **Note**   Ensure that your Ubuntu machine (physical or virtual) has a static IP (Internet Protocol) address for its main (etho) interface. Do that either by configuring the etho interface in Ubuntu or by configuring the DHCP (Dynamic Host Configuration Protocol) reservation with your hypervisor (if you chose to use a VM).

Having installed Ubuntu on that machine, the user can connect to the VM using a simple ssh client and get to a command-line prompt as shown in Figure 2-2. Most of the operations that you will be performing in the installation are done from this command line.

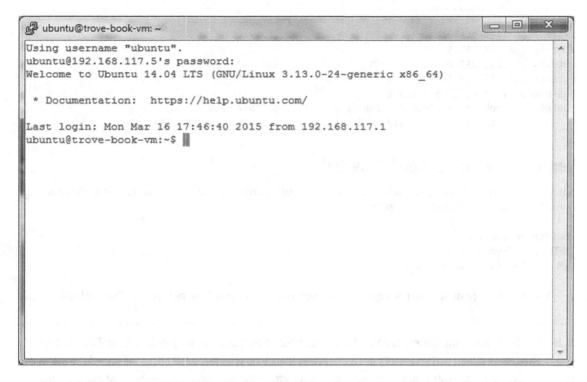

Figure 2-2. *A shell connection to the Ubuntu Guest VM*

Install Some Basic Packages

In addition to things like your favorite editor, make sure that you also have the git-core, ntp, openssh-server, and other convenience packages installed.

```
root@trove-book:~# apt-get update
root@trove-book:~# apt-get install emacs git-core ntp openssh-server cpu-checker -y
```

Verify Your Setup

Next, ensure that your machine is properly set up; this will prevent much costlier problems later on in the process.

Verify the Static IP Address

You configure the static IP by specifying the address in the file /etc/network/interfaces (or by using the NetworkManager applet).

```
root@trove-book:/etc/network# more interfaces
# interfaces(5) file used by ifup(8) and ifdown(8)
auto lo
iface lo inet loopback
```

```
auto eth0
iface eth0 inet static
address 192.168.117.5
netmask 255.255.255.0
gateway 192.168.117.2
dns-nameservers 8.8.8.8 8.8.4.4
root@trove-book:/etc/network# ifconfig eth0 | grep 'inet addr'
          inet addr:192.168.117.5  Bcast:192.168.117.255  Mask:255.255.255.0
```

Verify That Virtualization Is Enabled

Since you will be running OpenStack (and Trove) on your Ubuntu machine, you need to ensure that it is configured properly to enable virtualization.

```
root@trove-book:~# kvm-ok
INFO: /dev/kvm exists
KVM acceleration can be used
```

You may have to install the package cpu-checker as the command kvm-ok is part of that package.

■ **Note**   If you are using Ubuntu in a VM, it is a good habit to take periodic snapshots of your VM at known states. Storage is cheap and snapshots are a quick way to pick up where you left off, or roll back from some test gone wrong! While writing this book, we used a VM (with VMWare); Figure 2-3 shows what the snapshot page looked like, at one point.

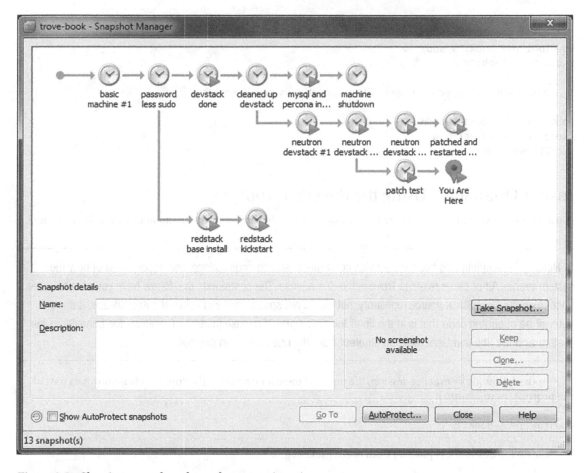

Figure 2-3. *Showing a number of snapshots at various times*

Enable Password-less sudo for the "*ubuntu*" User

Many commands executed during the install must be executed by the user root. Also, some OpenStack commands are run as the root user and they require password-less root access, which you need to enable next.

```
root@trove-book:~# visudo
root@trove-book:~# tail -n 4 /etc/sudoers

# this line gets added to the end of the file, /etc/sudoers
ubuntu ALL=(ALL) NOPASSWD: ALL
```

■ **Note**   Once you use `visudo` to make changes to the `sudo` configuration, you need to restart your session for the changes to take effect. Close the current shell session, reconnect to the machine, and then verify that the user ubuntu has password-less sudo access.

If your changes took effect, you should see the following:

```
ubuntu@trove-book:~$ sudo -s
root@trove-book:~#
```

If for some reason, your changes did not take effect, you will see this.

```
ubuntu@trove-book:~$ sudo -s
[sudo] password for ubuntu:
root@trove-book:~#
```

Install OpenStack Using the devstack Tool

Having connected to the shell, you can install a single-node development environment using the devstack tool.

■ **Note**   Throughout this book, we provide commands, source code listings, and descriptions of how the system works. All of these relate to Trove in the Kilo release. The commands that follow have you obtain source code from the OpenStack source repository, but we do not specify that you obtain the Kilo release. Rather, you will be obtaining code that is at the tip of the development release (master). Therefore, the behavior of the system and the line numbers could be different from the ones shown in this book.

In the following interactive session, the name of the user executing the commands is shown as part of the prompt (here *ubuntu*).

```
ubuntu@trove-book:~$
```

Clone the devstack repository from openstack.org.

```
ubuntu@trove-book:~$ git clone http://git.openstack.org/openstack-dev/devstack
Cloning into 'devstack'...
remote: Counting objects: 26464, done.
remote: Compressing objects: 100% (12175/12175), done.
remote: Total 26464 (delta 18846), reused 21351 (delta 14033)
Receiving objects: 100% (26464/26464), 5.28 MiB | 896.00 KiB/s, done.
Resolving deltas: 100% (18846/18846), done.
Checking connectivity... done.
```

Next, create a basic configuration file for devstack to use. This file, called localrc, is to be created in the devstack directory. The following code shows a sample localrc file:

```
ubuntu@trove-book:~/devstack$ more localrc
# Sample localrc file
# For use in installing Trove with devstack
# The various passwords below are just 20 character random passwords
# produced with makepasswd. The SWIFT_HASH is a unique string for a
# swift cluster and cannot be changed once established.
```

```
MYSQL_PASSWORD=07f1bff15e1cd3907c0f
RABBIT_PASSWORD=654a2b9115e9e02d6b8a
SERVICE_TOKEN=fd77e3eadc57a57d5470
ADMIN_PASSWORD=882f520bd67212bf9670
SERVICE_PASSWORD=96438d6980886000f90b
PUBLIC_INTERFACE=eth0
ENABLED_SERVICES+=,trove,tr-api,tr-tmgr,tr-cond

enable_plugin trove git://git.openstack.org/openstack/trove
enable_plugin python-troveclient git://git.openstack.org/openstack/python-troveclient

# Trove also requires Swift to be enabled for backup / restore
ENABLED_SERVICES+=,s-proxy,s-object,s-container,s-account
SWIFT_HASH=6f70656e737461636b2074726f766520627920616d72697468202620646f7567
```

You can now run the devstack tool by invoking stack.sh.

■ **Note**   When running long-running commands like stack.sh (which can take a while on the first invocation), it is a good idea to run them within a screen session. You may need to install screen.

```
ubuntu@trove-book:~$ cd ~/devstack
ubuntu@trove-book:~/devstack$ ./stack.sh

[. . . and a while later . . .]

This is your host ip: 192.168.117.5
Horizon is now available at http://192.168.117.5/
Keystone is serving at http://192.168.117.5:5000/
The default users are: admin and demo
The password: 882f520bd67212bf9670
2015-04-08 15:37:14.759 | stack.sh completed in 3186 seconds.
```

■ **Note**   If you are running Ubuntu in a VM, now is a good time to take a snapshot. We usually take a snapshot of the running VM, then stop all of OpenStack, shut down the Ubuntu operating system, and take another snapshot of the VM in that condition.

Listing the devstack screen Session

When devstack configures a system, it launches all the OpenStack processes in a screen session. You can list all the currently running screen sessions with the screen -ls command.

■ **Note**   Each invocation of the screen command is referred to as a screen session. You can have multiple screen sessions on your machine at one time, and each session can have a number of windows. Each window is an independent shell invocation.

```
ubuntu@trove-book:~/devstack$ screen -ls
There is a screen on:
        58568.stack     (04/08/2015 11:06:11 AM)           (Detached)
1 Socket in /var/run/screen/S-ubuntu.
```

As you can see from the previous command output, devstack launched a screen session, 58568.stack and you now attach to that screen session. Figure 2-4 shows you the screen session, and the window it displays is the one with the Trove Conductor process.

```
ubuntu@trove-book:~/devstack$ screen -dr 58568.stack
```

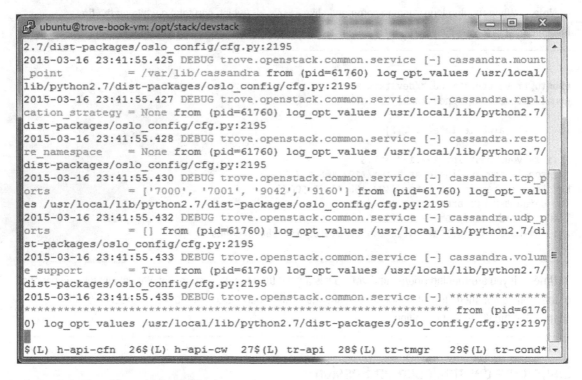

Figure 2-4. *Showing a window in the devstack screen session*

Within a single screen session, you can get a list of available windows using the list command (usually Ctrl-a-"). Figure 2-5 shows a list of screen windows.

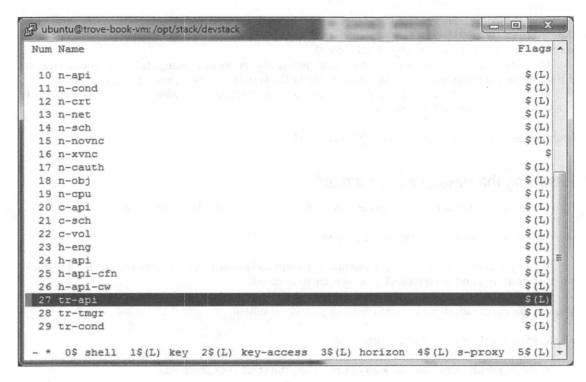

Figure 2-5. The devstack screen session showing a list of windows available

---

■ **Note**   The list command referenced here is used to list the available windows in a screen session. This is very different from the list command (screen -ls) which is used to list the screen sessions on the machine.

You can choose any one of these screen windows listed using the arrow keys and press Enter. The highlighted one in Figure 2-5 is the Trove API window.

Stopping and Restarting devstack

When launched with devstack, all the OpenStack services are launched in a screen session (as explained in the previous section).

Stopping devstack is merely a matter of closing that screen session and all the services therein.

One way to do this is by executing the command

```
screen -X -S 58568.stack quit
```

The -X option allows you to provide a command to be executed (in this case quit) and the -S option identifies the screen session. You would replace 58568.stack with the name of the screen session on your machine, obtained using the screen -ls command.

If you happen to make a configuration change to some service and you want to restart it, you find the right window in the devstack screen session and restart the service there.

One way to do this is to attach to the screen session as shown previously (screen -dr 58568.stack), then list the screen windows (Ctrl-a-") and use the arrow keys to navigate to the window for the service that you wish to restart (tr-api, tr-tmgr, and tr-cond).

On each window, you will be able to terminate the running service by pressing Ctrl-c and you can restart the service by just rerunning the previous command (the Up-Arrow key will get you the previous command).

If you shut down the machine on which you are running devstack, the easiest way to restart devstack is to use the rejoin-stack.sh command.

```
ubuntu@trove-book:~/devstack$ ./rejoin-stack.sh
```

Resetting the devstack Environment

Now is a good time to learn how to reset an OpenStack environment that has been launched with devstack.

```
ubuntu@trove-book:~/devstack$ ./unstack.sh
```

When you execute the unstack.sh command you will also notice that the screen session that devstack set up is destroyed and all OpenStack processes are terminated.

It is advisable to also clean up your setup before shutting down the machine and reinstalling devstack. You can use the clean.sh command to clean up your environment:

```
ubuntu@trove-book:~/devstack$ ./clean.sh
```

You can quickly restart devstack now by executing the stack.sh command.

```
ubuntu@trove-book:~/devstack$ ./stack.sh
```

Enable the Default Trove Public Key

■ **Note**   You must add a public key to a guest instance for the proper functioning of the guest image that will be installed by devstack.

When you launch a guest database instance using Trove, the default guest image needs to connect to the host and get some files. It does this using ssh and Trove's private key which is discussed in more detail in the Chapter 7. At this point go ahead and add the Trove public key to the authorized_keys file for the user *ubuntu*.

The Trove keypair is part of the trove-integration project so start by cloning this project into /opt/stack.

```
ubuntu@trove-book:~/devstack$ cd /opt/stack
ubuntu@trove-book:/opt/stack$ git clone http://git.openstack.org/openstack/trove-integration
Cloning into 'trove-integration'...
remote: Counting objects: 4663, done.
remote: Compressing objects: 100% (2008/2008), done.
remote: Total 4663 (delta 2985), reused 4132 (delta 2533)
Receiving objects: 100% (4663/4663), 1.48 MiB | 642.00 KiB/s, done.
Resolving deltas: 100% (2985/2985), done.
Checking connectivity... done.
```

You install the Trove public key in ~/.ssh as shown below. Observe that the public key is appended to the authorized_keys file.

```
ubuntu@trove-book:~$ cd .ssh
ubuntu@trove-book:~/.ssh$ cat /opt/stack/trove-integration/scripts/files/keys/
authorized_keys >> ~/.ssh/authorized_keys
ubuntu@trove-book:~$ chmod 700 ~/.ssh/authorized_keys
```

At this point, you are ready to start executing some basic Trove commands. This is also a good time to take a snapshot of your VM.

Authenticate with the System

Next, you execute a simple Trove command to list all running instances. Remember that the commands are being executed by the user *ubuntu*.

```
ubuntu@trove-book:~$ trove list
ERROR: You must provide a username via either --os-username or env[OS_USERNAME]
```

You just saw the attempt to execute the trove list command, which produced an error. This is because all commands require the user to provide valid credentials to OpenStack.

The following example demonstrates how you can specify these credentials from the command line.

```
ubuntu@trove-book:~$ trove --os-username admin \
> --os-password 882f520bd67212bf9670 \
> --os-auth-url http://192.168.117.5:5000/v2.0 \
> --os-tenant-name admin list
+----+------+-----------+-------------------+--------+-----------+------+
| ID | Name | Datastore | Datastore Version | Status | Flavor ID | Size |
+----+------+-----------+-------------------+--------+-----------+------+
+----+------+-----------+-------------------+--------+-----------+------+
```

What exactly are all of these things you just provided on the command line?

The username and password are the same ones that you saw at the very end of the output of the devstack command. The password is the one you provided in the localrc file when you ran the stack.sh command that installed and configured devstack.

```
[. . .]
Examples on using novaclient command line is in exercise.sh
The default users are: admin and demo
The password: 882f520bd67212bf9670
This is your host ip: 192.168.117.5
[. . .]
```

You specify these as the --os-username, --os-password and --os-tenant-name parameters. The auth-url is the end point for the Keystone (identity) service which will be discussed in more detail later in the book. The username (--os-username) and tenant name (--os-tenant-name) help identify the user admin who is a part of the admin tenant.

Since it is quite cumbersome to specify these credentials from the command line, the trove command allows you to establish several environment variables that will be used in place of the command line parameters. This is described in detail in Appendix B.

You can establish those credentials as environment variables using the convenient openrc command as shown next.

```
ubuntu@trove-book:~$ source ~/devstack/openrc admin admin
```

Now you can retry the trove list command.

```
ubuntu@trove-book:~$ trove list
+----+------+-----------+-------------------+--------+-----------+------+
| ID | Name | Datastore | Datastore Version | Status | Flavor ID | Size |
+----+------+-----------+-------------------+--------+-----------+------+
+----+------+-----------+-------------------+--------+-----------+------+
```

Launch Your First Trove Database

The devstack configuration that you performed earlier configured not only all of the required OpenStack services, including the three Trove services (trove-api, trove-conductor, and trove-taskmanager), but also a default MySQL guest instance which you can now launch.

To launch a new Trove instance, you will use the trove create command.

```
ubuntu@trove-book:~$ trove help create
usage: trove create <name> <flavor_id>
                    [--size <size>]
                    [--databases <databases> [<databases> ...]]
                    [--users <users> [<users> ...]] [--backup <backup>]
                    [--availability_zone <availability_zone>]
                    [--datastore <datastore>]
                    [--datastore_version <datastore_version>]
                    [--nic <net-id=net-uuid,v4-fixed-ip=ip-addr,port-id=port-uuid>]
                    [--configuration <configuration>]
                    [--replica_of <source:id>]

Creates a new instance.

Positional arguments:
  <name>                       Name of the instance.
  <flavor_id>                  Flavor of the instance.

Optional arguments:
  --size <size>                Size of the instance disk volume in GB.
                               Required when volume support is enabled.
  --databases <databases> [<databases> ...]
                               Optional list of databases.
  --users <users> [<users> ...]  Optional list of users in the form
                               user:password.
  --backup <backup>            A backup ID.
  --availability_zone <availability_zone>
                               The Zone hint to give to nova.
  --datastore <datastore>      A datastore name or ID.
```

```
--datastore_version <datastore_version>
                            A datastore version name or ID.
--nic <net-id=net-uuid,v4-fixed-ip=ip-addr,port-id=port-uuid>
                            Create a NIC on the instance. Specify option
                            multiple times to create multiple NICs. net-
                            id: attach NIC to network with this ID
                            (either port-id or net-id must be
                            specified), v4-fixed-ip: IPv4 fixed address
                            for NIC (optional), port-id: attach NIC to
                            port with this ID (either port-id or net-id
                            must be specified).
--configuration <configuration>
                            ID of the configuration group to attach to
                            the instance.
--replica_of <source:id>    ID of an existing instance to replicate
                            from.
```

Help is available for most Trove commands by executing trove help <command>.

The required arguments when you create a Trove instance are a name and a flavor id, and you can provide other optional arguments. Next, you create a Trove instance using the Trove flavor id 2 (m1.small).

```
ubuntu@trove-book:~$ trove flavor-list
+-----+-----------+-------+
|  ID | Name      |  RAM  |
+-----+-----------+-------+
|   1 | m1.tiny   |   512 |
|   2 | m1.small  |  2048 |
|   3 | m1.medium |  4096 |
|   4 | m1.large  |  8192 |
|   5 | m1.xlarge | 16384 |
|  42 | m1.nano   |    64 |
|  84 | m1.micro  |   128 |
| 451 | m1.heat   |   512 |
+-----+-----------+-------+

ubuntu@trove-book:~$ trove flavor-show 2
+----------+----------+
| Property | Value    |
+----------+----------+
| id       | 2        |
| name     | m1.small |
| ram      | 2048     |
| str_id   | 2        |
+----------+----------+
```

```
ubuntu@trove-book:~$ trove create m1 2 --size 1
+-------------------+--------------------------------------+
| Property          | Value                                |
+-------------------+--------------------------------------+
| created           | 2015-04-08T16:28:09                  |
| datastore         | mysql                                |
| datastore_version | 5.6                                  |
| flavor            | 2                                    |
| id                | e7a420c3-578e-4488-bb51-5bd08c4c3cbb |
| name              | m1                                   |
| status            | BUILD                                |
| updated           | 2015-04-08T16:28:09                  |
| volume            | 1                                    |
+-------------------+--------------------------------------+
```

The command succeeded and Trove will now attempt to create a database instance (called m1), which will run the default MySQL version 5.6 data store using Trove flavor 2 (m1.small) and a 1 GB volume from Cinder.

You can inquire on the status of this request using the trove list or the trove show command.

```
ubuntu@trove-book:~$ trove show e7a420c3-578e-4488-bb51-5bd08c4c3cbb
+-------------------+--------------------------------------+
| Property          | Value                                |
+-------------------+--------------------------------------+
| created           | 2015-04-08T16:28:09                  |
| datastore         | mysql                                |
| datastore_version | 5.6                                  |
| flavor            | 2                                    |
| id                | e7a420c3-578e-4488-bb51-5bd08c4c3cbb |
| ip                | 10.0.0.2                             |
| name              | m1                                   |
| status            | BUILD                                |
| updated           | 2015-04-08T16:28:21                  |
| volume            | 1                                    |
+-------------------+--------------------------------------+
```

After a few minutes, Trove reports that the database instance is in fact running. The status field is highlighted and has the value ACTIVE.

```
ubuntu@trove-book:~$ trove show e7a420c3-578e-4488-bb51-5bd08c4c3cbb
+-------------------+--------------------------------------+
| Property          | Value                                |
+-------------------+--------------------------------------+
| created           | 2015-04-08T16:28:09                  |
| datastore         | mysql                                |
| datastore_version | 5.6                                  |
| flavor            | 2                                    |
| id                | e7a420c3-578e-4488-bb51-5bd08c4c3cbb |
| ip                | 10.0.0.2                             |
| name              | m1                                   |
```

```
| status        | ACTIVE                  |
| updated       | 2015-04-08T16:28:21     |
| volume        | 1                       |
| volume_used   | 0.1                     |
+-----------------+-------------------------------------+
```

You can now create a database on that instance, and a user who can access that database.

```
ubuntu@trove-book:~$ trove database-create e7a420c3-578e-4488-bb51-5bd08c4c3cbb trove-book
ubuntu@trove-book:~$ trove user-create e7a420c3-578e-4488-bb51-5bd08c4c3cbb \
> demo password --databases trove-book
```

In the commands, we refer to the database instance by its id, as illustrated in the output from Trove just shown.

Finally, let's connect to the database. we do this using the mysql command line interface and specifying the username of demo, the password of password, and the host name of 10.0.0.2, the public IP address assigned to the instance m2 and shown previously in the output of the trove list command.

```
ubuntu@trove-book:~$ mysql -u demo -ppassword -h 10.0.0.2
[. . .]
mysql>
```

Using Neutron with devstack

OpenStack supports two projects that implement networking: Neutron and Nova Networking. By default, at the time of writing this book, devstack configures the system using Nova Networking. Neutron is a newer project, and provides some additional networking capabilities. Should you wish to use those, in this section we show you how to configure your system to use Neutron instead.

Selecting Neutron Instead of Nova Networking

The following additional lines are required in the localrc file in order to select Neutron instead of Nova Networking.

First, disable Nova Networking, then enable the various Neutron services.

```
disable_service n-net

enable_service neutron
enable_service q-svc
enable_service q-agt
enable_service q-dhcp
enable_service q-l3
enable_service q-meta
```

Configuring Private and Public Networks

Before running devstack, export these variables for proper functioning of the public and private networks. You must use 10.0.0.1 and 10.0.0.0/24.

```
export PUBLIC_NETWORK_GATEWAY=10.0.0.1
export FLOATING_RANGE=10.0.0.0/24
```

Before running devstack also export these variables. we have used the 172.24.4.0/24 network and chosen the address of 172.24.4.1 for the gateway. You can use any address that doesn't conflict with 10.0.0.0/24 chosen previously.

```
export NETWORK_GATEWAY=172.24.4.1
export FIXED_RANGE=172.24.4.0/24
```

If you don't make these changes, you will not be able to launch a Trove instance successfully. This is because of the way the default guest images used by devstack are built at this time.

We explore this issue in more detail in Chapter 7, but we provide a brief description here.

The guest images used by devstack are intended for development purposes only. Therefore, the images do not have any of the Trove code that runs on the guest agent and communicates with the datastore (guest database) on the image. Instead, they obtain that code at launch time as part of the bootstrapping process. This is ideal for development because you can make a small change and just launch a new instance, and that instance will reflect your latest change. This is not a configuration that is recommended for production use.

In order to obtain the trove code, the image has an job that is run at boot time that will copy the Trove guest agent code from a fixed location on the devstack machine whose IP address is 10.0.0.1.

The default devstack configuration makes 10.0.0.1 the private network and does not set up rules that allow the guest instance to copy (using rsync) from it. Making 10.0.0.1 the public interface (just swapping them is what I've shown previously) allows the process just described to work.

Trove Configuration for Neutron

In order to use Neutron, you need to make specific changes to configuration in both trove.conf and trove-taskmanager.conf.

■ **Note** In the Kilo release, neither is being done and the bug 1435612 was entered to track this (see https://bugs.launchpad.net/devstack/+bug/1435612).

This bug has been fixed after the Kilo release was shipped. So, if you obtain fresh code for devstack and Trove, you will be able to configure localrc as above and just run stack.sh. If the bug has not been fixed in the devstack or Trove that you have cloned, you will need to make the following corrections to your Trove configuration.

```
[. . .]
network_label_regex = .*
ip_regex = .*
black_list_regex = ^10.0.1.*
default_neutron_networks = 38c98a90-2c8c-4893-9f07-90a53b22000e
network_driver = trove.network.neutron.NeutronDriver
```

The UUID (universally unique identifier) 38c98a90-2c8c-4893-9f07-90a53b22000e shown previously is for the purpose of illustration only. On your machine, you will need to find the network ID for the private network as shown next.

```
ubuntu@trove-book:~$ source ~/devstack/openrc admin admin
ubuntu@trove-book:~$ neutron net-list | grep private | awk '{print $2}'
38c98a90-2c8c-4893-9f07-90a53b22000e
ubuntu@trove-book:~$
```

The UUID you will see on your system will be different. Use the UUID you see in your environment in trove.conf.

In the file /etc/trove-taskmanager.conf you need to add the following line in the DEFAULT section:

```
[DEFAULT]
[. . .]
network_driver = trove.network.neutron.NeutronDriver
```

In the same file, you also need to add the following line in a [mysql] section:

```
[mysql]
tcp_ports = 22,3306
```

Once you make these changes, you need to restart the three Trove services, tr-api, tr-cond, and tr-tmgr.

One way to do this is to attach to the screen session as shown previously (screen -dr 58568.stack), then list the screen windows (Ctrl-a ") and use the arrow keys to navigate to the window for tr-api, tr-tmgr, and tr-cond.

In each window, you will be able to terminate the running service by pressing Ctrl-c and you can restart the service by just rerunning the previous command (the Up-Arrow key will get you the previous command).

Accessing the Dashboard

Since your installation configured all of the base OpenStack services, including Horizon (dashboard component), you can now also connect to the dashboard.

To do that, point your browser at the Ubuntu development environment, and log in using the credentials set up by devstack.

	User Name	Password
Admin tenant	Admin	882f520bd67212bf9670
Demo tenant	Demo	882f520bd67212bf9670

These passwords are the same ones that were specified previously in the localrc file. For the purpose of this exercise, log in as admin.

You can navigate to the Database section under the Project tab (when you are logged in as admin (see Figure 2-6). The table lists all running Trove database instances on a running system (see Figure 2-7).

Figure 2-6. *Showing the Horizon (dashboard) log-in screen*

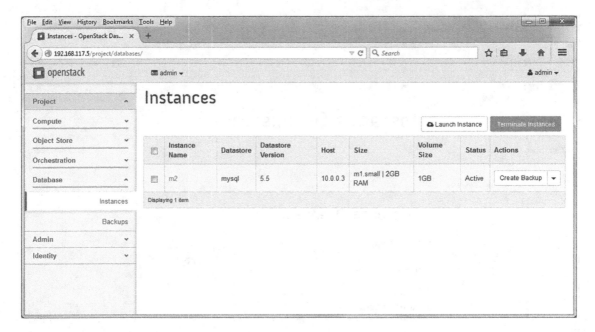

Figure 2-7. *Showing the Horizon dashboard Instance tab*

Clicking the instance name (m2) provides you with details about that instance as shown in Figure 2-8.

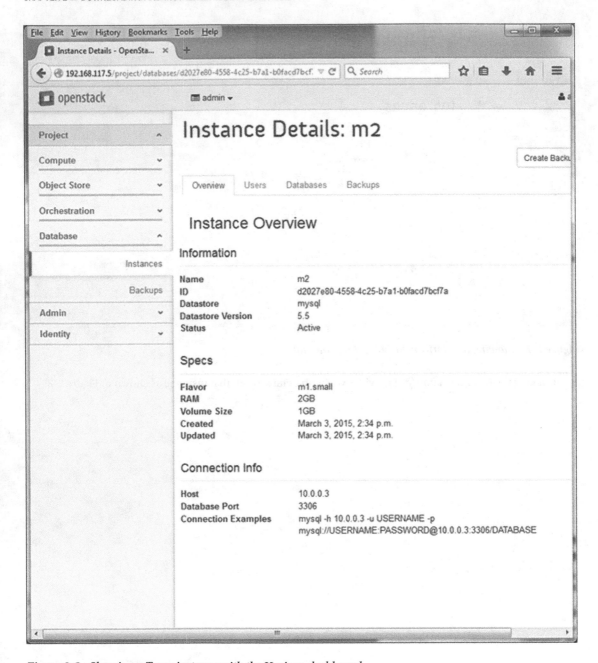

Figure 2-8. *Showing a Trove instance with the Horizon dashboard*

Deploying Trove in a Multinode OpenStack Environment

If you have an existing multinode OpenStack environment with the Ubuntu operating system and would like to add Trove to that environment, we have outlined the process in this section.

You can always find the most up-to-date instructions on how to install Trove on the OpenStack documentation page. For example, for the Juno release, the Trove installation documentation is available at

```
http://docs.openstack.org/juno/install-guide/install/apt/content/trove-install.html
```

Prerequisites

To operate Trove you need to have the following OpenStack components installed, configured, and operational:

- Keystone (Identity Service)
- Glance (Image Service)
- Neutron or Nova-Networking (Networking)
- Nova (Compute)

The following components are optional and may be required by some datastores, or to perform some specific Trove operations.

- Cinder (Block Storage)
- Swift (Object Storage)

To manage the system using the web-based UI, you require the following component to be installed, configured, and operational.

- Horizon (Dashboard)

Also gather the following information because you will require it later in the installation process:

- Controller host name
- Trove infrastructure database connection string
- RabbitMQ host
- RabbitMQ password
- Admin tenant password
- Default region name

Install the Required Packages

On the Trove controller node, install all the required packages. Since there are dependencies between OpenStack components and Trove, we assume that the OpenStack deployment is of the same version as the Trove that is being installed.

```
root@trove-controller:~$ apt-get install python-trove python-troveclient \
> python-glanceclient \
> trove-common \
> trove-api \
> trove-taskmanager
```

Create the Trove User

The majority of the installation commands will be run by the `trove` user, and the `trove` user will also be the one who will run the various Trove services. First create the user.

```
root@trove-controller:/$: useradd -m trove -s /bin/bash
```

Create the Trove Operational Database

Like the other OpenStack services, Trove stores operational information in a database. By default this database is a MySQL database. You therefore create the Trove operational database and provide access to the user that Trove will use to access this database.

```
root@trove-controller:~$ mysql -u root -p -s
mysql> create database trove;
mysql> grant all privileges on trove.* TO trove@'localhost' \
identified by '07f1bff15e1cd3907c0f';
mysql> grant all privileges on trove.* TO trove@'%' \
identified by '07f1bff15e1cd3907c0f';
```

Observe that in this configuration you're using the same passwords we used in the `devstack` configuration earlier. If you are going to operate Trove in a different environment, you change these passwords.

Configure OpenStack for Trove

You will need to be authenticated as the administrator with OpenStack. You typically accomplish this by sourcing a shell script that contains all the required settings.

```
ubuntu@trove-controller:~$ sudo su trove
trove@trove-controller:~$ source <path>/openrc-admin.sh
```

Trove requires service users defined in Keystone. The password provided for the service user `trove` (with the `--pass` command line parameter) is 96438d6980886000f90b which was provided in the `localrc` file earlier as the field SERVICE_PASSWORD.

```
trove@trove-controller:~$ keystone user-create --name trove --pass 96438d6980886000f90b
trove@trove-controller:~$ keystone user-role-add --user trove --tenant service --role admin
```

Configure the Trove Services

Next, you need to configure the Trove services.

- `/etc/trove/trove-conductor.conf`
- `/etc/trove/trove.conf`
- `/etc/trove/trove-taskmanager.conf`
- `/etc/trove/trove-guestagent.conf`

We look at each of these files individually. In the next few sections, we highlight the important and salient changes tying the Trove installation to the underlying OpenStack environment, as well as settings that will help in troubleshooting and debugging.

Sample configuration files are distributed with Trove. You can use them as a starting point to configure Trove.

- /etc/trove/trove.conf.sample
- /etc/trove/trove-taskmanager.conf.sample
- /etc/trove/trove.conf.test
- /etc/trove/trove-conductor.conf.sample
- /etc/trove/trove-guestagent.conf.sample

The file /etc/trove/trove-conductor.conf

The trove-conductor.conf file is the configuration for the Trove conductor service.

```
[DEFAULT]
use_syslog = False
debug = True
control_exchange = trove
trove_auth_url = http://192.168.117.5:35357/v2.0
nova_proxy_admin_pass =
nova_proxy_admin_tenant_name = trove
nova_proxy_admin_user = radmin
sql_connection = mysql://root:07f1bff15e1cd3907c0f@127.0.0.1/trove?charset=utf8
rabbit_password = 654a2b9115e9e02d6b8a
rabbit_userid = stackrabbit
```

The file /etc/trove/trove.conf

The file trove.conf contains general configuration for the Trove API service.

```
[DEFAULT]
trove_api_workers = 2

use_syslog = False
debug = True
default_datastore = mysql
sql_connection = mysql://root:07f1bff15e1cd3907c0f@127.0.0.1/trove?charset=utf8
rabbit_password = 654a2b9115e9e02d6b8a
rabbit_userid = stackrabbit

[keystone_authtoken]
signing_dir = /var/cache/trove
cafile = /opt/stack/data/ca-bundle.pem
auth_uri = http://192.168.117.5:5000
project_domain_id = default
project_name = service
user_domain_id = default
password = 96438d6980886000f90b
username = trove
auth_url = http://192.168.117.5:35357
auth_plugin = password
```

The file /etc/trove/trove-taskmanager.conf

The file trove-taskmanager.conf contains configuration options for the Trove Task Manager service.

```
[DEFAULT]
use_syslog = False
debug = True
trove_auth_url = http://192.168.117.5:35357/v2.0
nova_proxy_admin_pass =
nova_proxy_admin_tenant_name = trove
nova_proxy_admin_user = radmin
taskmanager_manager = trove.taskmanager.manager.Manager
sql_connection = mysql://root:07f1bff15e1cd3907c0f@127.0.0.1/trove?charset=utf8
rabbit_password = 654a2b9115e9e02d6b8a
rabbit_userid = stackrabbit
```

Observe that the passwords configured here are identical to the passwords you set up in the localrc file for the devstack install.

The file trove-guestagent.conf

This file, normally stored in /etc/trove (on the Trove controller) is actually used by the guest agent, not by the host. It gets sent to the guest instance at launch time by the Trove Task Manager. It contains the information used by the guest agent when it is launched on the guest.

The trove-guestagent.conf file ends up /etc/trove on the guest (shown here on a guest instance, m2).

```
ubuntu@m2:/etc/trove$ more trove-guestagent.conf

[DEFAULT]
use_syslog = False
debug = True
log_file = trove-guestagent.log
log_dir = /tmp/
ignore_users = os_admin
control_exchange = trove
trove_auth_url = http://192.168.117.5:35357/v2.0
nova_proxy_admin_pass =
nova_proxy_admin_tenant_name = trove
nova_proxy_admin_user = radmin
rabbit_password = 654a2b9115e9e02d6b8a
rabbit_host = 10.0.0.1
rabbit_userid = stackrabbit
```

Initialize the Trove Operational Database

Since you have created the Trove Operational Database and the user, and the configuration files properly point to this database, you can now initialize the database.

```
ubuntu@trove-controller:~$ sudo su trove
trove@trove-controller:~$ trove-manage db_sync
trove@trove-controller:~$ trove-manage datastore_update mysql
```

Configure the Trove Endpoint in Keystone

The final step before restarting the Trove services is to advertise the Trove service in Keystone by defining the end point.

```
trove@trove-controller:~$ keystone service-create --name trove \
        --type database \
        --description "Trove: The OpenStack Database Service"

# This command will give you the service-id of the newly created service.
# Make a note of that. Also, the first step (gathering information) had
# you record the default region. You will use that here.

trove@trove-controller:~$ keystone endpoint-create \
  --service-id <SERVICE_ID> \
  --publicurl http://192.168.117.5:8779/v1.0/%\(tenant_id\)s \
  --internalurl http://192.168.117.5:8779/v1.0/%\(tenant_id\)s \
  --adminurl http://192.168.117.5:8779/v1.0/%\(tenant_id\)s \
  --region <REGION_NAME>
```

Restart the Trove Services

Now you can restart the Trove services for your changes to take effect.

```
ubuntu@trove-controller:~$ sudo service trove-api restart
ubuntu@trove-controller:~$ sudo service trove-taskmanager restart
ubuntu@trove-controller:~$ sudo service trove-conductor restart
```

Download or Build a Trove Guest Image

In order to use Trove, you need a database guest image. In the previous setup, we described how to configure Trove to run MySQL as the default guest database. Chapter 7 covers in detail the steps to build a guest image.

You can also download Trove guest images for most supported databases from providers like Tesora (www.tesora.com). On the main page you will find a Download section, under the Products tab. Once you register, you will be able to download the Tesora DBaaS (Database as a Service) Platform and guest images.

The guest images used by devstack are also available for public download at http://tarballs. openstack.org/trove/images/ubuntu (see Figure 2-9).

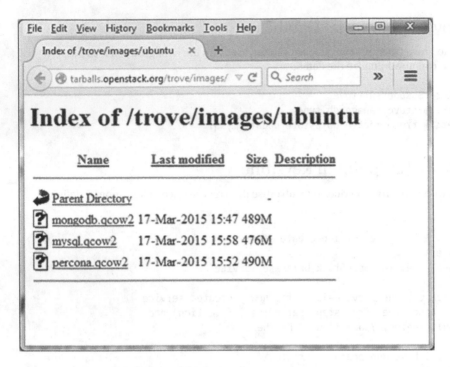

Figure 2-9. *Showing a listing of the devstack guest images*

Next, we will walk you through the process of downloading and installing a guest image on the Ubuntu host machine using the Percona (a MySQL variant) image.

In the following example, you download the image into the directory ~/downloaded-images on your local machine from the URL http://tarballs.openstack.org/trove/images/ubuntu/percona.qcow2.

■ **Note**   We are outlining how you can install and configure an image. You are using an image provided on tarballs.openstack.org. **Do not use these images in production.** In chapter 7 we will show you how to build a guest image for production use, and where you can get production-ready guest images.

```
ubuntu@trove-controller:~/downloaded-images$ wget http://tarballs.openstack.org/trove/
images/ubuntu/percona.qcow2
--2015-03-18 08:44:43--  http://tarballs.openstack.org/trove/images/ubuntu/percona.qcow2
Resolving tarballs.openstack.org (tarballs.openstack.org)... 192.237.219.31
Connecting to tarballs.openstack.org (tarballs.openstack.org)|192.237.219.31|:80
HTTP request sent, awaiting response... 200 OK
Length: 513343488 (490M)
Saving to: 'percona.qcow2'

100%[=====================================================================>] 513,343,488
873KB/s   in 9m 54s

2015-03-18 08:54:38 (843 KB/s) - 'percona.qcow2' saved [513343488/513343488]
```

First load the image into Glance. The output that follows lists the ID of the instance in Glance (here 80137e59-f2d6-4570-874c-4e9576624950); save that for later commands.

```
ubuntu@trove-controller:~/downloaded-images$ glance image-create --name percona \
> --disk-format qcow2 \
> --container-format bare --is-public True < ./percona.qcow2
+------------------+--------------------------------------+
| Property         | Value                                |
+------------------+--------------------------------------+
| checksum         | 963677491f25a1ce448a6c11bee67066     |
| container_format | bare                                 |
| created_at       | 2015-03-18T13:19:18                  |
| deleted          | False                                |
| deleted_at       | None                                 |
| disk_format      | qcow2                                |
| id               | 80137e59-f2d6-4570-874c-4e9576624950 |
| is_public        | True                                 |
| min_disk         | 0                                    |
| min_ram          | 0                                    |
| name             | percona                              |
| owner            | 979bd3efad6f42448ffa55185a122f3b     |
| protected        | False                                |
| size             | 513343488                            |
| status           | active                               |
| updated_at       | 2015-03-18T13:19:30                  |
| virtual_size     | None                                 |
+------------------+--------------------------------------+
```

Configure the *datastore* and *datastore version*

In order to identify this guest image to Trove and allow you to specify it in the trove create command later, we execute the following commands. In Chapter 7 we will go into detail about what these commands actually do and why they are required.

```
ubuntu@trove-controller:~/downloaded-images$ trove-manage datastore_update percona ''
2015-03-18 09:23:24.469 INFO trove.db.sqlalchemy.session [-] Creating SQLAlchemy engine with
args: {'pool_recycle': 3600, 'echo': False}
Datastore 'percona' updated.

ubuntu@trove-controller:~/downloaded-images$ trove-manage datastore_version_update percona
5.5 \
> percona 80137e59-f2d6-4570-874c-4e9576624950 \
> "percona-server-server-5.5" 1
2015-03-18 09:25:17.610 INFO trove.db.sqlalchemy.session [-] Creating SQLAlchemy engine with
args: {'pool_recycle': 3600, 'echo': False}
Datastore version '5.5' updated.

ubuntu@trove-controller:~/downloaded-images$ trove-manage datastore_update percona 5.5
2015-03-18 09:26:12.875 INFO trove.db.sqlalchemy.session [-] Creating SQLAlchemy engine with
args: {'pool_recycle': 3600, 'echo': False}
Datastore 'percona' updated.
```

```
ubuntu@trove-controller:~/downloaded-images$ trove-manage db_load_datastore_config_parameters \
> percona 5.5 ./validation_rules.json
2015-03-18 09:27:47.524 INFO trove.db.sqlalchemy.session [-] Creating SQLAlchemy engine with
args: {'pool_recycle': 3600, 'echo': False}
```

Finally, change the default datastore that Trove will launch in the trove.conf file (which is /etc/trove/trove.conf).

```
ubuntu@trove-controller:~/downloaded-images$ cp /etc/trove/trove.conf ./trove.conf.original
ubuntu@trove-controller:~/downloaded-images$ cp /etc/trove/trove.conf ./trove.conf
ubuntu@trove-controller:~/downloaded-images$ sed -i \
> 's/default_datastore = mysql/default_datastore = percona/' \
> ./trove.conf
ubuntu@trove-controller:~/downloaded-images$ diff ./trove.conf.original ./trove.conf
10c10
< default_datastore = mysql
---
> default_datastore = percona
```

And then install that file into /etc/trove where it belongs.

```
ubuntu@trove-controller:~/downloaded-images$ sudo cp ./trove.conf /etc/trove/
```

You are now able to launch your Percona instance with the trove commands shown in the following example:

```
ubuntu@trove-controller:~/downloaded-images$ trove datastore-list
+--------------------------------------+--------------------+
| ID                                   | Name               |
+--------------------------------------+--------------------+
| 170c8cce-15c0-497c-a148-d9120cc0630f | mysql              |
| c523235f-f977-45a5-b5bd-8a3a1e486e3e | percona            |
+--------------------------------------+--------------------+

ubuntu@trove-controller:~/downloaded-images$ trove datastore-version-list percona
+--------------------------------------+------+
| ID                                   | Name |
+--------------------------------------+------+
| 2417d4bb-79ae-48cd-96bf-854d381466ff | 5.5  |
+--------------------------------------+------+

ubuntu@trove-controller:~/downloaded-images$ trove datastore-version-show 5.5 \
> --datastore percona
+-----------+------------------------------------------+
| Property  | Value                                    |
+-----------+------------------------------------------+
| active    | True                                     |
| datastore | c523235f-f977-45a5-b5bd-8a3a1e486e3e     |
| id        | 2417d4bb-79ae-48cd-96bf-854d381466ff     |
| image     | 80137e59-f2d6-4570-874c-4e9576624950     |
| name      | 5.5                                      |
| packages  | percona-server-server-5.5                |
+-----------+------------------------------------------
```

```
ubuntu@trove-controller:~/downloaded-images$ trove create p1 2 --size 1 \
> --datastore percona --datastore_version 5.5
+-------------------+-------------------------------------+
| Property          | Value                               |
+-------------------+-------------------------------------+
| created           | 2015-03-18T13:36:10                 |
| datastore         | percona                             |
| datastore_version | 5.5                                 |
| flavor            | 2                                   |
| id                | 706c441b-7c54-4afd-8942-db8ff3450f66 |
| name              | p1                                  |
| status            | BUILD                               |
| updated           | 2015-03-18T13:36:10                 |
| volume            | 1                                   |
+-------------------+-------------------------------------+
```

After a brief period, you will notice that the Trove instance has transitioned to an active state.

```
ubuntu@trove-controller:~/downloaded-images$ trove show 706c441b-7c54-4afd-8942-db8ff3450f66
+-------------------+-------------------------------------+
| Property          | Value                               |
+-------------------+-------------------------------------+
| created           | 2015-03-18T13:36:10                 |
| datastore         | percona                             |
| datastore_version | 5.5                                 |
| flavor            | 2                                   |
| id                | 706c441b-7c54-4afd-8942-db8ff3450f66 |
| ip                | 10.0.0.2                            |
| name              | p1                                  |
| status            | ACTIVE                              |
| updated           | 2015-03-18T13:36:20                 |
| volume            | 1                                   |
| volume_used       | 0.1                                 |
+-------------------+-------------------------------------+
```

Now that the Percona database has been provisioned, You can execute various management commands against it and connect to it with a database client.

```
ubuntu@trove-controller:~/downloaded-images$ trove database-create \
> 706c441b-7c54-4afd-8942-db8ff3450f66 little-db

ubuntu@trove-controller:~/downloaded-images$ trove user-create \
> 706c441b-7c54-4afd-8942-db8ff3450f66 someone paper \
> --databases little-db
```

```
ubuntu@trove-controller:~/downloaded-images$ mysql -u someone -ppaper -h 10.0.0.2
[. . .]
mysql> show databases;
+--------------------+
| Database           |
+--------------------+
| information_schema |
| little-db          |
| test               |
+--------------------+
3 rows in set (0.01 sec)

mysql> select @@version_comment;
+-------------------------------------------------------+
| @@version_comment                                     |
+-------------------------------------------------------+
| Percona Server (GPL), Release 37.1, Revision 39acee0  |
+-------------------------------------------------------+
1 row in set (0.00 sec)

mysql>
```

Summary

This chapter demonstrates two ways in which you can install Trove, the OpenStack Database as a Service component.

First, you learned to install and configure Trove in a development environment using the 'devstack' tool. Note that the configuration steps provided here are essentially for a development environment and should not be used in a production situation. You also learned how Trove could be installed on an existing OpenStack environment and how to download and install a guest image for a database and then launch a database with that guest image.

Subsequent chapters will look more closely at the architecture of Trove and show how the various pieces configured previously work together.

CHAPTER 3

∎ ∎ ∎

Basic Trove Operations

The previous chapters introduced the concept of a Database as a Service (DBaaS) and showed how to download and install the software. This chapter builds on that and goes into more detail about Trove and describes some of the basic operations that you can perform with Trove. These include

- Interacting with RESTful services using `curl`
- How applications interact with OpenStack services
- Listing instances
- Launching instances
- Managing multiple datastores
- Managing users and databases

This chapter, and subsequent chapters, discuss interactive sessions where commands are being executed and, in some cases, show the results of these commands and highlight specific fields.

This chapter assumes that the reader is able to follow along and execute these commands on a working Trove deployment. In the interactive sessions, we use a `devstack` environment setup as described in Chapter 2. These operations work identically on a production OpenStack deployment with Trove.

Interacting with RESTful Services using `curl`

During the course of this book, there are going to be times when we describe the API (application programming interface) exposed by an OpenStack service in terms of the REST URI (uniform resource identifier). While it is often possible to use a CLI (command-line interface) or a GUI (graphical user interface) to interact with the service, there are times when it is easiest to inspect the responses using a simple `curl` session. We begin by describing how to do this.

The ability to interact with the services with `curl` is also very useful thing to know when attempting to debug some issue, or automate some activity using a customized script.

There are also some debugging capabilities that are only exposed via an API call (no CLI or web interface) and for those you will have to resort to this approach.

Interacting with a RESTful service in OpenStack consists of two steps.

- Establishing your identity and getting a token from Keystone
- Interacting with the RESTful URI with the token

Consider, for example, the request to obtain a list of datastores registered with Trove. Trove exposes this at the end point.

```
http://[host]:8779/v1.0/[tenant]/datastores
```

Appendix C provides a complete list of end points exposed as part of the Trove API.

Obtain a Token from Keystone

Using the username and password that was specified in localrc when launching devstack (or the appropriate username and password for your OpenStack setup) you can execute the following command:

```
curl -s -d '{"auth": {"tenantName": "admin", "passwordCredentials": \
> {"username" : "admin", "password": "882f520bd67212bf9670"}}}' \
> -H 'Content-Type: application/json' http://192.168.117.5:5000/v2.0/tokens \
> | python -m json.tool
```

The foregoing command accesses the Keystone public API (which is typically at host:5000) and the end point /v2.0/tokens. The system responds with a JSON (JavaScript Object Notation) response similar to the one shown in the following example. The response has been edited and some fields highlighted.

First, in the section listing endpoints, we look for the endpoint for the database service (type: database) and locate the adminURL associated with it. Then we look at the section called token and find the token id.

```
{
    "access": {
        "metadata": {
            "is_admin": 0,
            "roles": [
                "0fc2083997de44ee95a350a405790312"
            ]
        },
        "serviceCatalog": [
[. . .]
            {
                "endpoints": [
                    {
                        "adminURL": "http://192.168.117.5:8779/v1.0/979bd3efad6f42448ffa551
                        85a122f3b",
                        "id": "566ac5c0da564e88974e77504275a1a5",
                        "internalURL": "http://192.168.117.5:8779/v1.0/979bd3efad6f42448ffa
                        55185a122f3b",
                        "publicURL": "http://192.168.117.5:8779/v1.0/979bd3efad6f42448ffa55
                        185a122f3b",
                        "region": "RegionOne"
                    }
                ],
                "endpoints_links": [],
                "name": "trove",
                "type": "database"
            },
[. . .]
        ],
```

```json
    "token": {
        "audit_ids": [
            "OCg2NHfARzStxMCmYTcO5A"
        ],
        "expires": "2015-03-18T20:34:09Z",
        "id": "4290e975687444458526996337B9f92b",
        "issued_at": "2015-03-18T19:34:09.785685",
        "tenant": {
            "description": null,
            "enabled": true,
            "id": "979bd3efad6f42448ffa55185a122f3b",
            "name": "admin",
            "parent_id": null
        }
    },
    "user": {
        "id": "a69a4af4c4844253b8a1658f8e53ac23",
        "name": "admin",
        "roles": [
            {
                "name": "admin"
            }
        ],
        "roles_links": [],
        "username": "admin"
    }
  }
}
```

Use the Token to Interact with the RESTful Service

Armed with the URI and the token, you can now interact with the Trove service and request the information on the datastores as shown next.

```
ubuntu@trove-book-vm:~$ curl -H "X-Auth-Token: 4290e975687444458526996337B9f92b"
http://192.168.117.5:8779/v1.0/979bd3efad6f42448ffa55185a122f3b/datastores
```

We construct the foregoing command line by specifying the tenant-id
(979bd3efad6f42448ffa55185a122f3b), and appending "/datastores" to the adminURL from the previous command.

This produces the following response:

```json
{"datastores": [{"default_version": "79c5e43b-d7d0-4137-af20-84d75c485c56", "versions":
[{"name": "5.5", "links": [{"href": "https://192.168.117.5:8779/v1.0/979bd3efad6f424
48ffa55185a122f3b/datastores/versions/79c5e43b-d7d0-4137-af20-84d75c485c56", "rel":
"self"}, {"href": "https://192.168.117.5:8779/datastores/versions/79c5e43b-d7d0-4137-
af20-84d75c485c56", "rel": "bookmark"}], "image": "bc014926-31df-4bff-8d4e-a6547d56af02",
"active": 1, "packages": "mysql-server-5.5", "id": "79c5e43b-d7d0-4137-af20-84d75c485c56"},
{"name": "inactive_version", "links": [{"href": "https://192.168.117.5:8779/v1.0/979bd3efa
```

d6f42448ffa55185a122f3b/datastores/versions/fd8cf5a2-c456-4ba9-9ad2-d2c4390dccfb", "rel": "self"}, {"href": "https://192.168.117.5:8779/datastores/versions/fd8cf5a2-c456-4ba9-9ad2-d2c4390dccfb", "rel": "bookmark"}], "image": "bc014926-31df-4bff-8d4e-a6547d56af02", "active": 0, "packages": "", "id": "fd8cf5a2-c456-4ba9-9ad2-d2c4390dccfb"}], "id": "170c8cce-15c0-497c-a148-d9120cc0630f", "links": [{"href": "https://192.168.117.5:8779/v1.0/979bd3efad6f42448ffa55185a122f3b/datastores/170c8cce-15c0-497c-a148-d9120cc0630f", "rel": "self"}, {"href": "https://192.168.117.5:8779/datastores/170c8cce-15c0-497c-a148-d9120cc0630f", "rel": "bookmark"}], "name": "mysql"}, {"versions": [], "id": "79aae6a5-5beb-47b3-931f-c885dc590436", "links": [{"href": "https://192.168.117.5:8779/v1.0/979bd3efad6f424 48ffa55185a122f3b/datastores/79aae6a5-5beb-47b3-931f-c885dc590436", "rel": "self"}, {"href": "https://192.168.117.5:8779/datastores/79aae6a5-5beb-47b3-931f-c885dc590436", "rel": "bookmark"}], "name": "Inactive_Datastore"}, {"default_version": "2417d4bb-79ae-48cd-96bf-854d381466ff", "versions": [{"name": "5.5", "links": [{"href": "https://192.168.117.5:8779/v1.0/979bd3efad6f42448ffa55185a122f3b/datastores/versions/2417d4bb-79ae-48cd-96bf-854d381466ff", "rel": "self"}, {"href": "https://192.168.117.5:8779/datastores/versions/2417d4bb-79ae-48cd-96bf-854d381466ff", "rel": "bookmark"}], "image": "80137e59-f2d6-4570-874c-4e9576624950", "active": 1, "packages": "percona-server-server-5.5", "id": "2417d4bb-79ae-48cd-96bf-854d381466ff"}], "id": "c523235f-f977-45a5-b5bd-8a3a1e486e3e", "links": [{"href": "https://192.168.117.5:8779/v1.0/979bd3efad6f42448ffa55185a122f3b/datastores/c523235f-f977-45a5-b5bd-8a3a1e486e3e", "rel": "self"}, {"href": "https://192.168.117.5:8779/datastores/c523235f-f977-45a5-b5bd-8a3a1e486e3e", "rel": "bookmark"}], "name": "percona"}]}

Since Trove exposes the list of running instances at the end point—http://[host]:8779/v1.0/[tenant]/instances, you could list all running instances using the following command:

```
ubuntu@trove-book-vm:~$ curl -H "X-Auth-Token: 4290e975687444458526996337 89f92b"
http://192.168.11bd3efad6f42448ffa55185a122f3b/instances | python -m json.tool
```

This produces a JSON output as follows:

```
{
    "instances": [ . . .]
}
```

Although you won't have to interact with Trove (or any other OpenStack service) often in this way, it doesn't hurt to know and understand how this can be done. It also helps to know how to authenticate with services when using normal CLIs and web UIs, as explained in the following section.

Understanding How Applications and OpenStack Services Interact

This section examines how a client establishes its identity with OpenStack and how the various services handle this, as well as how applications can interact with OpenStack services.

In order to interact with an OpenStack service a client (requestor) must provide its identity so the service can validate the requestor and establish that the requestor has the requisite privileges.

The Keystone service handles identity management in OpenStack. In addition to user access credentials, it also houses the service catalog and a list of all active tokens. All this information is typically stored in the OpenStack infrastructure database. When interacting with OpenStack through the dashboard, establishing identity is merely a matter of entering a username and password on the sign-in screen.

When working with the CLI you can provide the requested credentials through command-line parameters as follows:

```
ubuntu@trove-book-vm:~$ trove --os-username admin \
> --os-password 882f520bd67212bf9670 \
> --os-auth-url http://192.168.117.5:5000/v2.0 \
> --os-tenant-name admin list
+----+------+-----------+------------------+--------+-----------+------+
| ID | Name | Datastore | Datastore Version | Status | Flavor ID | Size |
+----+------+-----------+------------------+--------+-----------+------+
+----+------+-----------+------------------+--------+-----------+------+
```

Optionally you can set environment variables like the ones that follow to eliminate the need to supply them on the command line.

```
OS_TENANT_NAME=admin
OS_USERNAME=admin
ADMIN_PASSWORD=882f520bd67212bf9670
OS_PASSWORD=882f520bd67212bf9670
OS_AUTH_URL=http://192.168.117.5:5000/v2.0
```

When a user executes a command like `trove list`, the code for this command need only know that Trove exposes an API to list instances at `http://[IP:PORT]/v1.0/{tenant_id}/instances` to be able to then perform the following sequence of operations:

- Authenticate with Keystone at `OS_AUTH_URL` using the `OS_USERNAME` and `OS_PASSWORD` and obtain the token

- Using that token, the command could then construct the end point from the service catalog and the URI /instances and access the following end point: `http://192.168.117.5:8779/v1.0/979bd3efad6f42448ffa55185a122f3b/instances`

Using the `--debug` command-line argument provides more information on how this all happens, as shown in the following response:

```
ubuntu@trove-book-vm:~$ trove --debug list
DEBUG (session:195) REQ: curl -g -i -X GET http://192.168.117.5:5000/v2.0 -H "Accept:
application/json" -H "User-Agent: python-keystoneclient"
DEBUG (retry:155) Converted retries value: 0 -> Retry(total=0, connect=None, read=None,
redirect=0)
INFO (connectionpool:203) Starting new HTTP connection (1): 192.168.117.5
DEBUG (connectionpool:383) "GET /v2.0 HTTP/1.1" 200 339
DEBUG (session:223) RESP: [200] content-length: 339 vary: X-Auth-Token server: Apache/2.4.7
(Ubuntu) date: Wed, 18 Mar 2015 22:25:08 GMT content-type: application/json x-openstack-
request-id: req-66e34191-6c96-4139-b8e5-aa9ec139ed51
RESP BODY: {"version": {"status": "stable", "updated": "2014-04-17T00:00:00Z", "media-
types": [{"base": "application/json", "type": "application/vnd.openstack.identity-
v2.0+json"}], "id": "v2.0", "links": [{"href": "http://192.168.117.5:5000/v2.0/",
"rel": "self"}, {"href": "http://docs.openstack.org/", "type": "text/html", "rel":
"describedby"}]}}
```

DEBUG (v2:76) Making authentication request to http://192.168.117.5:5000/v2.0/tokens
DEBUG (retry:155) Converted retries value: 0 -> Retry(total=0, connect=None, read=None, redirect=0)
DEBUG (connectionpool:383) "POST /v2.0/tokens HTTP/1.1" 200 4575
DEBUG (iso8601:184) Parsed 2015-03-18T23:25:08Z into {'tz_sign': None, 'second_fraction': None, 'hour': u'23', 'daydash': u'18', 'tz_hour': None, 'month': None, 'timezone': u'Z', 'second': u'08', 'tz_minute': None, 'year': u'2015', 'separator': u'T', 'monthdash': u'03', 'day': None, 'minute': u'25'} with default timezone <iso8601.iso8601.Utc object at 0x7fb7247648d0>
[. . .]
DEBUG (session:195) REQ: curl -g -i -X GET http://192.168.117.5:8779/v1.0/979bd3efad6f4244 8ffa55185a122f3b/instances -H "User-Agent: python-keystoneclient" -H "Accept: application/ json" -H "X-Auth-Token: {SHA1}7a8693593cc9fa0d612b064041515fc8a31c4d7a"
DEBUG (retry:155) Converted retries value: 0 -> Retry(total=0, connect=None, read=None, redirect=0)
INFO (connectionpool:203) Starting new HTTP connection (1): 192.168.117.5
DEBUG (connectionpool:383) **"GET /v1.0/979bd3efad6f42448ffa55185a122f3b/instances HTTP/1.1"** 200 17
DEBUG (session:223) RESP: [200] date: Wed, 18 Mar 2015 22:25:09 GMT content-length: 17 content-type: application/json
RESP BODY: {"instances": []}

```
+-----+------+-----------+-------------------+--------+-----------+------+
| ID  | Name | Datastore | Datastore Version | Status | Flavor ID | Size |
+-----+------+-----------+-------------------+--------+-----------+------+
+-----+------+-----------+-------------------+--------+-----------+------+
```

Scripting with the Trove CLI

By default, Trove CLIs provide tabular output. To facilitate scripting with the Trove CLI, you can also specify a JSON output format.

Consider the following listing of instances with the trove list command:

```
ubuntu@trove-book-vm:~$ trove list
+-----------------+------+-----------+-------------------+--------+-----------+------+
| ID              | Name | Datastore | Datastore Version | Status | Flavor ID | Size |
+-----------------+------+-----------+-------------------+--------+-----------+------+
| [instance uuid] | m1   | mysql     | 5.5               | BUILD  | 2         |    3 |
+-----------------+------+-----------+-------------------+--------+-----------+------+
```

You could modify the output format using the --json argument as follows:

```
ubuntu@trove-book-vm:~$ trove --json list
[
  {
    "status": "ACTIVE",
    "name": "m2",
[. . .]
```

```
    "ip": [
      "172.24.4.4"
    ],
    "volume": {
      "size": 2
    },
    "flavor": {
      "id": "2",
[. . .]
    },
    "id": "41037bd2-9a91-4d5c-b291-612ad833a6d5",
    "datastore": {
      "version": "5.5",
      "type": "mysql"
    }
  },
  {
    "status": "ACTIVE",
    "name": "m1",
[. . .]
    "ip": [
      "172.24.4.3"
    ],
    "volume": {
      "size": 3
    },
    "flavor": {
      "id": "2",
[. . .]
    },
    "id": "fc7bf8f0-8333-4726-85c9-2d532e34da91",
    "datastore": {
      "version": "5.5",
      "type": "mysql"
    }
  }
]
```

This is of course ideally suited for scripting using the CLI; take, for example, the following simple python program (names.py):

```
#!/usr/bin/env python
# names.py
#
# a simple python script to parse the output of
# the trove list command
#
# invoke it as
#
# trove --json list | ./names.py
#
```

```
import sys
import json

data = json.loads("".join(sys.stdin))

for obj in data:
    print obj['id'], obj['name'], obj['status']
```

You can invoke this as

```
ubuntu@trove-book-vm:~$ trove --json list | ./names.py
41037bd2-9a91-4d5c-b291-612ad833a6d5 m2 ACTIVE
fc7bf8f0-8333-4726-85c9-2d532e34da91 m1 ACTIVE
```

This is a very useful way of wrapping the CLI with a Python script that does some customized processing.

Listing Instances

One of the most commonly executed trove commands is the one to list instances and display their current statuses. The simplest version of the list command is trove list.

```
ubuntu@trove-book-vm:~$ trove list
+-----------------+------+-----------+------------------+--------+-----------+------+
| ID              | Name | Datastore | Datastore Version | Status | Flavor ID | Size |
+-----------------+------+-----------+------------------+--------+-----------+------+
| [instance uuid] | m1   | mysql     | 5.5              | BUILD  | 2         |    3 |
+-----------------+------+-----------+------------------+--------+-----------+------+
```

I modified (deleted the UUID) the preceding output to fit on the page.

When you have a large number of instances, you can also specify the --limit command-line option. You can accomplish pagination of results using the --limit and --marker options.

On the first invocation, provide just a --limit argument. On a subsequent invocation provide the last instance id returned in a previous invocation as the --marker argument. Consider the following illustration with two instances:

```
ubuntu@trove-book-vm:~$ trove list
+--------------------------------------+------+-----------+------------------+--------+
| ID                                   | Name | Datastore | Datastore Version | Status |
+--------------------------------------+------+-----------+------------------+--------+
| 41037bd2-9a91-4d5c-b291-612ad833a6d5 | m2   | mysql     | 5.5              | ACTIVE |
| fc7bf8f0-8333-4726-85c9-2d532e34da91 | m1   | mysql     | 5.5              | ACTIVE |
+--------------------------------------+------+-----------+------------------+--------+
```

```
ubuntu@trove-book-vm:~$ trove list --limit 1
+---------------------------------------+------+-----------+-------------------+--------+
| ID                                    | Name | Datastore | Datastore Version | Status |
+---------------------------------------+------+-----------+-------------------+--------+
| 41037bd2-9a91-4d5c-b291-612ad833a6d5  | m2   | mysql     | 5.5               | ACTIVE |
+---------------------------------------+------+-----------+-------------------+--------+

ubuntu@trove-book-vm:~$ trove list --marker 41037bd2-9a91-4d5c-b291-612ad833a6d5
+---------------------------------------+------+-----------+-------------------+--------+
| ID                                    | Name | Datastore | Datastore Version | Status |
+---------------------------------------+------+-----------+-------------------+--------+
| fc7bf8f0-8333-4726-85c9-2d532e34da91  | m1   | mysql     | 5.5               | ACTIVE |
+---------------------------------------+------+-----------+-------------------+--------+
```

Launching Instances

In Chapter 2, you learned how to launch instances as part of the demonstration of the installation process. This section provides more detail on the launch operation.

Consider the most basic way to launch an instance, which is to use the trove create command and pass in

- An instance name

- A flavor ID (indicating the various characteristics of an instance such as the RAM, the root volume size, etc.)

- The persistent volume size.

```
ubuntu@trove-book-vm:~$ trove create m1 2 --size 1
+-------------------+--------------------------------------+
| Property          | Value                                |
+-------------------+--------------------------------------+
| created           | 2015-03-18T18:12:09                  |
| datastore         | mysql                                |
| datastore_version | 5.5                                  |
| flavor            | 2                                    |
| id                | c1f25efa-8cea-447c-a70a-6360bc403d19 |
| name              | m1                                   |
| status            | BUILD                                |
| updated           | 2015-03-18T18:12:09                  |
| volume            | 1                                    |
+-------------------+--------------------------------------+
```

After a short while, the instance becomes active.

```
ubuntu@trove-book-vm:~$ trove show m1
+-------------------+------------------------------------+
| Property          | Value                              |
+-------------------+------------------------------------+
| datastore         | mysql                              |
| datastore_version | 5.5                                |
| flavor            | 2                                  |
| id                | c1f25efa-8cea-447c-a70a-6360bc403d19 |
| ip                | 10.0.0.2                           |
| name              | m1                                 |
| status            | ACTIVE                             |
| volume            | 1                                  |
+-------------------+------------------------------------+
```

The Trove instance created here is an instance of flavor 2 and has a 1 GB volume attached to it. It uses the default datastore configured on the system.

The Trove instance is based on a Nova instance (which by default has the same name).

```
ubuntu@trove-book-vm:~$ nova show m1
+-------------------------------------+-------------------------------------------------------+
| Property                            | Value                                                 |
+-------------------------------------+-------------------------------------------------------+
| OS-DCF:diskConfig                   | MANUAL                                                |
| OS-EXT-AZ:availability_zone         | nova                                                  |
| OS-EXT-SRV-ATTR:host                | trove-book-vm                                         |
| OS-EXT-SRV-ATTR:hypervisor_hostname | trove-book-vm                                         |
| OS-EXT-SRV-ATTR:instance_name       | instance-00000002                                     |
| OS-EXT-STS:power_state              | 1                                                     |
| OS-EXT-STS:task_state               | -                                                     |
| OS-EXT-STS:vm_state                 | active                                                |
| OS-SRV-USG:launched_at              | 2015-03-18T18:13:13.000000                            |
| OS-SRV-USG:terminated_at            | -                                                     |
| accessIPv4                          |                                                       |
| accessIPv6                          |                                                       |
| config_drive                        | True                                                  |
| created                             | 2015-03-18T18:12:16Z                                  |
| flavor                              | m1.small (2)                                          |
| hostId                              | fe06450ecc746eff0bf2fed26883f39c21c81c1ed8af633f..    |
| id                                  | b0ef5aac-04e9-49a6-809a-781425474628                  |
| image                               | mysql (bc014926-31df-4bff-8d4e-a6547d56af02)          |
| key_name                            | -                                                     |
| metadata                            | {}                                                    |
| name                                | m1                                                    |
| os-extended-volumes:volumes_attached| [{"id": "2be99c22-3b09-4061-95bb-81b5a19320f3"}]      |
| private network                     | 10.0.0.2                                              |
| progress                            | 0                                                     |
| security_groups                     | SecGroup_c1f25efa-8cea-447c-a70a-6360bc403d19         |
| status                              | ACTIVE                                                |
| tenant_id                           | 979bd3efad6f42448ffa55185a122f3b                      |
| updated                             | 2015-03-18T18:13:13Z                                  |
| user_id                             | a69a4af4c4844253b8a1658f8e53ac23                      |
+-------------------------------------+-------------------------------------------------------+
```

On a system with multiple datastores configured, you can specify the datastore from the command line as follows:

```
ubuntu@trove-book-vm:~$ trove datastore-list
+----------------------------------------+-------------------+
| ID                                     | Name              |
+----------------------------------------+-------------------+
| 170c8cce-15c0-497c-a148-d9120cc0630f   | mysql             |
| c523235f-f977-45a5-b5bd-8a3a1e486e3e   | percona           |
+----------------------------------------+-------------------+
ubuntu@trove-book-vm:~$ trove datastore-version-list 170c8cce-15c0-497c-a148-d9120cc0630f
+----------------------------------------+------------------+
| ID                                     | Name             |
+----------------------------------------+------------------+
| 79c5e43b-d7d0-4137-af20-84d75c485c56   | 5.5              |
+----------------------------------------+------------------+
ubuntu@trove-book-vm:~$ trove datastore-version-list c523235f-f977-45a5-b5bd-8a3a1e486e3e
+----------------------------------------+------+
| ID                                     | Name |
+----------------------------------------+------+
| 2417d4bb-79ae-48cd-96bf-854d381466ff   | 5.5  |
+----------------------------------------+------+

ubuntu@trove-book-vm:~$ trove create m1 2 --size 3 --datastore mysql --datastore_version 5.5
+-------------------+--------------------------------------+
| Property          | Value                                |
+-------------------+--------------------------------------+
| created           | 2015-03-18T18:14:43                  |
| datastore         | mysql                                |
| datastore_version | 5.5                                  |
| flavor            | 2                                    |
| id                | d92c7a01-dc16-48d4-80e0-cb57d8a5040a |
| name              | m1                                   |
| status            | BUILD                                |
| updated           | 2015-03-18T18:14:43                  |
| volume            | 3                                    |
+-------------------+--------------------------------------+
```

At this point, you know how to launch a Trove instance by specifying datastores and versions. In the section "Configuring Multiple Datastores," you will learn how to configure a datastore.

Restarting an Instance

Once launched, you can restart an instance using the `trove restart` command. This command only restarts the database service (the database program) running on the Nova instance that was provisioned by Trove. It does not restart the Nova instance.

```
ubuntu@trove-book-vm:~$ trove restart 64f32200-9da1-44af-b6c6-5e5b01ec0398

ubuntu@trove-book-vm:~$ trove show 64f32200-9da1-44af-b6c6-5e5b01ec0398
+-------------------+--------------------------------------+
| Property          | Value                                |
+-------------------+--------------------------------------+
| created           | 2015-03-18T18:19:55                  |
| datastore         | mysql                                |
| datastore_version | 5.5                                  |
| flavor            | 2                                    |
| id                | 64f32200-9da1-44af-b6c6-5e5b01ec0398 |
| ip                | 10.0.0.3                             |
| name              | m6                                   |
| status            | REBOOT                               |
| updated           | 2015-03-18T21:59:56                  |
| volume            | 2                                    |
+-------------------+--------------------------------------+

ubuntu@trove-book-vm:~$ trove show 64f32200-9da1-44af-b6c6-5e5b01ec0398
+-------------------+--------------------------------------+
| Property          | Value                                |
+-------------------+--------------------------------------+
| created           | 2015-03-18T18:19:55                  |
| datastore         | mysql                                |
| datastore_version | 5.5                                  |
| flavor            | 2                                    |
| id                | 64f32200-9da1-44af-b6c6-5e5b01ec0398 |
| ip                | 10.0.0.3                             |
| name              | m6                                   |
| status            | ACTIVE                               |
| updated           | 2015-03-18T22:00:15                  |
| volume            | 2                                    |
| volume_used       | 0.17                                 |
+-------------------+--------------------------------------+
```

Deleting an Instance

You can permanently delete an instance using the `trove delete` command. The `delete` command is irreversible and once you `delete` an instance, you will have no access to it and all data that was on that instance is lost.

```
ubuntu@trove-book-vm:~$ trove delete 64f32200-9da1-44af-b6c6-5e5b01ec0398
```

After a short while, the instance is completely deleted and no longer accessible.

```
ubuntu@trove-book-vm:~$ trove show 64f32200-9da1-44af-b6c6-5e5b01ec0398
ERROR: No instance with a name or ID of '64f32200-9da1-44af-b6c6-5e5b01ec0398' exists.
```

Configuring Multiple Datastores

A user can set up multiple datastores and multiple datastore versions for each datastore. For example, you could have MySQL versions 5.5, 5.6, and 5.7 alongside Percona 5.5 and MariaDB 5.6 and 10.0, and also some NoSQL datastores.

Configuring Datastores

The Trove infrastructure database, in the datastores and datastore_versions tables, stores information about datastores and datastore versions. Connect to the infrastructure database using the mysql command-line utility. The password used here is the password for the user root in the infrastructure database. Chapter 2 specified this password as MYSQL_PASSWORD in the localrc file. You specify the name of the database (trove) on the command line.

```
ubuntu@trove-book-vm:~$ mysql -uroot -p07f1bff15e1cd3907c0f trove
[. . .]
mysql> describe datastores;
+--------------------+--------------+------+-----+---------+-------+
| Field              | Type         | Null | Key | Default | Extra |
+--------------------+--------------+------+-----+---------+-------+
| id                 | varchar(36)  | NO   | PRI | NULL    |       |
| name               | varchar(255) | YES  | UNI | NULL    |       |
| default_version_id | varchar(36)  | YES  |     | NULL    |       |
+--------------------+--------------+------+-----+---------+-------+
3 rows in set (0.01 sec)

mysql> describe datastore_versions;
+--------------+--------------+------+-----+---------+-------+
| Field        | Type         | Null | Key | Default | Extra |
+--------------+--------------+------+-----+---------+-------+
| id           | varchar(36)  | NO   | PRI | NULL    |       |
| datastore_id | varchar(36)  | YES  | MUL | NULL    |       |
| name         | varchar(255) | YES  |     | NULL    |       |
| image_id     | varchar(36)  | NO   |     | NULL    |       |
| packages     | varchar(511) | YES  |     | NULL    |       |
| active       | tinyint(1)   | NO   |     | NULL    |       |
| manager      | varchar(255) | YES  |     | NULL    |       |
+--------------+--------------+------+-----+---------+-------+
7 rows in set (0.00 sec)
```

```
mysql> select d.name, dv.name from datastores d, datastore_versions dv where d.default_
version_id = dv.id;
+---------+------+
| name    | name |
+---------+------+
| mysql   | 5.5  |
| percona | 5.5  |
+---------+------+
2 rows in set (0.00 sec)
```

You configure a datastore after installing the image in Glance. For example, the percona datastore shown previously was configured like this (as described in Chapter 2).

First, load the image into Glance. The following response lists the ID of the instance in Glance; save that for later commands:

```
ubuntu@trove-controller:~/downloaded-images$ glance image-create --name percona \
> --disk-format qcow2 \
> --container-format bare --is-public True < ./percona.qcow2
+------------------+-------------------------------------+
| Property         | Value                               |
+------------------+-------------------------------------+
[...]
| id               | 80137e59-f2d6-4570-874c-4e9576624950 |
[...]
+------------------+-------------------------------------+
```

Next, create a datastore for Trove called percona.

```
ubuntu@trove-controller:~/downloaded-images$ trove-manage datastore_update percona ''
2015-03-18 09:23:24.469 INFO trove.db.sqlalchemy.session [-] Creating SQLAlchemy engine with
args: {'pool_recycle': 3600, 'echo': False}
Datastore 'percona' updated.
ubuntu@trove-controller:~/downloaded-images$
```

Next, use the trove-manage command to tie the datastore and version to a specific image and package set. The UUID here is the Glance image-id shown when the image was loaded into Glance (in the preceding code, the field is called id in the output of the glance image-create command). Appendix B describes the trove-manage command in detail.

```
ubuntu@trove-controller:~/downloaded-images$ trove-manage datastore_version_update percona 5.5 \
> percona 80137e59-f2d6-4570-874c-4e9576624950 \
> "percona-server-server-5.5" 1
2015-03-18 09:25:17.610 INFO trove.db.sqlalchemy.session [-] Creating SQLAlchemy engine with
args: {'pool_recycle': 3600, 'echo': False}
Datastore version '5.5' updated.
ubuntu@trove-controller:~/downloaded-images$
```

Next, set the default datastore version for the Percona datastore.

```
ubuntu@trove-controller:~/downloaded-images$ trove-manage datastore_update percona 5.5
2015-03-18 09:26:12.875 INFO trove.db.sqlalchemy.session [-] Creating SQLAlchemy engine with
args: {'pool_recycle': 3600, 'echo': False}
Datastore 'percona' updated.
ubuntu@trove-controller:~/downloaded-images$
```

Finally, load the configuration parameters for the datastore. This file is typically found in the /trove/templates/<datastore-name> directory wherever your software is installed. For more details, see Chapter 5, which covers the configuration groups in more detail.

```
ubuntu@trove-controller:~/downloaded-images$ trove-manage db_load_datastore_config_
parameters \
> percona 5.5 ./validation_rules.json
2015-03-18 09:27:47.524 INFO trove.db.sqlalchemy.session [-] Creating SQLAlchemy engine with
args: {'pool_recycle': 3600, 'echo': False}
ubuntu@trove-controller:~/downloaded-images$
```

You provide the validation_rules.json file in the final command along with the datastore (in this case, the Percona datastore) and the datastore version (5.5). The file contains the valid configuration parameters that can be used by configuration groups that configuration groups can use for this datastore. More on the use of configuration groups in Chapter 5.

Here is some information from the validation_rules.json file for the Percona datastore.

```
{
    "configuration-parameters": [
        {
            "name": "innodb_file_per_table",
            "restart_required": true,
            "max": 1,
            "min": 0,
            "type": "integer"
        },
        {
            "name": "autocommit",
            "restart_required": false,
            "max": 1,
            "min": 0,
            "type": "integer"
        },
        {
            "name": "local_infile",
            "restart_required": false,
            "max": 1,
            "min": 0,
            "type": "integer"
        },
```

```
      {
          "name": "key_buffer_size",
          "restart_required": false,
          "max": 4294967296,
          "min": 0,
          "type": "integer"
      },
[. . .]
```

Specifying the Default Datastore

If you have multiple datastores on your system, and a user does not specify a particular datastore on the
trove create command line, then the system uses the default datastore.

The trove.conf configuration file specifies the default datastore. If you change this, you have to restart
the Trove services.

```
ubuntu@trove-book-vm:~$ grep default_datastore /etc/trove/trove.conf
default_datastore = percona
```

Each datastore can have multiple versions; if a version is not specified, use the default version for the
datastore.

```
ubuntu@trove-book-vm:~$ trove --json datastore-show c523235f-f977-45a5-b5bd-8a3a1e486e3e
{
  "default_version": "2417d4bb-79ae-48cd-96bf-854d381466ff",
  "name": "percona",
  "id": "c523235f-f977-45a5-b5bd-8a3a1e486e3e",
  "versions": [
    {
      "name": "5.5",
[. . .]
      "image": "80137e59-f2d6-4570-874c-4e9576624950",
      "active": 1,
      "packages": "percona-server-server-5.5",
      "id": "2417d4bb-79ae-48cd-96bf-854d381466ff"
    }
  ]
}
```

```
ubuntu@trove-book-vm:~$ trove datastore-version-show 2417d4bb-79ae-48cd-96bf-854d381466ff
+-----------+--------------------------------------+
| Property  | Value                                |
+-----------+--------------------------------------+
| active    | True                                 |
| datastore | c523235f-f977-45a5-b5bd-8a3a1e486e3e |
| id        | 2417d4bb-79ae-48cd-96bf-854d381466ff |
| image     | 80137e59-f2d6-4570-874c-4e9576624950 |
| name      | 5.5                                  |
| packages  | percona-server-server-5.5            |
+-----------+--------------------------------------+
```

Creating Users and Databases

Users who connect to a datastore store their data in databases (typically in Relational Database Management Systems, or RDBMSs). Trove therefore provides the ability to create and manage users and databases. This section explores this ability, taking a MySQL instance as an example.

```
ubuntu@trove-book-vm:~$ trove show d92c7a01-dc16-48d4-80e0-cb57d8a5040a
+-------------------+----------------------------------------+
| Property          | Value                                  |
+-------------------+----------------------------------------+
| created           | 2015-03-18T18:14:43                    |
| datastore         | mysql                                  |
| datastore_version | 5.5                                    |
| flavor            | 2                                      |
| id                | d92c7a01-dc16-48d4-80e0-cb57d8a5040a   |
| ip                | 10.0.0.2                               |
| name              | m1                                     |
| status            | ACTIVE                                 |
| updated           | 2015-03-18T18:14:49                    |
| volume            | 3                                      |
| volume_used       | 0.17                                   |
+-------------------+----------------------------------------+
```

Enabling the Database *root* User

Databases like MySQL have a *superuser* (called root) and by default the root user is disabled for a Trove database instance. In this section you learn how to enable the root user. You have two options: you can enable the root user on a running instance or system-wide for all instances.

Enabling the *root* User on a Running Instance

Assume that you have a running Trove instance and you would like to access the instance with the root database user. You could enable the root user with the root-enable command.

```
ubuntu@trove-book-vm:~$ trove root-enable  d92c7a01-dc16-48d4-80e0-cb57d8a5040a
+----------+------------------------------------+
| Property | Value                              |
+----------+------------------------------------+
| name     | root                               |
| password | dAyPj7X24acJAgWtCsTjACEgPX2g6c4cGvhR |
+----------+------------------------------------+
```

Note that the output from the trove root-enable command includes the username (root) and the password (dAyPj7X24acJAgWtCsTjACEgPX2g6c4cGvhR). With this you are now able to connect to the MySQL database using the root account as shown next. The preceding output of trove shows the IP address of the instance (10.0.0.2).

```
ubuntu@trove-book-vm:~$ mysql -uroot -pdAyPj7X24acJAgWtCsTjACEgPX2g6c4cGvhR -h10.0.0.2 -s
mysql>
```

You can interrogate the status of the root account with the root-show command.

```
ubuntu@trove-book-vm:~$ trove root-show d92c7a01-dc16-48d4-80e0-cb57d8a5040a
+-----------------+-------+
| Property        | Value |
+-----------------+-------+
| is_root_enabled | True  |
+-----------------+-------+
```

If the root account is not enabled, you will see the following:

```
ubuntu@trove-book-vm:~$ trove root-show d92c7a01-dc16-48d4-80e0-cb57d8a5040a
+-----------------+-------+
| Property        | Value |
+-----------------+-------+
| is_root_enabled | False |
+-----------------+-------+
```

If the root account is enabled but you don't recall the password, you can execute the root-enable command again and you will get a new password.

```
ubuntu@trove-book-vm:~$ trove root-enable  d92c7a01-dc16-48d4-80e0-cb57d8a5040a
+----------+--------------------------------------+
| Property | Value                                |
+----------+--------------------------------------+
| name     | root                                 |
| password | TykqjpFAwjG8sXcjC4jUycwJQBkjznGgDpA2 |
+----------+--------------------------------------+
```

```
ubuntu@trove-book-vm:~$ mysql -uroot -pTykqjpFAwjG8sXcjC4jUycwJQBkjznGgDpA2 -h10.0.0.2 -s
mysql>
```

Enabling the *root* User by Default

In addition to being able to enable the root user on an existing database instance, you can also enable the root user by default (on instance creation). To do this, set root_on_create to True in the [mysql] section of trove.conf. Note that you will have to restart the Trove services first for your change to take effect. After restart, all instances will have the root user enabled when launched.

```
ubuntu@trove-book-vm:/etc/trove$ tail /etc/trove.conf
project_name = service
user_domain_id = default
password = 96438d6980886000f90b
username = trove
auth_url = http://192.168.117.5:35357
auth_plugin = password
```

```
[mysql]
root_on_create = True
```

After restarting the Trove services, launch a database instance.

```
ubuntu@trove-book-vm:~$ trove create m5 2 --size 3 --datastore mysql
+------------------+---------------------------------------+
| Property         | Value                                 |
+------------------+---------------------------------------+
| created          | 2015-03-18T18:12:40                   |
| datastore        | mysql                                 |
| datastore_version| 5.5                                   |
| flavor           | 2                                     |
| id               | 9507b444-2a62-4d21-ba64-2fa165c8892c  |
| name             | m5                                    |
| password         | eddtAKH2erH4Msdkujq7rcuTJskkj9MygFtc  |
| status           | BUILD                                 |
| updated          | 2015-03-18T18:12:40                   |
| volume           | 3                                     |
+------------------+---------------------------------------+
```

The password for the root user is returned as part of the response to the create command. A few minutes later, when the database instance is ACTIVE, you can immediately connect to it using the password provided previously.

```
ubuntu@trove-book-vm:~$ trove show 9507b444-2a62-4d21-ba64-2fa165c8892c
+------------------+---------------------------------------+
| Property         | Value                                 |
+------------------+---------------------------------------+
| created          | 2015-03-18T18:12:40                   |
| datastore        | mysql                                 |
| datastore_version| 5.5                                   |
| flavor           | 2                                     |
| id               | 9507b444-2a62-4d21-ba64-2fa165c8892c  |
| ip               | 10.0.0.2                              |
| name             | m5                                    |
| status           | ACTIVE                                |
| updated          | 2015-03-18T18:12:47                   |
| volume           | 3                                     |
| volume_used      | 0.17                                  |
+------------------+---------------------------------------+
ubuntu@trove-book-vm:~$ mysql -uroot -peddtAKH2erH4Msdkujq7rcuTJskkj9MygFtc -h 10.0.0.2 -s
mysql>
```

Manipulating Databases

Some datastores support the ability to create databases through Trove. In Trove, databases are manipulated using the database-create, database-delete, and database-list commands.

Listing Databases

You use the Trove command `database-list` to list the databases on an instance as shown next.

```
ubuntu@trove-book-vm:~$ trove database-list d92c7a01-dc16-48d4-80e0-cb57d8a5040a
+--------------------+
| Name               |
+--------------------+
| performance_schema |
+--------------------+
```

Suppressing Some Databases from Showing

Often a system has some internal databases that are not to be exposed to the user via the `trove database-list` command. You can suppress these databases by setting the `ignore_dbs` parameter in `trove.conf`.

The default value of `ignore_dbs` is `lost+found`, `mysql`, and `information_schema`. If you connect to the database and list the databases there, you see the following:

```
mysql> show databases;
+--------------------+
| Database           |
+--------------------+
| information_schema |
| #mysql50#lost+found |
| mysql              |
| performance_schema |
+--------------------+
4 rows in set (0.03 sec)
```

If you change the value of `ignore_dbs` you need to restart Trove services.

Creating a Database on a Running Instance

You can create a database on a running instance by using the `trove database-create` command, as shown next.

```
ubuntu@trove-book-vm:~$ trove database-create d92c7a01-dc16-48d4-80e0-cb57d8a5040a
chapter_3_db
ubuntu@trove-book-vm:~$ trove database-list d92c7a01-dc16-48d4-80e0-cb57d8a5040a
+--------------------+
| Name               |
+--------------------+
| chapter_3_db       |
| performance_schema |
+--------------------+
```

Creating Databases During Instance Creation

The trove create command also lets you create databases at the same time you are creating an instance. You can specify any number of databases and associated users as shown here.

```
ubuntu@trove-booktrove create m6 2 --size 2 --datastore mysql --databases \
> chapter_3_db_1 chapter_3_db_2 --users user1:password1 user2:password2
+-------------------+--------------------------------------+
| Property          | Value                                |
+-------------------+--------------------------------------+
| created           | 2015-03-18T18:19:55                  |
| datastore         | mysql                                |
| datastore_version | 5.5                                  |
| flavor            | 2                                    |
| id                | 64f32200-9da1-44af-b6c6-5e5b01ec0398 |
| name              | m6                                   |
| password          | xQ6wyJCUZzhjVrkNeRtQpCYeh2XcQEfbY8Cf |
| status            | BUILD                                |
| updated           | 2015-03-18T18:19:55                  |
| volume            | 2                                    |
+-------------------+--------------------------------------+
```

Once the instance comes online you can list the databases.

```
ubuntu@trove-book-vm:~$ trove database-list 64f32200-9da1-44af-b6c6-5e5b01ec0398
+--------------------+
| Name               |
+--------------------+
| chapter_3_db_1     |
| chapter_3_db_2     |
| performance_schema |
+--------------------+
```

Manipulating Users

There are a number of commands to manipulate users, and they can be broadly grouped into commands for

- Listing

- Creation and deletion

- Access control

This chapter discusses each in turn. In the previous section, you learned how to create an instance m6 with multiple users and databases at launch time. You use the same instance for this exercise.

Creating Users at Instance Creation Time

The following command creates an instance and two users (and two databases):

```
ubuntu@trove-booktrove create m6 2 --size 2 --datastore mysql --databases \
> chapter_3_db_1 chapter_3_db_2 --users user1:password1 user2:password2
+-------------------+--------------------------------------+
| Property          | Value                                |
+-------------------+--------------------------------------+
| created           | 2015-03-18T18:19:55                  |
| datastore         | mysql                                |
| datastore_version | 5.5                                  |
| flavor            | 2                                    |
| id                | 64f32200-9da1-44af-b6c6-5e5b01ec0398 |
| name              | m6                                   |
| password          | xQ6wyJCUZzhjVrkNeRtQpCYeh2XcQEfbY8Cf |
| status            | BUILD                                |
| updated           | 2015-03-18T18:19:55                  |
| volume            | 2                                    |
+-------------------+--------------------------------------+
```

Listing Users

You can list registered users on an instance using the user-list command.

```
ubuntu@trove-book-vm:~$ trove user-list 64f32200-9da1-44af-b6c6-5e5b01ec0398
+-------+------+-------------------------------+
| Name  | Host | Databases                     |
+-------+------+-------------------------------+
| user1 | %    | chapter_3_db_1, chapter_3_db_2 |
| user2 | %    | chapter_3_db_1, chapter_3_db_2 |
+-------+------+-------------------------------+
```

The value % in the host column is the SQL wildcard character indicating that the user may connect from any host.

Creating a User on a Running Instance

You can also create a user on a running instance and provide access to a specific database (or databases).

```
ubuntu@trove-book-vm:~$ trove user-create 64f32200-9da1-44af-b6c6-5e5b01ec0398 \
> user3 password3 --databases chapter_3_db_1
```

When you use the trove user-list command, you get the following output:

```
ubuntu@trove-book-vm:~$ trove user-list 64f32200-9da1-44af-b6c6-5e5b01ec0398
+-------+------+-------------------------------+
| Name  | Host | Databases                     |
+-------+------+-------------------------------+
| user1 | %    | chapter_3_db_1, chapter_3_db_2 |
| user2 | %    | chapter_3_db_1, chapter_3_db_2 |
| user3 | %    | chapter_3_db_1                 |
+-------+------+-------------------------------+
```

Access control is now enforced directly by the database as shown next. If the user user3 attempts to access the database chapter_3_db_2, MySQL will prevent this as expected.

```
ubuntu@trove-book-vm:~$ mysql -uuser3 -ppassword3 -h 10.0.0.3 -s chapter_3_db_1
mysql>

ubuntu@trove-book-vm:~$ mysql -uuser3 -ppassword3 -h 10.0.0.3 -s chapter_3_db_2
ERROR 1044 (42000): Access denied for user 'user3'@'%' to database 'chapter_3_db_2'
```

Deleting Users

You delete users on an instance using the Trove user-delete command.

```
ubuntu@trove-book-vm:~$ trove user-list 64f32200-9da1-44af-b6c6-5e5b01ec0398
+-------+------+-------------------------------+
| Name  | Host | Databases                     |
+-------+------+-------------------------------+
| user1 | %    | chapter_3_db_1, chapter_3_db_2 |
| user2 | %    | chapter_3_db_1, chapter_3_db_2 |
| user3 | %    | chapter_3_db_1                 |
+-------+------+-------------------------------+
ubuntu@trove-book-vm:~$ trove user-delete 64f32200-9da1-44af-b6c6-5e5b01ec0398 user3
ubuntu@trove-book-vm:~$ trove user-list 64f32200-9da1-44af-b6c6-5e5b01ec0398
+-------+------+-------------------------------+
| Name  | Host | Databases                     |
+-------+------+-------------------------------+
| user1 | %    | chapter_3_db_1, chapter_3_db_2 |
| user2 | %    | chapter_3_db_1, chapter_3_db_2 |
+-------+------+-------------------------------+
ubuntu@trove-book-vm:~$ mysql -uuser3 -ppassword3 -h 10.0.0.3 -s chapter_3_db_1
ERROR 1045 (28000): Access denied for user 'user3'@'10.0.0.1' (using password: YES)
```

Managing User Access Control

You manage user access control by using the Trove user-grant-access, user-revoke-access, and user-show-access as illustrated here.

Listing User Access

The user-show-access command shows the access granted to a user.

```
ubuntu@trove-book-vm:~$ trove user-show-access 64f32200-9da1-44af-b6c6-5e5b01ec0398 user1
+----------------+
| Name           |
+----------------+
| chapter_3_db_1 |
| chapter_3_db_2 |
+----------------+
```

Suppressing Users from user-list

Some databases have internal users that should not be displayed to the user. You can suppress specific users from the user-list by adding them to the Trove configuration.

You use the ignore_users parameter in the datastore specific section of trove.conf for datastores other than MySQL (and in the [DEFAULT] section for MySQL) to suppress users from the output of the user-list command. The default value for this parameter is datastore specific.

```
#
# [DEFAULT]
# ignore_users = os_admin,root
#
# [postgresql]
# ignore_users = os_admin,postgres,root
#
```

If you make a change to this parameter, you must restart the Trove services before it takes effect.

Granting a User Access

You can grant access to a database using the user-grant-access command, as shown next, using a newly created account for a user, user5.

First, create the new user.

```
ubuntu@trove-book-vm:~$ trove user-create 64f32200-9da1-44af-b6c6-5e5b01ec0398 user5
password5
```

The user has been created; however, the user has no access to any databases on the machine, as can be demonstrated with the user-show-access command.

```
ubuntu@trove-book-vm:~$ trove user-show-access 64f32200-9da1-44af-b6c6-5e5b01ec0398 user5
+------+
| Name |
+------+
+------+
```

Access control and database visibility are handled by MySQL as shown here. The user, user5 does not see any of the databases on the instance.

```
ubuntu@trove-book-vm:~$ mysql -uuser5 -ppassword5 -h 10.0.0.3 -s
mysql> show databases;
+--------------------+
| Database           |
+--------------------+
| information_schema |
+--------------------+
1 row in set (0.02 sec)
```

You can grant access to a database using the user-grant-access command. The user is then able to see the database when connected to MySQL.

```
ubuntu@trove-book-vm:~$ trove user-grant-access 64f32200-9da1-44af-b6c6-5e5b01ec0398 \
> user5 chapter_3_db_1
ubuntu@trove-book-vm:~$ mysql -uuser5 -ppassword5 -h 10.0.0.3 -s
mysql> show databases;
+--------------------+
| Database           |
+--------------------+
| information_schema |
| chapter_3_db_1     |
+--------------------+
2 rows in set (0.02 sec)
```

Revoking User Access

You use the user-revoke-access command to revoke a user's access to a database.

```
ubuntu@trove-book-vm:~$ trove user-revoke-access 64f32200-9da1-44af-b6c6-5e5b01ec0398 \
>  user5 chapter_3_db_1
ubuntu@trove-book-vm:~$ trove user-show-access 64f32200-9da1-44af-b6c6-5e5b01ec0398  user5
+------+
| Name |
+------+
+------+
```

Summary

This chapter provided an introduction to some basic operations with Trove, including how to interact with the service using the CLI and the REST API and how to create, list, and manipulate instances, datastores, users, and databases.

Trove exposes a RESTful API and users can interact with these services using a simple `curl` command. To do this, users must authenticate with Keystone and obtain a token. Users then use this token to interact with Trove.

Trove CLIs and applications (including Horizon) interact with Trove and other OpenStack services in exactly this way.

Many Trove CLI commands provide the user with tabular output, but the `--json` option will generate JSON output. This is ideally suited for scripting.

Users can create, delete, and restart Trove database instances by using the `create`, `delete`, and `restart` commands.

You can configure a system to have multiple datastores and multiple versions of each datastore. You can specify a default datastore (via the `trove.conf` configuration file), and each datastore has an associated default version.

Some datastores support the specification of users, databases, and access control. With these datastores, you can specify users and databases either when you are creating the Trove instance or after the instance is up and running. Commands are available for manipulating user access to databases, as well as for deleting users and databases.

CHAPTER 4

■ ■ ■

Concepts and Architecture

Previously you learned how to configure and install OpenStack Trove and how to perform some basic operations, including launching, restarting, and deleting instances. We also discussed registering and using datastores as well as manipulating databases and users. In previous chapters we also showed how one could interact with Trove using an API (application programming interface) or CLI (command-line identifier).

In this chapter we look at the internals and the architecture of Trove. Trove consists of multiple services: the Trove API, the Trove conductor, and the Trove task manager. In addition, each Trove instance has a guest agent that helps Trove provide a database-agnostic set of services while in fact being able to support a number of relational and nonrelational databases.

You will learn how these services work together to process user requests, and how Trove handles the basic operations discussed in previous chapters. In Chapter 5 we will also look at more complex operations like backup and restore, replication, and clustering.

We begin with a high-level architecture overview, which is followed by a more detailed description of some key concepts in the Trove architecture.

- Trove services
- Internal Trove guest agent API
- Mechanisms for extending the Trove framework
- Trove guest agents
- Trove guest image
- Trove message queue
- Trove infrastructure database
- Trove public API

High-Level Trove Architecture

At a high level, Trove is a service like every other OpenStack service. It exposes a RESTful public API and stores some persistent data in an infrastructure database (see Figure 4-1).

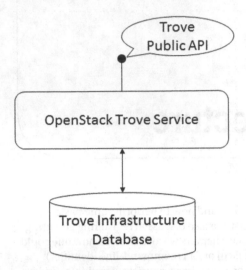

Figure 4-1. *A high-level representation of the OpenStack Trove service*

All clients of Trove, including the CLI and the Horizon dashboard, interact with Trove via this public API. The infrastructure database can be shared with the other OpenStack services, or it could be a dedicated database. For security reasons, and as a matter of service isolation, however, it is strongly advised that production deployments of Trove have a dedicated infrastructure database, not shared with other services.

Typically this database is MySQL (or some variant thereof), but in theory it could be any database supported by SQLAlchemy. MySQL is the most commonly used back end for the infrastructure database, and is also the most widely tested. It is strongly advised that you use MySQL for this purpose. If you want to use some other database as the back end, you may need to take some additional steps specific to that database.

Trove is a client of other OpenStack services like Nova (for compute), Cinder (for block storage) and Swift (for object storage), Keystone (for identity management), and so on. In each instance where Trove interacts with one of these other services, it does so by making requests on their respective public APIs as shown in Figure 4-2.

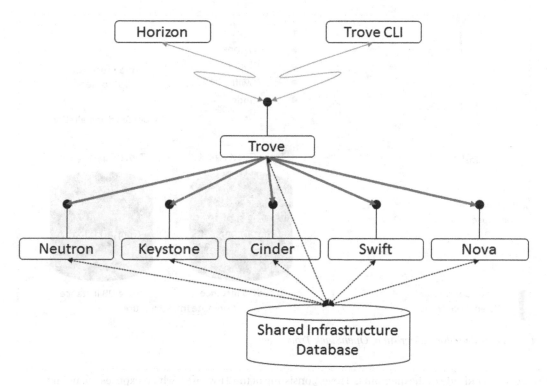

Figure 4-2. *The OpenStack Trove service in the context of other OpenStack services*

OpenStack Trove consists of three services: the Trove API, the Trove conductor, and the Trove task manager. In addition, each Trove instance has a guest agent that is specific to the datastore on that instance.

The block diagram in Figure 4-3 represents the Trove services and the OpenStack services with which they interact.

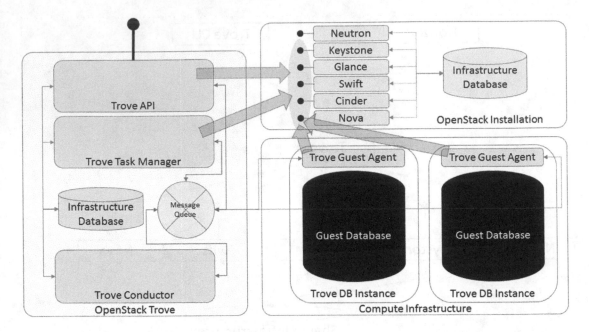

Figure 4-3. *A detailed block diagram of OpenStack Trove*

On the left-hand side of the diagram is Trove, consisting of the Trove API, which exposes the public Trove API, the Trove task manager, and the Trove conductor. The Trove services store persistent data in an infrastructure database.

On the upper-right-hand side of the diagram is the OpenStack installation including the basic services and an infrastructure database for these services. Below this is the compute infrastructure including servers and storage on which Nova, Cinder, Swift, and Neutron provision compute, storage, and networking resources.

The Trove API and Trove task manager are both clients of the various OpenStack services and as depicted they interact with these services on their respective public APIs.

When Nova spawns a compute instance, it does this on the compute infrastructure (lower right of Figure 4-3). A Trove instance is a special case of a Nova instance, which contains a guest database and a Trove guest agent.

The Trove guest agent performs actions on the Trove guest instance on behalf of the Trove services and communicates with the Trove services over a message queue (shown in Figure 4-3 as part of OpenStack Trove on the left of the picture).

The rest of this chapter covers the Trove services in more detail and explains how they work together with the Trove guest agent to enable the DBaaS (Database as a Service) functionality within OpenStack.

Trove Concepts

In this section we look at some basic Trove concepts, including

- a high-level description of the Trove services

- the Trove guest agent internal Remote Procedure Call (RPC) "API"

- Trove strategies that provide a framework for extending Trove

- a classification model for guest agents and strategies
- the Trove guest image
- the Trove message queue
- the Trove infrastructure database abstraction
- the Trove public API

The Trove Services

We now examine the three Trove services and the Trove guest agent at a high level and describe their roles and purpose. In later sections we will examine these services in more detail.

The Trove API Service

Like all OpenStack services, Trove exposes a standard contract with which clients can interact with the service. It provides this as a RESTful API, just like the other OpenStack services.

The Trove API implements a WSGI (Web Server Gateway Interface) and interacts with all clients wishing to interact with Trove. When the Trove API receives a request, it authenticates the requester using one of the configured authentication mechanisms (default is the Keystone service) and if the requester is authenticated, the credentials are associated with the request. These are the requester's *context* and will be used throughout the processing. Some simple requests are processed completely by the Trove API. Other requests may require the involvement of other services.

The Trove API runs on the Trove controller node.

The Trove Manager Service

The task manager performs the majority of the complex operations in Trove.

It listens on the message queue for a specific topic and behaves like an RPC server. Requesters post messages to the task manager and the task manager executes these requests by invoking the appropriate routines in the *context* of the requester. The task manager handles operations involving instance creation; deletion; interactions with other services like Nova, Cinder, and Swift; and more complex Trove operations like replication and clustering, and the management of an instance throughout its life cycle. The Trove task manager entry point is defined by the `taskmanager_manager` entry in the configuration file `trove-taskmanager.conf`. There is only one implementation in the Trove code base and this configuration entry provided for extensibility.

```
ubuntu@trove-book-vm:/etc/trove$ grep taskmanager_manager trove-taskmanager.conf
taskmanager_manager = trove.taskmanager.manager.Manager
```

■ **Note** There is no default value for the Trove `taskmanager_manager` setting in the code and this setting must be provided in `trove-taskmanager.conf`. `devstack` automatically configures a value and it is almost invariably `trove.taskmanager.manager.Manager`.

The Trove task manager runs on the Trove controller node.

The Trove Conductor Service

The primary purpose of the Trove conductor is to receive and handle various types of status updates from the guest agent. These status updates are handled in some cases by updating the Trove Infrastructure database or by providing information to other services.

It listens on the message queue for a specific topic and behaves like an RPC server. Guest agents post messages to the conductor and the conductor executes these requests by invoking the appropriate routines. The conductor handles such messages as guest agent heartbeats and backup status. The conductor_manager entry in the configuration file trove-conductor.conf defines the Trove conductor entry point. If one is not specified, the default value of trove.conductor.manager.Manager is used. As with the Trove task manager, there is only one implementation in the Trove code base and this configuration entry provided for extensibility.

The Trove conductor runs on the Trove controller node.

The Trove Guest Agent Service

Trove aims to provide a database-agnostic set of capabilities and a framework within which these can be implemented and extended.

The framework that Trove establishes relies on a guest agent to provide database-specific capabilities that are implemented by code on the guest instance and invoked by the task manager when required. The primary purpose of the Trove guest agent is to act as an RPC server enabling the other Trove services to execute operations on the Trove guest instance. It listens on the message queue for a specific topic and locally executes code within to carry out database-specific tasks. The Trove task manager posts messages to the guest agent and the guest agent executes these requests by invoking the appropriate routines. The guest agent handles all operations on the guest like prepare() (which is invoked during the initial setup of the guest), restart(), and other control operations. It also handles operations to create and manage users and databases, to initiate backups, and so on.

The Trove guest agent entry point is defined based on the datastore_manager configuration parameter that is set by the task manager during instance creation.

```
ubuntu@m2:~$ more /etc/trove/conf.d/guest_info.conf
[DEFAULT]
guest_id=41037bd2-9a91-4d5c-b291-612ad833a6d5
datastore_manager=mysql
tenant_id=cde807e8ca304a7fb04691928edea019
```

And in the guest agent we find the following mapping that identifies the manager for each specific datastore:

```
defaults = {
    'mysql':      'trove.guestagent.datastore.mysql.manager.Manager',
    'percona':    'trove.guestagent.datastore.mysql.manager.Manager',
    'redis':      'trove.guestagent.datastore.experimental.redis.manager.Manager',
    'cassandra':  'trove.guestagent.datastore.experimental.cassandra.manager.Manager',
    'couchbase':  'trove.guestagent.datastore.experimental.couchbase.manager.Manager',
    'mongodb':    'trove.guestagent.datastore.experimental.mongodb.manager.Manager',
    'postgresql': 'trove.guestagent.datastore.experimental.postgresql.manager.Manager',
    'vertica':    'trove.guestagent.datastore.experimental.vertica.manager.Manager',
    'db2':        'trove.guestagent.datastore.experimental.db2.manager.Manager',
}
```

The Trove guest agent runs on the Trove guest instance.

The Trove Guest Agent API

The Trove task manager causes the Trove guest agent to execute specific operations. However, the intent is that the Trove task manager be (as far as possible) database agnostic, and the Trove guest agent be the implementation of the database-specific code.

In that regard, the Trove guest agent can be viewed as the implementation of an API that is invoked by the task manager. This is an internal API, entirely within Trove. It is not a RESTful API but rather implemented by having the guest agent act as an RPC server for the task manager.

The guest agent manager for MySQL is implemented in trove.guestagent.datastore.mysql. manager.Manager (as shown in the mapping earlier). It provides methods like, for example, prepare(), change_password(), list_users(), stop_db(), get_replication_snapshot(), and so on. In a similar way, the MongoDB implementation also provides implementations for these methods, but in some cases the implementation may merely be to indicate that the operation is not supported.

Following is the implementation of the delete_user() method in trove.guestagent.datastore. mysql.manager.Manager:

```
def delete_user(self, context, user):
    MySqlAdmin().delete_user(user)
```

And following is the implementation of the delete_user() method in trove.guestagent.datastore. experimental.mongodb.manager.Manager:

```
def delete_user(self, context, user):
    LOG.debug("Deleting user.")
    raise exception.DatastoreOperationNotSupported(
        operation='delete_user', datastore=MANAGER)
```

As described previously, the guest agent is a RPC server that acts on behalf of the task manager. When the task manager makes a guest agent API call, it does this by posting a message to the guest agent on the message queue with the name of the method to be invoked on the guest agent, and the RPC dispatcher invokes this method.

Trove Strategies

Trove aims to provide a database-agnostic set of capabilities, and a framework within which these can be implemented and extended.

Strategies are a design construct within Trove that allows developers to extend Trove by supporting new implementations of specified abstractions that Trove has established as part of the overall framework.

It is reasonable to assume that all databases provide some mechanism to back up the data that they store. This is, broadly speaking, true of all databases. MySQL, PostgreSQL, and other relational databases support this operation, and MongoDB, Cassandra, Couchbase, and many other NoSQL databases support the operation as well. However, each of them has a different method by which to actually generate a backup, and in some cases a single database may have more than one way in which to generate a backup.

Figure 4-4 illustrates these various concepts. A client makes a request to Trove via the Trove API. The Trove API service messages the task manager, which in turn messages the guest agent.

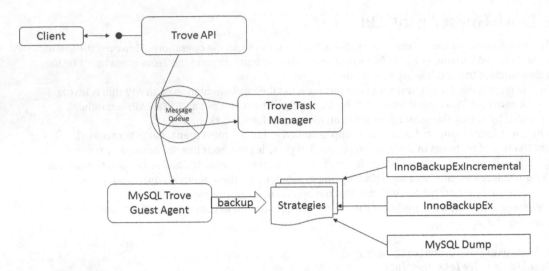

Figure 4-4. *Illustration of the flow of messages from the client through to a backup strategy on the guest agent*

In some cases, there is only one implementation for a given action, but in others there may be many alternative implementations. The mechanism of strategies allows developers to extend Trove and to add new implementations.

For example, there are currently three implementations of the backup strategy for MySQL: MySQLDump, InnoBackupEx, and InnoBackupExIncremental.

When you initiate a backup, you invoke the currently configured strategy. Initially, there were two strategies, MySQLDump and InnoBackupEx. Later, when Trove added InnoBackupExIncremental, reconfiguring the backup strategy meant that you could immediately use the new implementation.

There are currently strategies for backup, replication, storage, and clustering. Strategies are defined as configuration options. We describe the concept with the definition of the backup strategies.

```
435     cfg.StrOpt('backup_strategy', default='InnoBackupEx',
436             help='Default strategy to perform backups.',
437             deprecated_name='backup_strategy',
438             deprecated_group='DEFAULT'),

455     cfg.StrOpt('backup_namespace',
456             default='trove.guestagent.strategies.backup.mysql_impl',
457             help='Namespace to load backup strategies from.',
458             deprecated_name='backup_namespace',
459             deprecated_group='DEFAULT'),

469     cfg.DictOpt('backup_incremental_strategy',
470              default={'InnoBackupEx': 'InnoBackupExIncremental'},
471              help='Incremental Backup Runner based on the default '
472              'strategy. For strategies that do not implement an '
473              'incremental backup, the runner will use the default full '
474              'backup.',
475              deprecated_name='backup_incremental_strategy',
476              deprecated_group='DEFAULT'),
```

The preceding configuration options (from `trove/common/cfg.py`) define the backup strategy and namespace for the MySQL datastore to be InnoBackupEx, which is located in `trove.guestagent. strategies.backup.mysql_impl`.

Correspondingly, in `trove/guestagent/strategies/backup/mysql_impl.py` you find the class InnoBackupEx.

```
46   class InnoBackupEx(base.BackupRunner):
47       """Implementation of Backup Strategy for InnoBackupEx."""
48       __strategy_name__ = 'innobackupex'
```

The configuration option `backup_strategy` defines the name of the class and the `backup_namespace` defines the object within which to find the implementation. If you do not implement a backup strategy, it is initialized to None as shown in the following code for MongoDB:

```
690      cfg.StrOpt('backup_strategy', default=None,
691              help='Default strategy to perform backups.',
692              deprecated_name='backup_strategy',
693              deprecated_group='DEFAULT'),

730      cfg.StrOpt('backup_namespace', default=None,
731              help='Namespace to load backup strategies from.',
732              deprecated_name='backup_namespace',
733              deprecated_group='DEFAULT'),
```

Strategies are also used to extend Trove and implement replication and clustering. In the OpenStack Kilo release, Trove supports replication for MySQL and clustering for MongoDB.

The default in the Kilo release is to enable GTID-based replication. Since GTID (global transaction identifier) support was only introduced in MySQL version 5.6, take particular care about this if you are using MySQL version 5.5. For more details, refer to the section "Replication in Trove" in Chapter 5.

You define your replication strategy by setting the `replication_strategy` and `replication_namespace` options in the `trove-guestagent.conf` file. These options are located in the `[mysql]` section of the file.

```
439      cfg.StrOpt('replication_strategy', default='MysqlGTIDReplication',
440              help='Default strategy for replication.'),
441      cfg.StrOpt('replication_namespace',
442                  default='trove.guestagent.strategies.replication.mysql_gtid',
443                  help='Namespace to load replication strategies from.'),
```

In a system with MySQL version 5.5 you would have to override this with settings like the ones that follow, placed in the `trove-guestagent.conf` file:

```
[mysql]

# Override the default configuration for mysql replication
replication_strategy = MysqlBinlogReplication
replication_namespace = trove.guestagent.strategies.replication.mysql_binlog
```

The `binlog` module provides `binlog` replication, whereas the GTID module provides GTID-based replication.

Strategies are used to implement clustering by extending the guest agent, the API, and the task manager. The settings that follow show the extensions to the API, the task manager, and the guest agent for MongoDB:

```
716     cfg.StrOpt('api_strategy',
717             default='trove.common.strategies.cluster.experimental.'
718             'mongodb.api.MongoDbAPIStrategy',
719             help='Class that implements datastore-specific API logic.'),
720     cfg.StrOpt('taskmanager_strategy',
721             default='trove.common.strategies.cluster.experimental.mongodb.'
722             'taskmanager.MongoDbTaskManagerStrategy',
723             help='Class that implements datastore-specific task manager '
724                 'logic.'),
725     cfg.StrOpt('guestagent_strategy',
726             default='trove.common.strategies.cluster.experimental.'
727             'mongodb.guestagent.MongoDbGuestAgentStrategy',
728             help='Class that implements datastore-specific Guest Agent API '
729                 'logic.'),
```

In a similar way, the implementation for Vertica clustering added these configuration settings. They define the strategies that are used to implement the Vertica specific code for clustering.

```
862     cfg.StrOpt('api_strategy',
863             default='trove.common.strategies.cluster.experimental.vertica.'
864                     'api.VerticaAPIStrategy',
865             help='Class that implements datastore-specific API logic.'),
866     cfg.StrOpt('taskmanager_strategy',
867             default='trove.common.strategies.cluster.experimental.vertica.'
868                     'taskmanager.VerticaTaskManagerStrategy',
869             help='Class that implements datastore-specific task manager '
870                 'logic.'),
871     cfg.StrOpt('guestagent_strategy',
872             default='trove.common.strategies.cluster.experimental.vertica.'
873                     'guestagent.VerticaGuestAgentStrategy',
874             help='Class that implements datastore-specific Guest Agent API '
875                 'logic.'),
```

Trove Extensions

Trove also supports some database-specific operations (called *extensions*). These include commands like root-show, root-enable, database-list, database-create, database-delete, user-list, user-create, user-delete, user-grant-access, user-revoke-access, and user-show-access.

Trove uses Paste Deploy (http://pythonpaste.org/deploy/), and the configuration file api-paste.ini shown next defines the pipeline of operations to be performed by the API WSGI server when it receives a message.

```
 9  [pipeline:troveapi]
10  pipeline = faultwrapper osprofiler authtoken authorization contextwrapper ratelimit
        extensions troveapp

13  [filter:extensions]
14  paste.filter_factory = trove.common.extensions:factory
```

```
36  [app:troveapp]
37  paste.app_factory = trove.common.api:app_factory
```

The pipeline established here provides a list of handlers that the Trove API service will invoke to process a request. You can find the `extension` commands in the `extensions` module. Implementation for commands like `list` and `create` that we have used earlier are in the `troveapp` module.

The definition of each filter, and finally the app (`troveapp`), provides the name of the module where you can find the implementation. It shows (line 36) that you can find `troveapp` in `trove.common.api`. Similarly, the `extensions` filter (see line 13) is in `trove.common.extensions`.

You can find the extension for the `database-list` command in `trove.extensions.routes.mysql` and this defines the `SchemaController` to be the handler for the `database-list` command.

When the WSGI server receives a command like `database-list`, it will invoke the handler in `trove/extensions/mysql/service.py`.

Classification Model for Guest Agents and Strategies

Prior to the Kilo release, Trove treated all guest agents and strategies equally and provided no indication of their relative maturity or applicability for general use.

The Kilo release implemented a classification model for guest agents and strategies (`https://review.openstack.org/#/c/154119/`). Accordingly, guest agents are now classified as "stable," "technical-preview," or "experimental," and strategies are either "stable" or "experimental."

The following definitions and criteria were established as part of this classification mechanism (see `http://git.openstack.org/cgit/openstack/trove-specs/tree/specs/kilo/experimental-datastores.rst`).

Experimental

A datastore will be considered for merging in the experimental stage if it includes the following items:

- implementation of a basic subset of the Trove API including create and delete

- elements in the `trove-integration` project that will allow a user to create a guest image

- a definition of supported operating systems

- basic unit tests that will verify the operation of the guest agent and a test suite that is nonvoting

Note that it is not required that the datastore implement all features (resize, backup, replication, clustering, etc.) to meet this classification.

A strategy will be considered experimental if it provides an implementation and includes basic unit tests to verify operation of the strategy. A passing and nonvoting test suite should also be provided.

Technical Preview

A datastore will be considered for "technical preview" if it meets the requirements of "experimental" and provides APIs required to implement the capabilities of the datastore as defined in the datastore compatibility matrix at `https://wiki.openstack.org/wiki/Trove/DatastoreCompatibilityMatrix`:

- Launch

- Reboot

- Terminate

- Resize

- Backup

- Restore

- Replication and clustering if they are relevant to the datastore

You can find the preceding list of capabilities at `https://wiki.openstack.org/wiki/Trove/DatastoreCompatibilityMatrix`.

The "technical preview" datastore must also provide nonvoting gate tests for all capabilities and a mechanism to build a guest image that will allow a user to exercise these capabilities.

Stable

A datastore will be considered "stable" if it meets the requirements of "technical-preview" and also has stable voting tests as part of the gate.

A strategy will be considered "stable" if it meets the requirements of "experimental" and also has stable voting tests as part of the gate.

Implementation of the Classification Model

The classification model is implemented by placing components that are not stable in a directory named experimental or technical-preview.

For example, the following list shows currently supported guest agents:

- mysql: `trove.guestagent.datastore.mysql.manager.Manager`

- percona: `trove.guestagent.datastore.mysql.manager.Manager`

- redis: `trove.guestagent.datastore.experimental.redis.manager.Manager`

- cassandra: `trove.guestagent.datastore.experimental.cassandra.manager.Manager`

- couchbase: `trove.guestagent.datastore.experimental.couchbase.manager.Manager`

- mongodb: `trove.guestagent.datastore.experimental.mongodb.manager.Manager`

- postgresql: `trove.guestagent.datastore.experimental.postgresql.manager.Manager`

- vertica: `trove.guestagent.datastore.experimental.vertica.manager.Manager`

- db2: `trove.guestagent.datastore.experimental.db2.manager.Manager`

This mechanism makes the classification of a guest agent (and similarly for strategies) apparent from the qualified name of the implementation.

The Trove Guest Image

When a client requests a new Trove instance, Trove provisions an instance through Nova and asks Nova to boot that instance with a specified Glance image.

This Glance image contains an operating system, the database specified by the client, and the guest agent for that specific database.

Once launched, it is important that the guest agent be started, establish connectivity to the message queue, and begin to process the commands sent to it by the task manager.

The Trove 'create' request identifies the database to be launched by specifying the various attributes of the datastore property as shown.

```
"datastore": {
    "type": "object",
    "additionalProperties": True,
    "properties": {
        "type": non_empty_string,
        "version": non_empty_string
    }
}
```

The trove create command produces the following API call:

```
ubuntu@trove-book-vm:$ trove create m3 2 --size 1 --datastore mysql --datastore_version 5.5
+-------------------+--------------------------------------+
| Property          | Value                                |
+-------------------+--------------------------------------+
| created           | 2015-03-24T22:28:47                  |
| datastore         | mysql                                |
| datastore_version | 5.5                                  |
| flavor            | 2                                    |
| id                | 6e7ef470-ca4f-4bfd-9b67-7482991f3b96 |
| name              | m3                                   |
| status            | BUILD                                |
| updated           | 2015-03-24T22:28:47                  |
| volume            | 1                                    |
+-------------------+--------------------------------------+
```

```
{
    "instance": {
        "volume": {
            "size": 1
        },
        "flavorRef": "2",
        "name": "m3",
        "datastore": {
            "version": "5.5",
            "type": "mysql"
        }
    }
}
```

If a datastore is not specified, the default datastore is used (for details on how to set the default datastore see Chapter 3). If a version is not specified, Trove uses the default version for the datastore. With the datastore and the version identified, Trove can translate that into a Glance image ID and provide that to Nova.

In later chapters we describe how to build guest images for Trove.

The Trove Message Queue and the Trove Internal API

The Trove message queue is the transport mechanism used for communication among the Trove services. In the Kilo release, Trove was changed to use oslo.messaging as the underlying messaging system. The Trove task manager, conductor, and guest agent are RPC servers and communication is over the Trove message queue.

Each of these servers also exposes an API, and clients wishing to post a message to each of these servers use this API. We look closer at this API mechanism now.

■ **Note**   The APIs described here are Trove's internal APIs that use the message queue as a transport, not the Trove public API, which is Trove's public RESTful API.

Consider the Trove conductor, which exposes an API in the form of the implementation at trove.conductor.api.API.

A slightly edited listing of this entire API follows. We've retained the line numbers, so you can easily see where code has been removed from these listings.

```
26  class API(object):
27      """API for interacting with trove conductor."""
28
29      def __init__(self, context):

32
33          target = messaging.Target(topic=CONF.conductor_queue,
34                                    version=rpc_version.RPC_API_VERSION)
35

38          self.client = self.get_client(target, self.version_cap)
39
40      def get_client(self, target, version_cap, serializer=None):
41          return rpc.get_client(target,
42                                version_cap=version_cap,
43                                serializer=serializer)
44
45      def heartbeat(self, instance_id, payload, sent=None):

48
49          cctxt = self.client.prepare(version=self.version_cap)
50          cctxt.cast(self.context, "heartbeat",
51                     instance_id=instance_id,
52                     sent=sent,
53                     payload=payload)
54
```

```
55      def update_backup(self, instance_id, backup_id, sent=None,
56                          **backup_fields):

59
60          cctxt = self.client.prepare(version=self.version_cap)
61          cctxt.cast(self.context, "update_backup",
62                      instance_id=instance_id,
63                      backup_id=backup_id,
64                      sent=sent,
65                      **backup_fields)
66
67      def report_root(self, instance_id, user):

70          cctxt = self.client.prepare(version=self.version_cap)
71          cctxt.cast(self.context, "report_root",
72                      instance_id=instance_id,
73                      user=user)
```

This is the API exposed by the Trove conductor. The guest agent, which is the *only* component that invokes this API currently, can issue the heartbeat(), update_backup(), and report_root() calls. The cast() mechanism performs the actual RPC and causes the specified method to be executed in the context of the server with the appropriate parameters. Note that cast() shown here is an asynchronous method while a similar call() is available that will synchronously execute the RPC call and return.

The task manager and the guest agent expose similar APIs and these can be found in trove. guestagent.api.API and trove.taskmanager.api.API, respectively.

A simple example of this API mechanism over the message queue is shown next. We demonstrate the regular heartbeat sent by a guest to the controller. On the guest we have the following code (trove/guestagent/datastore/service.py):

```
105     def set_status(self, status):
106         """Use conductor to update the DB app status."""

111         heartbeat = {
112             'service:status': status.description,
113         }
114         conductor_api.API(ctxt).heartbeat(CONF.guest_id,
115                                             heartbeat,
116                                             sent=timeutils.float_utcnow())

120     def update(self):
121         """Find and report status of DB on this machine.
122         The database is updated and the status is also returned.
123         """
124         if self.is_installed and not self._is_restarting:
125             LOG.debug("Determining status of DB server.")
126             status = self._get_actual_db_status()
127             self.set_status(status)
128         else:
129             LOG.info(_("DB server is not installed or is in restart mode, so "
130                        "for now we'll skip determining the status of DB on "
131                        "this instance."))
```

The heartbeat being invoked here is the heartbeat() method in the Trove conductor API, shown earlier. It merely invokes cast() to get the message across the queue.

On the Trove conductor (which is running on the Trove controller node), the heartbeat() method is implemented as shown (see trove/conductor/manager.py).

```
24  from trove.instance import models as t_models


84      def heartbeat(self, context, instance_id, payload, sent=None):
85          LOG.debug("Instance ID: %s" % str(instance_id))
86          LOG.debug("Payload: %s" % str(payload))
87          status = t_models.InstanceServiceStatus.find_by(
88              instance_id=instance_id)
89          if self._message_too_old(instance_id, 'heartbeat', sent):
90              return
91          if payload.get('service:status') is not None:
92              status.set_status(ServiceStatus.from_description(
93                  payload['service:status']))
94          status.save()
```

Next we see the implementation in the instance model (t_models) from trove/instance/models.py.

```
1153  class InstanceServiceStatus(dbmodels.DatabaseModelBase):
1154      _data_fields = ['instance_id', 'status_id', 'status_description',
1155                      'updated_at']

1179      def set_status(self, value):
1180          """
1181          Sets the status of the hosted service
1182          :param value: current state of the hosted service
1183          :type value: trove.common.instance.ServiceStatus
1184          """
1185          self.status_id = value.code
1186          self.status_description = value.description
1187
1188      def save(self):
1189          self['updated_at'] = utils.utcnow()
1190          return get_db_api().save(self)
1191
1192      status = property(get_status, set_status)
1193
```

The call to save() causes the Trove infrastructure database to be updated with the latest information from the payload of the heartbeat.

Each of the interactions among the Trove services follows this same pattern. The three RPC services expose their respective APIs and operate RPC servers on the message queue listening for specific topics.

Clients use the API that they expose to cast() a message onto the queue and the RPC server receives and executes the message. There is also support for a synchronous call() method, which will allow the requestor to block and receive a response to the RPC.

At various places in the preceding discussion we have mentioned the Trove infrastructure database. Next, we turn our attention to this database and how it is used.

The Trove Infrastructure Database

The Trove infrastructure database is set up during the installation of Trove. Trove interacts with this database through the `trove.db` abstraction.

In the earlier example of the `heartbeat()` message, the implementation in the Trove conductor caused the heartbeat to be stored into the infrastructure database with the following (from `trove/instance/models.py`).

```
33   from trove.db import get_db_api
```

```
1188      def save(self):
1189          self['updated_at'] = utils.utcnow()
1190          return get_db_api().save(self)
```

In this case, the method `save()` in `get_db_api()` is part of the `trove.db` abstraction for the Trove infrastructure database.

The `__init__.py` for trove.db provides the linkage to the Trove infrastructure database abstraction.

```
21   CONF = cfg.CONF
22
23   db_api_opt = CONF.db_api_implementation
24
25
26   def get_db_api():
27       return utils.import_module(db_api_opt)
28
```

The default value of the configuration `db_api_implementation` is `trove.db.sqlalchemy.api` as shown next.

```
ubuntu@trove-book-vm:/opt/stack/trove/trove/common$ grep -n db_api_implementation -A 1 cfg.
py
97:    cfg.StrOpt('db_api_implementation', default='trove.db.sqlalchemy.api',
98-            help='API Implementation for Trove database access.'),
```

The Trove infrastructure database abstraction is based on SQLAlchemy (`www.sqlalchemy.org/`) and accordingly the database schema itself is defined in the form of a SQLAlchemy migration repo.

At the time of this writing, the current version of the Trove infrastructure database is 35. You can see the base schema (which is version 1) and the 35 versions that come after it in `/opt/stack/trove/trove/db/sqlalchemy/migrate_repo/versions`.

SQLAlchemy will establish an infrastructure database at the location pointed to by the connection string in the Trove configuration setting `connection` in the `database` section as shown next in `db/sqlalchemy/session.py`.

```
76   def _create_engine(options):
77       engine_args = {
78           "pool_recycle": CONF.database.idle_timeout,
79           "echo": CONF.database.query_log
80       }
81       LOG.info(_("Creating SQLAlchemy engine with args: %s") % engine_args)
82       db_engine = create_engine(options['database']['connection'], **engine_args)
```

```
83        if CONF.profiler.enabled and CONF.profiler.trace:sqlalchemy:
84            osprofiler.sqlalchemy.add_tracing(sqlalchemy, db_engine, "db")
85        return db_engine
```

While the default value for connection is to use a SQLite database,

```
402-database_opts = [
403:    cfg.StrOpt('connection',
404-                default='sqlite:///trove_test.sqlite',
405-                help='SQL Connection.',
406-                secret=True,
407:                deprecated_name='sql_connection',
408-                deprecated_group='DEFAULT'),
409-    cfg.IntOpt('idle_timeout',
410-                default=3600,
```

this is rarely sufficient for a Trove installation of any size. In our sample Trove installation using devstack, we see that connection is set as in /etc/trove.conf.

```
19  [database]
20  connection = mysql://root:07f1bff15e1cd3907c0f@127.0.0.1/trove?charset=utf8
```

According to this setting, all data relating to Trove in the infrastructure database is stored in a database called trove on a MySQL server running on the host 127.0.0.1 (localhost) and access to this uses the root user with a password of 07f1bff15e1cd3907c0f. The password, as you will recall, came from the setting in the localrc file that was used to drive the devstack installation in Chapter 2.

The Trove Public API

We conclude the section on Trove concepts by describing the Trove public API and the Trove API service. Note that unlike the other services, which are all RPC servers, the Trove API service implements a WSGI server.

The API class defined in trove/common/api.py implements the Trove public API.

```
28
29  class API(wsgi.Router):
30      """Defines the API routes."""
```

The public API of Trove is a RESTful API. Clients interact with Trove by issuing requests to specific URIs. Appendix C describes the complete public API; in this section we describe how the public API and the Trove API service work.

We use these three routes in the instance router to illustrate the working of the Trove public API (again from trove/common/api.py).

```
64      def _instance_router(self, mapper):
65          instance_resource = InstanceController().create_resource()
66          mapper.connect("/{tenant_id}/instances",
67                          controller=instance_resource,
68                          action="index",
69                          conditions={'method': ['GET']})
70          mapper.connect("/{tenant_id}/instances",
71                          controller=instance_resource,
```

```
72                              action="create",
73                              conditions={'method': ['POST']})
74          mapper.connect("/{tenant_id}/instances/{id}",
75                              controller=instance_resource,
76                              action="show",
77                              conditions={'method': ['GET']})
```

These three routes define the action to be taken when we invoke the specified APIs.

URI	Condition	Action
/{tenant_id}/instances	GET	index
/{tenant_id}/instances	POST	create
/{tenant_id}/instances/{id}	GET	show

The first two actions, index and create, are performed against the same URI; one of them is a GET and one of them is a POST. The show action is a GET against a URI that includes the id of the instance on which the operation is being invoked.

The preceding code (_instance_router()) defines a mapping for each URI by identifying the controller. The routes define the action as being handled by a controller called instance_resource. The code earlier initializes instance_resource to be an instance of the InstanceController class (see line 65).

The Trove API defines a GET on /{tenant_id}/instances/{id} to be a request to show details about a specific instance (identified by {id}).

In response to a GET on the /{tenant_id}/instances/{id} URI, the API will invoke the show() method defined by the InstanceController class. trove/instance/service.py defines the InstanceController class.

```
41   class InstanceController(wsgi.Controller):

159      def show(self, req, tenant_id, id):
160          """Return a single instance."""
161          LOG.info(_LI("Showing database instance '%(instance_id)s' for tenant "
162                       "'%(tenant_id)s'"),
163                   {'instance_id': id, 'tenant_id': tenant_id})
164          LOG.debug("req : '%s'\n\n", req)
165
166          context = req.environ[wsgi.CONTEXT_KEY]
167          server = models.load_instance_with_guest(models.DetailInstance,
168                                                    context, id)
169          return wsgi.Result(views.InstanceDetailView(server,
170                                                    req=req).data(), 200)
```

The show() method is provided the tenant_id and id parameters and the complete request from the user (req).

We invoke the trove show command on a known instance and show next the output from the command and the output logged by the Trove API service (in the log file /opt/stack/logs/tr-api.log).

```
ubuntu@trove-book-vm:~$ trove show 41037bd2-9a91-4d5c-b291-612ad833a6d5
+-------------------+-------------------------------------+
| Property          | Value                               |
+-------------------+-------------------------------------+
| created           | 2015-03-24T19:33:07                 |
| datastore         | mysql                               |
| datastore_version | 5.5                                 |
| flavor            | 2                                   |
| id                | 41037bd2-9a91-4d5c-b291-612ad833a6d5 |
| ip                | 172.24.4.4                          |
| name              | m2                                  |
| status            | ACTIVE                              |
| updated           | 2015-03-24T19:33:12                 |
| volume            | 2                                   |
| volume_used       | 0.17                                |
+-------------------+-------------------------------------+
```

The output from the log of the Trove API service (shown next) has been annotated. Following are sections of the error log, followed by short explanations.

```
2015-03-25 22:26:25.966 INFO eventlet.wsgi [-] (30165) accepted ('192.168.117.5', 41543)
```

```
[. . . authentication . . .]
```

```
2015-03-25 22:26:26.121 INFO trove.instance.service [-] Showing database instance '41037bd2-
9a91-4d5c-b291-612ad833a6d5' for tenant 'cde807e8ca304a7fb04691928edea019'
```

```
2015-03-25 22:26:26.121 DEBUG trove.instance.service [-] req : 'GET /v1.0/
cde807e8ca304a7fb04691928edea019/instances/41037bd2-9a91-4d5c-b291-612ad833a6d5 HTTP/1.0
[. . . rest of request deleted . . .]
 from (pid=30165) show /opt/stack/trove/trove/instance/service.py:164
```

At this point, the request has been authenticated and will now be processed. In order to produce the required output we need to get information about the instance. We invoke the method load_instance_with_guest() for this.

```
2015-03-25 22:26:27.760 DEBUG trove.instance.models [-] Instance 41037bd2-9a91-4d5c-b291-
612ad833a6d5 service status is running. from (pid=30165) load_instance_with_guest /opt/
stack/trove/trove/instance/models.py:482
```

The reason we use load_instance_with_guest() here is that one of the things that is sought to be shown in the output of the show command is the amount of disk space used on the guest. See the last line in the previous output, which shows 0.17.

In order to get volume information from the guest, the API service invokes the get_volume_info() API provided by the Trove guest agent. A synchronous call is made to the guest, which provides the required information. Next you see the interaction including the messages indicating the communication over AMQP (Advance Message Queuing Protocol).

```
2015-03-25 22:26:27.844 DEBUG trove.guestagent.api [-] Check Volume Info on instance
41037bd2-9a91-4d5c-b291-612ad833a6d5. from (pid=30165) get_volume_info /opt/stack/trove/
trove/guestagent/api.py:290
```

```
2015-03-25 22:26:27.845 DEBUG trove.guestagent.api [-] Calling get_filesystem_stats with
timeout 5 from (pid=30165) _call /opt/stack/trove/trove/guestagent/api.py:59
2015-03-25 22:26:27.847 DEBUG oslo_messaging._drivers.amqpdriver [-] MSG_ID is
2e414512490b48a9bdbd2ec942988ede from (pid=30165) _send /usr/local/lib/python2.7/dist-
packages/oslo_messaging/_drivers/amqpdriver.py:310
2015-03-25 22:26:27.849 DEBUG oslo_messaging._drivers.amqp [-] Pool creating new connection
from (pid=30165) create /usr/local/lib/python2.7/dist-packages/oslo_messaging/_drivers/amqp.
py:70
2015-03-25 22:26:27.854 INFO oslo_messaging._drivers.impl_rabbit [-] Connecting to AMQP
server on localhost:5672
2015-03-25 22:26:27.884 INFO oslo_messaging._drivers.impl_rabbit [-] Connected to AMQP
server on 127.0.0.1:5672
2015-03-25 22:26:27.909 DEBUG oslo_messaging._drivers.amqp [-] UNIQUE_ID is
eb16e7c436b148dc9a4008b5ccdc28d5. from (pid=30165) _add_unique_id /usr/local/lib/python2.7/
dist-packages/oslo_messaging/_drivers/amqp.py:226
```

And we have the following response from the guest agent:

```
2015-03-25 22:26:27.959 DEBUG trove.guestagent.api [-] Result is {u'total': 1.97, u'free':
1933627392, u'total_blocks': 516052, u'used': 0.17, u'free_blocks': 472077, u'block_size':
4096}. from (pid=30165) _call /opt/stack/trove/trove/guestagent/api.py:64
```

We assemble the rest of the instance information for the show command.

```
2015-03-25 22:26:27.966 DEBUG trove.instance.views [-] {'status': 'ACTIVE', 'name': u'm2',
'links': [{'href': u'https://192.168.117.5:8779/v1.0/cde807e8ca304a7fb04691928edea019/
instances/41037bd2-9a91-4d5c-b291-612ad833a6d5', 'rel': 'self'}, {'href': u'
https://192.168.117.5:8779/instances/41037bd2-9a91-4d5c-b291-612ad833a6d5',
'rel': 'bookmark'}], 'ip': [u'172.24.4.4'], 'id': u'41037bd2-9a91-4d5c-b291-
612ad833a6d5', 'volume': {'size': 2L}, 'flavor': {'id': '2', 'links': [{'href': u'htt
ps://192.168.117.5:8779/v1.0/cde807e8ca304a7fb04691928edea019/flavors/2', 'rel': 'self'},
{'href': 'https://192.168.117.5:8779/flavors/2', 'rel': 'bookmark'}]}, 'datastore':
{'version': u'5.5', 'type': u'mysql'}} from (pid=30165) data /opt/stack/trove/trove/
instance/views.py:55
```

And the following information gets sent back to the requester (in this case, the trove show client):

```
2015-03-25 22:26:27.971 INFO eventlet.wsgi [-] 192.168.117.5 - - [25/Mar/2015 22:26:27]
"GET /v1.0/cde807e8ca304a7fb04691928edea019/instances/41037bd2-9a91-4d5c-b291-612ad833a6d5
HTTP/1.1" 200 843 2.004077
```

Figure 4-5 represents the flow of the trove show command described previously. The trove show command issued by the client (at top left) translates into a GET request to the URI /v1.0/{tenant_id}/ instances/{id} against the Trove public API.

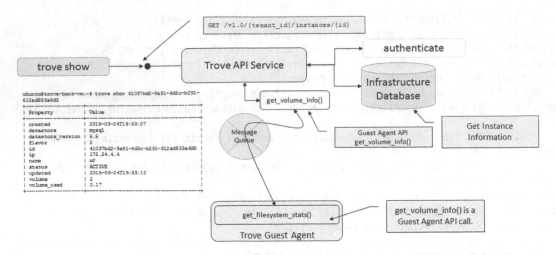

Figure 4-5. *The flow of the* trove show *command*

After authenticating the request (which is a whole ritual unto itself, involving API calls to Keystone, the retrieval of a service catalog, and the establishment of the users context), the Trove API service gets instance information from the infrastructure database and makes a synchronous call to the guest agent using the get_volume_info() API.

The get_volume_info() API exposed by the Trove guest agent translates into an RPC call to get_filesystem_stats() in the guest agent.

The Trove API service then computes the amount of free space and returns the information to the Trove client, which produces the output shown.

OpenStack Trove Architecture

With all of the preceding concepts as a background, we now begin to look at the Trove architecture as a whole, and understand how all the pieces fit together.

Using the example from the previous section, the trove show command, we will show how the command actually gets executed on the guest instance. We then explain how to implement more complex interactions with the system using the various concepts that have been described earlier. We discuss in more detail the instance, user, and database manipulation commands described in earlier chapters and set the stage for later chapters which will build further on these descriptions.

We begin by looking at the interactions during some simple invocations of the trove create command that we demonstrated in earlier chapters.

The trove create command (which is part of the python-troveclient repository) packages up all the command-line arguments provided by the user and issues a POST to the URI /v1.0/{tenant_id}/ instances/ as defined by the Trove public API.

```
ubuntu@trove-book-vm:/opt/stack/python-troveclient/troveclient$ cat -n v1/instances.py
    51      def create(self, name, flavor_id, volume=None, databases=None, users=None,
    52              restorePoint=None, availability_zone=None, datastore=None,
    53              datastore_version=None, nics=None, configuration=None,
    54              replica_of=None, slave_of=None, replica_count=None):
    55          """Create (boot) a new instance."""
    56
```

```
57              body = {"instance": {
58                  "name": name,
59                  "flavorRef": flavor_id
60              }}
61              datastore_obj = {}
62              if volume:
63                  body["instance"]["volume"] = volume
64              if databases:
65                  body["instance"]["databases"] = databases
66              if users:
67                  body["instance"]["users"] = users
68              if restorePoint:
69                  body["instance"]["restorePoint"] = restorePoint
70              if availability_zone:
71                  body["instance"]["availability_zone"] = availability_zone
72              if datastore:
73                  datastore_obj["type"] = datastore
74              if datastore_version:
75                  datastore_obj["version"] = datastore_version
76              if datastore_obj:
77                  body["instance"]["datastore"] = datastore_obj
78              if nics:
79                  body["instance"]["nics"] = nics
80              if configuration:
81                  body["instance"]["configuration"] = configuration
82              if replica_of or slave_of:
83                  body["instance"]["replica_of"] = base.getid(replica_of) or slave_of
84              if replica_count:
85                  body["instance"]["replica_count"] = replica_count
86
87              return self._create("/instances", body, "instance")
```

This request makes its way over to the Trove API service where a WSGI mapper defines the action to be taken in response to it.

```
ubuntu@trove-book-vm:/opt/stack/trove/trove/common$ cat -n api.py

64      def _instance_router(self, mapper):
65          instance_resource = InstanceController().create_resource()

70          mapper.connect("/{tenant_id}/instances",
71                          controller=instance_resource,
72                          action="create",
73                          conditions={'method': ['POST']})
```

The create request is passed along to the create() method in the controller (instance_resource) which is an instance of InstanceController.

```
ubuntu@trove-book-vm:/opt/stack/trove/trove/instance$ cat -n service.py

  185     def create(self, req, body, tenant_id):

  191         context = req.environ[wsgi.CONTEXT_KEY]

  228
  229         instance = models.Instance.create(context, name, flavor_id,
  230                                           image_id, databases, users,
  231                                           datastore, datastore_version,
  232                                           volume_size, backup_id,
  233                                           availability_zone, nics,
  234                                           configuration, slave_of_id)
  235
  236         view = views.InstanceDetailView(instance, req=req)
  237         return wsgi.Result(view.data(), 200)
  238
```

After unpacking and making sense of the arguments received in req and body, the information is passed along to the create() method in the model (at line 229).

The code in models.py (along with service.py) implement most of the functionality of the create() call. The code of the create() method is annotated as follows:

```
ubuntu@trove-book-vm:/opt/stack/trove/trove/instance$ cat -n models.py

  655     def create(cls, context, name, flavor_id, image_id, databases, users,
  656                 datastore, datastore_version, volume_size, backup_id,
  657                 availability_zone=None, nics=None, configuration_id=None,
  658                 slave_of_id=None, cluster_config=None):
  659
  660         datastore_cfg = CONF.get(datastore_version.manager)
```

Since the user specified a flavor, we check with Nova whether this flavor is a valid one or not.

```
  661         client = create_nova_client(context)
  662         try:
  663             flavor = client.flavors.get(flavor_id)
  664         except nova_exceptions.NotFound:
  665             raise exception.FlavorNotFound(uuid=flavor_id)
```

In later sections we describe the mechanism for launching an instance from an existing backup. When a user specifies a backup as a source for an instance, some validation is performed.

```
  684         if backup_id:
  685             backup_info = Backup.get_by_id(context, backup_id)
  686             if not backup_info.is_done_successfuly:
  687                 raise exception.BackupNotCompleteError(
  688                     backup_id=backup_id, state=backup_info.state)
  689
  690             if backup_info.size > target_size:
  691                 raise exception.BackupTooLarge(
```

```
692                         backup_size=backup_info.size, disk_size=target_size)
693
694             if not backup_info.check_swift_object_exist(
695                     context,
696                     verify_checksum=CONF.verify_swift_checksum_on_restore):
697                 raise exception.BackupFileNotFound(
698                     location=backup_info.location)
699
700             if (backup_info.datastore_version_id
701                     and backup_info.datastore.name != datastore.name):
702                 raise exception.BackupDatastoreMismatchError(
703                     datastore1=backup_info.datastore.name,
704                     datastore2=datastore.name)
705
```

In later sections we describe the mechanism for launching an instance as a replica of another instance. When a user attempts to launch a replica, some validation is performed.

```
706         if slave_of_id:
707             replication_support = datastore_cfg.replication_strategy
708             if not replication_support:
709                 raise exception.ReplicationNotSupported(
710                     datastore=datastore.name)
711             try:
712                 # looking for replica source
713                 replica_source = DBInstance.find_by(
714                     context,
715                     id=slave_of_id,
716                     deleted=False)
717                 if replica_source.slave_of_id:
718                     raise exception.Forbidden(
719                         _("Cannot create a replica of a replica %(id)s.")
720                         % {'id': slave_of_id})
721             except exception.ModelNotFoundError:
722                 LOG.exception(
723                     _("Cannot create a replica of %(id)s "
724                       "as that instance could not be found.")
725                     % {'id': slave_of_id})
726                 raise exception.NotFound(uuid=slave_of_id)
727
```

The _create_resource() method does much of the heavy lifting and is invoked in line 791.

```
734         def _create_resources():
735
```

The instance creation is recorded in the infrastructure database, and this instance is recorded in the InstanceTasks.BUILDING state.

```
742
743              db_info = DBInstance.create(name=name, flavor_id=flavor_id,
744                                    tenant_id=context.tenant,
745                                    volume_size=volume_size,
746                                    datastore_version_id=
747                                    datastore_version.id,
748                                    task_status=InstanceTasks.BUILDING,
749                                    configuration_id=configuration_id,
750                                    slave_of_id=slave_of_id,
751                                    cluster_id=cluster_id,
752                                    shard_id=shard_id,
753                                    type=instance_type)
```

If the user specified that a root password must be specified at launch, that password is generated here.

```
773              root_password = None
774              if cls.get_root_on_create(
775                      datastore_version.manager) and not backup_id:
776                  root_password = utils.generate_random_password()
777
```

At this point, the Trove API service makes a call to the Trove task manager to do the rest of the work. Notice the invocation task_api.API(context).create_instance(). It conveys to the task manager the context of the user requesting this instance and all the parameters that the client provided.

```
778              task_api.API(context).create_instance(db_info.id, name, flavor,
779                                          image_id, databases, users,
780                                          datastore_version.manager,
781                                          datastore_version.packages,
782                                          volume_size, backup_id,
783                                          availability_zone,
784                                          root_password, nics,
785                                          overrides, slave_of_id,
786                                          cluster_config)
```

When the create_instance() call here is completed, this _create_resources() call returns the instance, in this case to run_with_quotas() as shown.

```
788              return SimpleInstance(context, db_info, service:status,
789                                    root_password)

791          return run_with_quotas(context.tenant,
792                                  deltas,
793                                  _create_resources)
```

Since the Trove API made a request to the task manager, we pick up the processing with the task manager, starting at the API that was invoked.

```
ubuntu@trove-book-vm:/opt/stack/trove/trove/taskmanager$ cat -n api.py

135    def create_instance(self, instance_id, name, flavor,
136                            image_id, databases, users, datastore_manager,
137                            packages, volume_size, backup_id=None,
138                            availability_zone=None, root_password=None,
139                            nics=None, overrides=None, slave_of_id=None,
140                            cluster_config=None):
141
142        LOG.debug("Making async call to create instance %s " % instance_id)
143
144        cctxt = self.client.prepare(version=self.version_cap)
145        cctxt.cast(self.context, "create_instance",
146                    instance_id=instance_id, name=name,
147                    flavor=self._transform_obj(flavor),
148                    image_id=image_id,
149                    databases=databases,
150                    users=users,
151                    datastore_manager=datastore_manager,
152                    packages=packages,
153                    volume_size=volume_size,
154                    backup_id=backup_id,
155                    availability_zone=availability_zone,
156                    root_password=root_password,
157                    nics=nics,
158                    overrides=overrides,
159                    slave_of_id=slave_of_id,
160                    cluster_config=cluster_config)
```

The API merely takes all the information provided and makes an asynchronous cast() call to the task manager. Recall that a cast() is an asynchronous request and a call() is a synchronous request.

It specifies that the Trove task manager will take the additional information provided and execute the create_instance() method which is annotated starting at line 115.

```
ubuntu@trove-book-vm:/opt/stack/trove/trove/taskmanager$ cat -n manager.py

29  from trove.taskmanager.models import FreshInstanceTasks

93    def _create_replication_slave(self, context, instance_id, name, flavor,
94                            image_id, databases, users,
95                            datastore_manager, packages, volume_size,
96                            availability_zone,
97                            root_password, nics, overrides, slave_of_id):
98
99        instance_tasks = FreshInstanceTasks.load(context, instance_id)
100
101        snapshot = instance_tasks.get_replication_master_snapshot(context,
102                                                        slave_of_id)
103        try:
104            instance_tasks.create_instance(flavor, image_id, databases, users,
105                                            datastore_manager, packages,
```

```
106                                      volume_size,
107                                      snapshot['dataset']['snapshot_id'],
108                                      availability_zone, root_password,
109                                      nics, overrides, None)
110          finally:
111              Backup.delete(context, snapshot['dataset']['snapshot_id'])
112
113          instance_tasks.attach_replication_slave(snapshot, flavor)
114
115      def create_instance(self, context, instance_id, name, flavor,
116                          image_id, databases, users, datastore_manager,
117                          packages, volume_size, backup_id, availability_zone,
118                          root_password, nics, overrides, slave_of_id,
119                          cluster_config):
```

If the user is attempting to create a replica of an existing instance we invoke the _create_replication_ slave() method. This method just performs some setup and then invokes instance_tasks.create_ instance() (see preceding lines 93–113).

```
120          if slave_of_id:
121              self._create_replication_slave(context, instance_id, name,
122                                              flavor, image_id, databases, users,
123                                              datastore_manager, packages,
124                                              volume_size,
125                                              availability_zone, root_password,
126                                              nics, overrides, slave_of_id)
```

If the user is just creating a new instance, we invoke instance_tasks.create_instance() which is where we look next.

```
127          else:
128              instance_tasks = FreshInstanceTasks.load(context, instance_id)
129              instance_tasks.create_instance(flavor, image_id, databases, users,
130                                              datastore_manager, packages,
131                                              volume_size, backup_id,
132                                              availability_zone, root_password,
133                                              nics, overrides, cluster_config)
```

As shown by the import (at line 29), instance_tasks() is in trove.taskmanager.models. That code is annotated starting at line 246.

```
219  class FreshInstanceTasks(FreshInstance, NotifyMixin, ConfigurationMixin):
```

This _get_injected_files() is invoked from create_instance() at line 271. This method performs arguably the most crucial part of the processing in the create workflow. It generates the configuration files that will be then sent to the guest instance when it is launched and will provide the guest agent the information required to operate.

```
220      def _get_injected_files(self, datastore_manager):
```

The purpose of this method is to construct the files collection, and it contains two files, the guest_info file and the trove-guestagent.conf file. The contents of these two files are shown later in this section.

```
221            injected_config_location = CONF.get('injected_config_location')
222            guest_info = CONF.get('guest_info')
223

231
232            files = {guest_info_file: (
233                "[DEFAULT]\n"
234                "guest_id=%s\n"
235                "datastore_manager=%s\n"
236                "tenant_id=%s\n"
237                % (self.id, datastore_manager, self.tenant_id))}
238
239            if os.path.isfile(CONF.get('guest_config')):
240                with open(CONF.get('guest_config'), "r") as f:
241                    files[os.path.join(injected_config_location,
242                                "trove-guestagent.conf")] = f.read()
243
244            return files
245
```

This is create_instance() where the heavy lifting of instance creation gets done.

```
246        def create_instance(self, flavor, image_id, databases, users,
247                            datastore_manager, packages, volume_size,
248                            backup_id, availability_zone, root_password, nics,
249                            overrides, cluster_config):
250
251            LOG.info(_("Creating instance %s.") % self.id)
```

The first order of business is to get the files that must be sent over to the guest. The _get_injected_files() method (shown previously) does this.

```
271            files = self._get_injected_files(datastore_manager)
```

Depending on how the system is configured, you can invoke one of three methods to create a server and volume. These three are using heat, having Nova create the instance and volume, and creating the Nova instance and volume individually. Observe that in each case, the configuration files are passed along (destined for the Nova call).

```
273            if use_heat:
274                volume_info = self._create_server_volume_heat(
275                    flavor,

281                    files)
282            elif use_nova_server_volume:
283                volume_info = self._create_server_volume(
284                    flavor['id'],
```

```
291                    files)
292        else:
293            volume_info = self._create_server_volume_individually(
294                flavor['id'],

301                    files)
```

The call that follows to self._guest_prepare() is an extremely important operation that will be described later. This call eventually translates into a guest API call that invokes the method prepare() on the guest agent.

```
315            self._guest_prepare(flavor['ram'], volume_info,
316                                packages, databases, users, backup_info,
317                                config.config_contents, root_password,
318                                config_overrides.config_contents,
319                                cluster_config)
```

Next, we look at the mechanism for creating servers and volumes, using _create_server_volume(). The other two are similar. First, observe that the files described earlier are received as the last argument.

```
486    def _create_server_volume(self, flavor_id, image_id, security_groups,
487                                datastore_manager, volume_size,
488                                availability_zone, nics, files):
489        LOG.debug("Begin _create_server_volume for id: %s" % self.id)
490        try:
```

First, prepare user data (the user data used in the Nova call), using the following code:

```
491            userdata = self._prepare_userdata(datastore_manager)
```

Then call Nova (on its public API) to create an instance.

```
498            server = self.nova_client.servers.create(
499                name, image_id, flavor_id,
500                files=files, volume=volume_ref,
501                security_groups=security_groups,
502                availability_zone=availability_zone,
503                nics=nics, config_drive=config_drive,
504                userdata=userdata)
```

Following is _prepare_userdata() and its purpose is to generate the user data that must be passed to Nova.

```
740    def _prepare_userdata(self, datastore_manager):
741        userdata = None
742        cloudinit = os.path.join(CONF.get('cloudinit_location'),
743                                 "%s.cloudinit" % datastore_manager)
744        if os.path.isfile(cloudinit):
745            with open(cloudinit, "r") as f:
746                userdata = f.read()
747        return userdata
```

The configuration files rendered by _get_injected_files() make their way over to the guest agent. On a running guest, following is what those files contain:

```
ubuntu@m1:/etc/trove/conf.d$ cat guest_info.conf
[DEFAULT]
guest_id=fc7bf8f0-8333-4726-85c9-2d532e34da91
datastore_manager=mysql
tenant_id=cde807e8ca304a7fb04691928edea019

ubuntu@m1:/etc/trove/conf.d$ cat trove-guestagent.conf
[DEFAULT]
[. . .]
debug = True
log_file = trove-guestagent.log
log_dir = /var/log/trove/
ignore_users = os_admin
control_exchange = trove
trove_auth_url = http://192.168.117.5:35357/v2.0
nova_proxy_admin_pass =
nova_proxy_admin_tenant_name = trove
nova_proxy_admin_user = radmin
rabbit_password = 654a2b9115e9e02d6b8a
rabbit_host = 10.0.0.1
rabbit_userid = stackrabbit
```

Finally, look at the prepare() guest agent call. The API implementation is shown here.

```
ubuntu@trove-book-vm:/opt/stack/trove/trove/guestagent$ cat -n api.py

212    def prepare(self, memory_mb, packages, databases, users,
213                device:path='/dev/vdb', mount_point='/mnt/volume',
214                backup_info=None, config_contents=None, root_password=None,
215                overrides=None, cluster_config=None):
216        """Make an asynchronous call to prepare the guest
217          as a database container optionally includes a backup id for restores
218        """
219        LOG.debug("Sending the call to prepare the Guest.")
```

First initialize the interprocess communication (IPC) mechanism that will communicate with the guest.

```
225        self._create_guest_queue()
```

And then _cast() a prepare() call onto this queue. This prepare() call will be picked up by the guest agent on the guest instance once it gets launched and attaches to the message queue.

```
228        self._cast(
229            "prepare", self.version_cap, packages=packages,
230            databases=databases, memory_mb=memory_mb, users=users,
231            device:path=device:path, mount_point=mount_point,
232            backup_info=backup_info, config_contents=config_contents,
233            root_password=root_password, overrides=overrides,
234            cluster_config=cluster_config)
```

The prepare() method in the guest agent is itself found in each of the guest agent implementations. The right guest agent code will be launched on the guest and this call gets executed there. The goal of the prepare() method is to configure the guest instance based on the parameters provided to the create command. At the completion of the prepare() call, the guest database should be ready for use.

The Trove guest agent is launched and reads its configuration file (shown previously) and has sufficient information to bootstrap itself and connect to the message queue.

We take a look at the implementation in the MySQL guest agent.

```
ubuntu@trove-book-vm:/opt/stack/trove/trove/guestagent/datastore/mysql$ cat -n manager.py

111     def prepare(self, context, packages, databases, memory_mb, users,
112                     device:path=None, mount_point=None, backup_info=None,
113                     config_contents=None, root_password=None, overrides=None,
114                     cluster_config=None):
```

If any packages need to be installed, that list is sent down from the task manager, so the guest agent will do that first. As part of the description of the trove-manage command, Appendix B will provide more details about how to specify packages.

```
119         app.install_if_needed(packages)
```

Since a volume on which to store data may have been specified, Trove may have to reconfigure MySQL to use that. Prepare, mount, and use that location.

```
120         if device:path:
```

Stop the database first, as the preceding installation step would have left the database running.

```
121             #stop and do not update database
122             app.stop_db()
```

Prepare the new location, migrate the data-dir, and remount the file system.

```
123             device = volume.VolumeDevice(device:path)
124             # unmount if device is already mounted
125             device.unmount_device(device:path)
126             device.format()
127             if os.path.exists(mount_point):
128                 #rsync exiting data
129                 device.migrate_data(mount_point)
130             #mount the volume
131             device.mount(mount_point)
132             LOG.debug("Mounted the volume.")
```

Now restart the MySQL database instance.

```
133         app.start_mysql()
```

If the user specified databases or users, create them now.

```
152        if databases:
153            self.create_database(context, databases)
154
155        if users:
156            self.create_user(context, users)
```

And that's all there is to it; log a message in the guest agent log file and indicate that the database is set up and ready.

```
157
158        LOG.info(_('Completed setup of MySQL database instance.'))
159
```

The code to actually install and get the database to a running state is database specific and the prepare() implementation is therefore in the appropriate guest agent.

Earlier in this chapter we described the Trove conductor and illustrated how the guest agent invokes the conductor API using the heartbeat() method as the example.

Periodic tasks running on the guest agent invoke this heartbeat() method and as part of that payload include the status of the database. Once the prepare() call completes, the database is ready to be marked ACTIVE and in the next heartbeat message sent by the guest agent to the conductor, the payload reflects this. This causes the conductor to update the infrastructure database with the ACTIVE status.

Figure 4-6 shows the complete create() flow. The user (at the top left of the diagram) executes the trove create command. This results in an API call to the Trove public API in the form of a POST to the /v1.0/{tenant_id}/instances URI. The Trove API service implements the Trove public API and after authenticating the request, makes a call to Nova (on its public API) to verify the flavor. It then records the instance creation in the infrastructure database and invokes the task manager create_instance() API. This invocation is asynchronous. Finally the Trove API returns the information about the instance from the infrastructure database to the client.

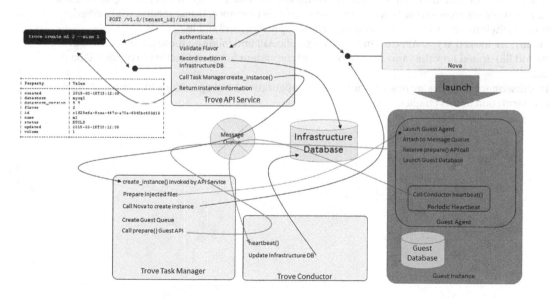

Figure 4-6. *The complete flow of a Trove create() call*

The Trove task manager receives the `create_instance()` call and prepares files for injection to the Trove guest instance. It then invokes Nova to launch a Trove guest instance with a specified image. Booting starts the Trove guest agent, which then reads the configuration files passed to it by the task manager. The task manager then creates the Trove guest queue and sends a `prepare()` message for the Trove guest to consume when it gets there.

The Trove guest agent gets launched when the guest instance boots and receives the injected configuration files. There it finds information about the message queue that it must connect to, and receives and processes the `prepare()` message sent to it by the task manager. When this completes, the guest database is up and running.

The periodic heartbeat from the guest agent invokes the `heartbeat()` method in the Trove conductor with a payload including the guest agent status. This causes the database status to be recorded in the infrastructure database.

Summary

This chapter provided a high-level introduction to the Trove architecture and a comprehensive look at some key Trove concepts before taking a very detailed look at how the various components of Trove fit together.

Trove is an OpenStack service like the other services; it exposes a public RESTful API and stores data in an infrastructure database. Internally Trove is a complex service consisting of three services (Trove API, Trove conductor, and Trove task manager) that run on the Trove controller node, and the Trove guest agent that runs on each Trove guest instance. Trove is also a client of other OpenStack services and interacts with them on their respective public APIs. Internally, each of the services exposes a private API.

The Trove services communicate among themselves over a message queue. The infrastructure database stores data about the present state of running Trove instances and other persistent information . This is typically a MySQL database.

Trove provides a mechanism for extensibility through strategies. Strategies are plug-ins that implement a specific aspect of the Trove abstraction. Strategies are classified according to their maturity in two types: experimental and stable.

Trove can be extended to support additional databases through the use of database-specific guest agents. Guest agents are a part of Trove that run on each guest instance. Guest agents are classified according to their maturity into experimental, technical-preview, and stable.

Finally, we looked at two API calls in the Trove public API and followed these requests through the system and illustrated how the various components of the system function together to provide DBaaS capability.

In subsequent chapters we describe advanced configurations and operations in Trove and build further on the information in this chapter.

CHAPTER 5

∎ ∎ ∎

Advanced Trove Operations

In previous chapters we demonstrated how to install and perform some basic configurations of Trove, as well as how to perform some basic operations with Trove. We have also looked in detail at the Trove architecture and how the various components of Trove work together.

This chapter builds on the earlier chapters and looks at more advanced Trove operations including

- Custom flavors
- Backup and restore
- Replication
- Clustering
- Configuration groups
- Instance resizing
- Terminating instances

Custom Flavors

When launching a Trove instance, you must specify a *flavor*. Flavors are a template for the virtual machine; they provide basic hardware configuration information such as amount of memory and disk space, number of virtual CPUs (vCPUs), and so on.

Nova creates default flavors during the installation process. These can be viewed using the trove flavor-list command. In addition, you can create a custom flavor to reflect a specific configuration that you would like to use. This is shown next. First, we look at the default flavors that Nova installs.

```
trovubuntu@trove-book:~$ nova flavor-list
+----+-----------+-----------+------+-----------+------+-------+-------------+-----------+
| ID | Name      | Memory_MB | Disk | Ephemeral | Swap | VCPUs | RXTX_Factor | Is_Public |
+----+-----------+-----------+------+-----------+------+-------+-------------+-----------+
| 1  | m1.tiny   | 512       | 1    | 0         |      | 1     | 1.0         | True      |
| 2  | m1.small  | 2048      | 20   | 0         |      | 1     | 1.0         | True      |
| 3  | m1.medium | 4096      | 40   | 0         |      | 2     | 1.0         | True      |
| 4  | m1.large  | 8192      | 80   | 0         |      | 4     | 1.0         | True      |
| 42 | m1.nano   | 64        | 0    | 0         |      | 1     | 1.0         | True      |
| 5  | m1.xlarge | 16384     | 160  | 0         |      | 8     | 1.0         | True      |
| 84 | m1.micro  | 128       | 0    | 0         |      | 1     | 1.0         | True      |
+----+-----------+-----------+------+-----------+------+-------+-------------+-----------+
```

Let's assume that you would like a new flavor that only uses 1 GB of memory. You can create your own flavor using the nova flavor-create command as shown next.

```
ubuntu@trove-book:~$ nova flavor-create m1.1gb 10 1024 20 1
+----+--------+-----------+------+-----------+------+-------+-------------+-----------+
| ID | Name   | Memory_MB | Disk | Ephemeral | Swap | VCPUs | RXTX_Factor | Is_Public |
+----+--------+-----------+------+-----------+------+-------+-------------+-----------+
| 10 | m1.1gb | 1024      | 20   | 0         |      | 1     | 1.0         | True      |
+----+--------+-----------+------+-----------+------+-------+-------------+-----------+
ubuntu@trove-book:~$ nova help flavor-create
usage: nova flavor-create [--ephemeral <ephemeral>] [--swap <swap>]
                          [--rxtx-factor <factor>] [--is-public <is-public>]
                          <name> <id> <ram> <disk> <vcpus>

Optional arguments:
  --ephemeral <ephemeral>  Ephemeral space size in GB (default 0)
  --swap <swap>            Swap space size in MB (default 0)
  --rxtx-factor <factor>   RX/TX factor (default 1)
  --is-public <is-public>  Make flavor accessible to the public (default true)
```

The foregoing command creates a new flavor with the name m1.1gb, with an ID of 10, 1 GB of memory, 20 GB of disk, and 1 virtual CPU. By default, flavors are accessible by all (--is-public defaults to true).

Backup and Restore in Trove

Trove implements a framework within which datastores can implement mechanisms to take a backup, and to launch new instances from the backup. This framework is based on the backup and restore strategies. For details about how strategies work, refer to the section "Trove Strategies" in Chapter 4. Trove itself does not perform the backup and restore. It relies on the strategies that implement database-specific commands that perform the backup and restore operations.

The settings in trove-guestagent.conf in the datastore-specific section (or the default values if they are not specified) of the configuration parameters backup_strategy, backup_namespace, restore_namespace, and backup_incremental_strategy control how backup and restore are handled. Shown next are the defaults for MySQL.

```
435    cfg.StrOpt('backup_strategy', default='InnoBackupEx',
436            help='Default strategy to perform backups.',

455    cfg.StrOpt('backup_namespace',
456            default='trove.guestagent.strategies.backup.mysql_impl',
457            help='Namespace to load backup strategies from.',

460    cfg.StrOpt('restore_namespace',
461            default='trove.guestagent.strategies.restore.mysql_impl',
462            help='Namespace to load restore strategies from.',

469    cfg.DictOpt('backup_incremental_strategy',
470            default={'InnoBackupEx': 'InnoBackupExIncremental'},
471            help='Incremental Backup Runner based on the default '
```

```
472                    'strategy. For strategies that do not implement an '
473                    'incremental backup, the runner will use the default full '
474                    'backup.',
```

Since backup and restore aren't (currently) supported by MongoDB, they are initialized (to None) as follows (in trove/common/cfg.py):

```
677    # MongoDB
678    mongodb_group = cfg.OptGroup(

690        cfg.StrOpt('backup_strategy', default=None,
691                    help='Default strategy to perform backups.',
692                    deprecated_name='backup_strategy',
693                    deprecated_group='DEFAULT'),
694        cfg.DictOpt('backup_incremental_strategy', default={},
695                    help='Incremental Backup Runner based on the default '
696                    'strategy. For strategies that do not implement an '
697                    'incremental, the runner will use the default full backup.',
698                    deprecated_name='backup_incremental_strategy',
699                    deprecated_group='DEFAULT'),

730        cfg.StrOpt('backup_namespace', default=None,
731                    help='Namespace to load backup strategies from.',
732                    deprecated_name='backup_namespace',
733                    deprecated_group='DEFAULT'),
734        cfg.StrOpt('restore_namespace', default=None,
735                    help='Namespace to load restore strategies from.',
736                    deprecated_name='restore_namespace',
737                    deprecated_group='DEFAULT'),
738    ]
```

You can initiate a backup of an instance using the trove backup-create command as shown next. Specify the instance ID and the backup name as arguments to the command.

```
ubuntu@trove-book:~$ trove backup-create ed77ec23-6444-427d-bc0c-56a8b202974e backup-1
+-------------+----------------------------------------------------------------+
| Property    | Value                                                          |
+-------------+----------------------------------------------------------------+
| created     | 2015-04-19T21:59:50                                            |
| datastore   | {u'version': u'5.6', u'type': u'mysql',                        |
|             | u'version_id': u'a5ec21dc-3a5b-41c8-97fe-4fc3ed007023'}       |
| description | None                                                           |
| id          | ff6398a6-e15f-4063-8c66-58f3a8528794                          |
| instance_id | ed77ec23-6444-427d-bc0c-56a8b202974e                          |
| locationRef | None                                                           |
| name        | backup-1                                                       |
| parent_id   | None                                                           |
| size        | None                                                           |
| status      | NEW                                                            |
| updated     | 2015-04-19T21:59:50                                            |
+-------------+----------------------------------------------------------------+
```

Trove also supports the creation of an incremental backup based on an existing backup. To do this, specify a parent backup using the --parent option. The following example also shows how you can add a description to a backup using the --description command-line argument.

```
ubuntu@trove-book:~$ trove backup-create ed77ec23-6444-427d-bc0c-56a8b202974e \
> backup-1-incremental \
> --parent ff6398a6-e15f-4063-8c66-58f3a8528794 --description "make an incremental backup"
+--------------+--------------------------------------------------------------------------+
| Property     | Value                                                                    |
+--------------+--------------------------------------------------------------------------+
| created      | 2015-04-19T22:07:16                                                      |
| datastore    | {u'version': u'5.6', u'type': u'mysql',                                  |
|              | u'version_id': u'a5ec21dc-3a5b-41c8-97fe-4fc3ed007023'}                  |
| description  | make an incremental backup                                              |
| id           | 496589a6-3f82-4ccc-a509-91fbfc2a3091                                    |
| instance_id  | ed77ec23-6444-427d-bc0c-56a8b202974e                                    |
| locationRef  | None                                                                     |
| name         | backup-1-incremental                                                    |
| parent_id    | ff6398a6-e15f-4063-8c66-58f3a8528794                                    |
| size         | None                                                                     |
| status       | NEW                                                                      |
| updated      | 2015-04-19T22:07:16                                                      |
+--------------+--------------------------------------------------------------------------+
```

In the Kilo release, the MySQL backup strategy has been configured to create backups using InnoBackupEx by default. You can use the storage strategy to determine where to store the backup. You can set a number of configuration options related to this in trove-guestagent.conf. These include the storage_strategy (the name of the class implementing storage), storage_namespace (the module implementing storage_strategy), and other options that indicate whether the backup should be compressed and encrypted. The default storage_strategy is SwiftStorage.

```
263    cfg.StrOpt('storage_strategy', default='SwiftStorage',
264               help="Default strategy to store backups."),
265    cfg.StrOpt('storage_namespace',
266               default='trove.guestagent.strategies.storage.swift',
267               help='Namespace to load the default storage strategy from.'),
268    cfg.StrOpt('backup_swift_container', default='database_backups',
269               help='Swift container to put backups in.'),
270    cfg.BoolOpt('backup_use_gzip_compression', default=True,
271                help='Compress backups using gzip.'),
272    cfg.BoolOpt('backup_use_openssl_encryption', default=True,
273                help='Encrypt backups using OpenSSL.'),
274    cfg.StrOpt('backup_aes_cbc_key', default='default_aes_cbc_key',
275               help='Default OpenSSL aes_cbc key.'),
```

The two backups that were just created were therefore stored on object storage provided by Swift.

```
ubuntu@trove-book:~$ swift list
swift database_backups
ubuntu@trove-book:~$ swift list database_backups
496589a6-3f82-4ccc-a509-91fbfc2a3091.xbstream.gz.enc
```

```
496589a6-3f82-4ccc-a509-91fbfc2a3091_00000000
ff6398a6-e15f-4063-8c66-58f3a8528794.xbstream.gz.enc
ff6398a6-e15f-4063-8c66-58f3a8528794_00000000
```

You can create a list of backups using the trove backup-list command.

```
ubuntu@trove-book:~$ trove --json backup-list
[
  {
    "status": "COMPLETED",
    "updated": "2015-04-19T22:07:28",
    "description": "make an incremental backup",
    "created": "2015-04-19T22:07:16",
    "name": "backup-1-incremental",
    "instance_id": "ed77ec23-6444-427d-bc0c-56a8b202974e",
    "parent_id": "ff6398a6-e15f-4063-8c66-58f3a8528794",
    "locationRef": "http://192.168.117.5:8080/v1/AUTH_7ce14db4c7914492ac17b29a310b7636/
    database_backups/496589a6-3f82-4ccc-a509-91fbfc2a3091.xbstream.gz.enc",
    "datastore": {
      "version": "5.6",
      "type": "mysql",
      "version_id": "a5ec21dc-3a5b-41c8-97fe-4fc3ed007023"
    },
    "id": "496589a6-3f82-4ccc-a509-91fbfc2a3091",
    "size": 0.11
  },
  {
    "status": "COMPLETED",
    "updated": "2015-04-19T21:59:59",
    "description": null,
    "created": "2015-04-19T21:59:50",
    "name": "backup-1",
    "instance_id": "ed77ec23-6444-427d-bc0c-56a8b202974e",
    "parent_id": null,
    "locationRef": "http://192.168.117.5:8080/v1/AUTH_7ce14db4c7914492ac17b29a310b7636/
    database_backups/ff6398a6-e15f-4063-8c66-58f3a8528794.xbstream.gz.enc",
    "datastore": {
      "version": "5.6",
      "type": "mysql",
      "version_id": "a5ec21dc-3a5b-41c8-97fe-4fc3ed007023"
    },
    "id": "ff6398a6-e15f-4063-8c66-58f3a8528794",
    "size": 0.11
  }
]
```

The output lists the incremental backup (id: 496589a6-3f82-4ccc-a509-91fbfc2a3091), which is stored on the Swift object database_backups/496589a6-3f82-4ccc-a509-91fbfc2a3091.xbstream.gz.enc, and the full backup (id: ff6398a6-e15f-4063-8c66-58f3a8528794), which is stored on the Swift object database_backups/ff6398a6-e15f-4063-8c66-58f3a8528794.xbstream.gz.enc.

Note that the output indicates that both the incremental backup and the full backup are of the same original instance (instance-id: ed77ec23-6444-427d-bc0c-56a8b202974e).

The operation of *restoring* a backup is accomplished by launching a new instance based on the backup. In Trove, you cannot *load* a backup onto an existing instance. Next, we will show how to create a new instance based on the incremental backup generated previously. Note that, regardless of how many incremental backups you may have, you simply use the --backup argument to pass in the BACKUP_ID of your most recent incremental backup. Trove handles the complexities of applying the chain of all previous incremental backups.

```
ubuntu@trove-book:~$ trove create from-backup 2 --size 2 --backup 496589a6-3f82-4ccc-a509-
91fbfc2a3091
+-------------------+------------------------------------------+
| Property          | Value                                    |
+-------------------+------------------------------------------+
| created           | 2015-04-19T22:29:34                       |
| datastore         | mysql                                    |
| datastore_version | 5.6                                      |
| flavor            | 2                                        |
| id                | f62e48fa-33f7-4bb4-bf2d-c8ef8ee4cb42     |
| name              | from-backup                              |
| status            | BUILD                                    |
| updated           | 2015-04-19T22:29:34                       |
| volume            | 2                                        |
+-------------------+------------------------------------------+
```

Soon thereafter the instance becomes active and the data stored in the initial backup (backup-1) and the incremental backup (backup-1-incremental) are now on the instance from-backup. First look at the databases on the instance from which Trove took the backup.

```
ubuntu@trove-book:~$ trove database-list ed77ec23-6444-427d-bc0c-56a8b202974e
+--------------------+
| Name               |
+--------------------+
| db1                |
| performance_schema |
+--------------------+
ubuntu@trove-book:~$ trove user-list ed77ec23-6444-427d-bc0c-56a8b202974e
+----------------+------+-----------+
| Name           | Host | Databases |
+----------------+------+-----------+
| amrith         | %    | db1       |
| andreas        | %    |           |
+----------------+------+-----------+
```

Next, execute the same commands on the new instance just launched from the backup. As shown in the following example, trove restored the databases and users onto the new instance.

```
ubuntu@trove-book:~$ trove database-list f62e48fa-33f7-4bb4-bf2d-c8ef8ee4cb42
+---------------------+
| Name                |
+---------------------+
| db1                 |
| performance_schema  |
+---------------------+
ubuntu@trove-book:~$ trove user-list f62e48fa-33f7-4bb4-bf2d-c8ef8ee4cb42
+-----------------+------+-----------+
| Name            | Host | Databases |
+-----------------+------+-----------+
| amrith          | %    | db1       |
| andreas         | %    |           |
+-----------------+------+-----------+
```

When creating an instance from a backup, Trove uses metadata stored with the backup to determine whether the storage volume being provisioned for the new instance will be big enough to accommodate the data in the backup.

You can find all backups for a specified instance by using the trove backup-list-instance command. You can delete backups using the trove backup-delete command.

Replication in Trove

Trove provides a framework within which datastores can implement and manage their own native replication capabilities. Trove does not (itself) perform the replication; that is left to the underlying database server.

Trove merely

- Configures and establishes the replication

- Maintains information to help it identify the members in the replication set

- Performs operations like failover if required

In this section we examine how implement replication in Trove and the operations that Trove can perform on a replicated database.

Support for Replication

The MySQL datastore (and variants like Percona and MariaDB) currently supports replication . The currently supported topology is master-slave; slaves are read-only and are asynchronously populated. The Juno release added support for master-slave binlog replication.

You can find more information about binlog replication with MySQL 5.5 at https://dev.mysql.com/doc/refman/5.5/en/replication-configuration.html. This support works with versions 5.5 of MySQL, Percona, and MariaDB.

The Kilo release extended replication support to also include GTID-based replication that is available with MySQL version 5.6. This support is also available with Percona Server 5.6. MariaDB version 10 supports GTID-based replication, but it is not compatible with MySQL and Percona. More information about GTID (global transaction identifier) replication can be found at https://dev.mysql.com/doc/refman/5.6/en/replication-configuration.html and https://mariadb.com/kb/en/mariadb/global-transaction-id/.

Creating a Replica

You can create a replica of an existing instance using the trove create command and specifying the
--replica_of command-line argument.

■ **Note**   This example uses a machine configured with the Trove code from the Kilo release (Kilo RC1) and
a MySQL 5.5 guest instance. Replication in MySQL 5.5 uses the binlog replication model. In Kilo, the default
replication is GTID-based replication and requires MySQL 5.6. Later in this section we demonstrate GTID-based
replication and failover on a system with MySQL 5.6.

Start by displaying information about the master.

```
ubuntu@trove-book-vm:/opt/stack/trove$ trove show 41037bd2-9a91-4d5c-b291-612ad833a6d5
+-------------------+------------------------------------+
| Property          | Value                              |
+-------------------+------------------------------------+
| created           | 2015-03-24T19:33:07                |
| datastore         | mysql                              |
| datastore_version | 5.5                                |
| flavor            | 2                                  |
| id                | 41037bd2-9a91-4d5c-b291-612ad833a6d5 |
| ip                | 172.24.4.4                         |
| name              | m2                                 |
| status            | ACTIVE                             |
| updated           | 2015-03-24T19:33:12                |
| volume            | 2                                  |
| volume_used       | 0.17                               |
+-------------------+------------------------------------+

ubuntu@trove-book-vm:/opt/stack/trove$ trove create m2-mirror 2 --size 2 \
>  --replica_of 41037bd2-9a91-4d5c-b291-612ad833a6d5
+-------------------+------------------------------------+
| Property          | Value                              |
+-------------------+------------------------------------+
| created           | 2015-03-24T19:49:50                |
| datastore         | mysql                              |
| datastore_version | 5.5                                |
| flavor            | 2                                  |
| id                | 091b1a9b-8b0c-44fc-814e-ade4fca4e9c6 |
| name              | m2-mirror                          |
| replica_of        | 41037bd2-9a91-4d5c-b291-612ad833a6d5 |
| status            | BUILD                              |
| updated           | 2015-03-24T19:49:50                |
| volume            | 2                                  |
+-------------------+------------------------------------+
```

After a brief period we see that the newly created instance has gone ACTIVE. One additional option (not
demonstrated earlier) is --replica-count, which allows you to create multiple replicas at the same time.
The default value of the --replica-count parameter is 1 and therefore in the preceding command, one
replica is created.

```
ubuntu@trove-book-vm:/opt/stack/trove$ trove show 091b1a9b-8b0c-44fc-814e-ade4fca4e9c6
+-------------------+-------------------------------------------+
| Property          | Value                                     |
+-------------------+-------------------------------------------+
| created           | 2015-03-24T19:49:50                       |
| datastore         | mysql                                     |
| datastore_version | 5.5                                       |
| flavor            | 2                                         |
| id                | 091b1a9b-8b0c-44fc-814e-ade4fca4e9c6      |
| ip                | 172.24.4.5                                |
| name              | m2-mirror                                 |
| replica_of        | 41037bd2-9a91-4d5c-b291-612ad833a6d5      |
| status            | ACTIVE                                    |
| updated           | 2015-03-24T19:50:23                       |
| volume            | 2                                         |
| volume_used       | 0.18                                      |
+-------------------+-------------------------------------------+
```

We now see how this appears to an end user by performing some database operations. Trove refers to these operations (like database-create, database-list, database-delete, user-create, user-list, and user-delete) as "database extensions." Chapter 4 describes details about how to implement extensions.

First, create a database on the master; note that the ID being provided to the database-create command is the ID of the master, 41037bd2-9a91-4d5c-b291-612ad833a6d5.

```
ubuntu@trove-book-vm:$ trove database-create 41037bd2-9a91-4d5c-b291-612ad833a6d5 db1
ubuntu@trove-book-vm:$ trove database-list 41037bd2-9a91-4d5c-b291-612ad833a6d5
+--------------------+
| Name               |
+--------------------+
| db1                |
| performance_schema |
+--------------------+
```

Next, execute a database-list command against the replica by providing the id of the replica 091b1a9b-8b0c-44fc-814e-ade4fca4e9c6.

```
ubuntu@trove-book-vm:$ trove database-list 091b1a9b-8b0c-44fc-814e-ade4fca4e9c6
+--------------------+
| Name               |
+--------------------+
| db1                |
| performance_schema |
+--------------------+
```

Since you created the database on the master and listed databases on the replica, it is clear that replication is in fact working as expected. If any rows of data were inserted into a table created on the master, they would also appear on the replica.

You can connect to the MySQL servers directly and on the replica you can execute some commands that show the current replication status. When you first connect to the replica, you will see the following:

```
mysql> show master status;
+------------------+----------+--------------+------------------+
| File             | Position | Binlog_Do_DB | Binlog_Ignore_DB |
+------------------+----------+--------------+------------------+
| mysql-bin.000001 |      332 |              |                  |
+------------------+----------+--------------+------------------+
1 row in set (0.00 sec)

mysql> show variables like 'server%';
+---------------+------------+
| Variable_name | Value      |
+---------------+------------+
| server_id     | 1236306658 |
+---------------+------------+
1 row in set (0.00 sec)
```

Next, when connecting to the master instance, you can execute the corresponding commands to interrogate the replication status.

```
mysql> show slave hosts;
+------------+------+------+-----------+
| Server_id  | Host | Port | Master_id |
+------------+------+------+-----------+
| 1236306658 |      | 3306 | 506806179 |
+------------+------+------+-----------+
1 row in set (0.00 sec)

mysql> show variables like 'server%';
+---------------+-----------+
| Variable_name | Value     |
+---------------+-----------+
| server_id     | 506806179 |
+---------------+-----------+
1 row in set (0.00 sec)
```

Covering MySQL replication in detail is beyond the scope of this book; for our purposes, the important thing to know is that Trove has set up a master and a replica database.

A system configured with MySQL version 5.6 and a running Trove instance for the master can create a replica using the same method as with MySQL version 5.5.

```
ubuntu@trove-book:/opt/stack/trove/trove$ trove create m12 2 --size 2 \
> --replica_of ed77ec23-6444-427d-bc0c-56a8b202974e
+-------------------+------------------------------------------+
| Property          | Value                                    |
+-------------------+------------------------------------------+
| created           | 2015-04-10T07:57:07                      |
| datastore         | mysql                                    |
| datastore_version | 5.6                                      |
| flavor            | 2                                        |
```

```
| id               | 7ac6d15f-75b8-42d7-a3d8-9338743cc9b7 |
| name             | m12                                  |
| replica_of       | ed77ec23-6444-427d-bc0c-56a8b202974e |
| status           | BUILD                                |
| updated          | 2015-04-10T07:57:07                  |
| volume           | 2                                    |
+------------------+--------------------------------------+
```

After the provisioning process completes, both the master (ed77ec23-6444-427d-bc0c-56a8b202974e) and the replica (7ac6d15f-75b8-42d7-a3d8-9338743cc9b7) are online.

Trove manages the process for generating a replica based on an existing instance. It does this by first generating a snapshot of the source (master) and then using that snapshot to launch the replica. The snapshot is a backup that is generated exactly the same way as a user-initiated backup created in response to a trove backup-create command.

Once the replica instance is launched based on the snapshot, the replication strategy executes commands to configure replication to connect the replica to the master. These commands depend on whether the replication strategy is binlog based or GTID based.

In the case of binlog replication, you can find the implementation of connect_to_master() in trove.guestagent.strategies.replication.mysql_binlog. Compare this with the instructions for setting up MySQL replication using binlog (at https://dev.mysql.com/doc/refman/5.5/en/replication-howto-slaveinit.html).

```
40      def connect_to_master(self, service, snapshot):
41          logging_config = snapshot['log_position']
42          logging_config.update(self._read_log_position())
43          change_master_cmd = (
44              "CHANGE MASTER TO MASTER_HOST='%(host)s', "
45              "MASTER_PORT=%(port)s, "
46              "MASTER_USER='%(user)s', "
47              "MASTER_PASSWORD='%(password)s', "
48              "MASTER_LOG_FILE='%(log_file)s', "
49              "MASTER_LOG_POS=%(log_pos)s" %
50              {
51                  'host': snapshot['master']['host'],
52                  'port': snapshot['master']['port'],
53                  'user': logging_config['replication_user']['name'],
54                  'password': logging_config['replication_user']['password'],
55                  'log_file': logging_config['log_file'],
56                  'log_pos': logging_config['log_position']
57              })
58          service.execute_on_client(change_master_cmd)
59          service.start_slave()
```

The corresponding implementation for GTID-based replication is found in trove.guestagent.strategies.replication.mysql_gtid as shown next. Compare this with the instructions for setting up MySQL replication using GTIDs (at https://dev.mysql.com/doc/refman/5.6/en/replication-gtids-howto.html) and observe that the command uses MASTER_AUTO_POSITION instead of MASTER_LOG_POS.

```
31      def connect_to_master(self, service, snapshot):
32          logging_config = snapshot['log_position']
33          LOG.debug("connect_to_master %s" % logging_config['replication_user'])
34          change_master_cmd = (
```

```
35          "CHANGE MASTER TO MASTER_HOST='%(host)s', "
36          "MASTER_PORT=%(port)s, "
37          "MASTER_USER='%(user)s', "
38          "MASTER_PASSWORD='%(password)s', "
39          "MASTER_AUTO_POSITION=1 " %
40          {
41              'host': snapshot['master']['host'],
42              'port': snapshot['master']['port'],
43              'user': logging_config['replication_user']['name'],
44              'password': logging_config['replication_user']['password']
45          })
46      service.execute_on_client(change_master_cmd)
47      service.start_slave()
```

Once replication is set up, the MySQL server on the replica will catch up with the master by getting and applying the effect of all transactions that occurred after the snapshot.

Figure 5-1 illustrates this process. The user issues a request which is handled by the Trove API service and a response is returned to the requester. The Trove task manager performs further processing in response to a message sent over the message queue. The task manager does four things: it first initiates a backup of the instance, then launches a new Nova instance, causes the backup to be loaded onto that instance, and finally establishes replication between the master and the replica.

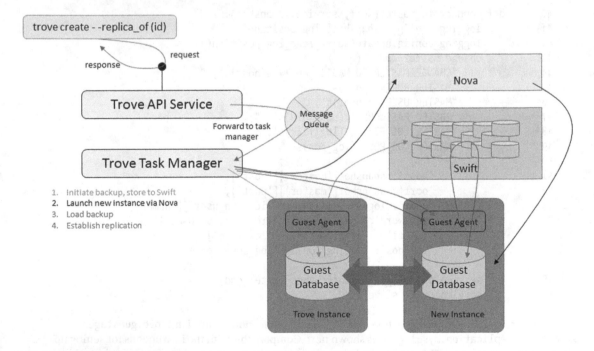

Figure 5-1. *An illustration of the steps involved in setting up replication*

The replication strategy contains some optimizations to minimize the time taken to launch a replica, including using an existing snapshot as the basis for an incremental snapshot. This is accomplished by specifying both --backup and --replica-of parameters when creating the instance.

Failover

In a replicated environment, you have one master and one or more replicas. It is possible for a user to cause a new master to be chosen from among the currently available replicas. This process is called a failover.

There are three commands that help users manage masters and replicas. These are detach-replica, eject-replica-source, and promote-to-replica-source. We begin with the configuration where the master is instance m1 (ed77ec23-6444-427d-bc0c-56a8b202974e) and the replicas are instances m12 (7ac6d15f-75b8-42d7-a3d8-9338743cc9b7), m13 (c9643f1c-8393-46cd-acb5-6fe85db16f0a), and m14 (22ac3792-0dd4-4b55-b4b4-b36a8a221ba8) as shown next in the output of the trove show command.

```
ubuntu@trove-book:~$ trove show ed77ec23-6444-427d-bc0c-56a8b202974e
+-------------------+-------------------------------------+
| Property          | Value                               |
+-------------------+-------------------------------------+
| created           | 2015-04-09T11:44:42                 |
| datastore         | mysql                               |
| datastore_version | 5.6                                 |
| flavor            | 2                                   |
| id                | ed77ec23-6444-427d-bc0c-56a8b202974e |
| ip                | 172.24.4.3                          |
| name              | m1                                  |
| replicas          | 22ac3792-0dd4-4b55-b4b4-b36a8a221ba8, |
|                   | 7ac6d15f-75b8-42d7-a3d8-9338743cc9b7, |
|                   | c9643f1c-8393-46cd-acb5-6fe85db16f0a |
| status            | ACTIVE                              |
| updated           | 2015-04-09T11:44:56                 |
| volume            | 2                                   |
| volume_used       | 0.11                                |
+-------------------+-------------------------------------+
```

We begin by looking at the command to perform an orderly failover.

Orderly Failover

In normal circumstances, the approach would be to use the commands detach-replica and promote-to-replica-source to handle failures. The current master can be replaced by using the promote-to-replica-source command as shown next.

```
ubuntu@trove-book:~$ trove promote-to-replica-source m14
```

The instances will all transition to the PROMOTE state and after a few minutes all instances will go back to ACTIVE state. Executing the trove show command against each of the instances m1, m12, m13, and m14 we see that m14 is indeed the master and the other three instances are now replicating from m14.

```
ubuntu@trove-book:~$ trove show m1
+-------------------+-------------------------------------+
| Property          | Value                               |
+-------------------+-------------------------------------+
| id                | ed77ec23-6444-427d-bc0c-56a8b202974e |
| ip                | 172.24.4.3                          |
| name              | m1                                  |
```

```
| replica_of           | 22ac3792-0dd4-4b55-b4b4-b36a8a221ba8 |
| status               | ACTIVE                               |
| updated              | 2015-04-20T00:50:15                  |
| volume               | 2                                    |
| volume_used          | 0.11                                 |
+----------------------+--------------------------------------+
ubuntu@trove-book:~$ trove show m12
+----------------------+--------------------------------------+
| Property             | Value                                |
+----------------------+--------------------------------------+
| created              | 2015-04-10T07:57:07                  |
| datastore            | mysql                                |
| datastore_version    | 5.6                                  |
| flavor               | 2                                    |
| id                   | 7ac6d15f-75b8-42d7-a3d8-9338743cc9b7 |
| ip                   | 172.24.4.4                           |
| name                 | m12                                  |
| replica_of           | 22ac3792-0dd4-4b55-b4b4-b36a8a221ba8 |
| status               | ACTIVE                               |
| updated              | 2015-04-20T00:50:15                  |
| volume               | 2                                    |
| volume_used          | 0.12                                 |
+----------------------+--------------------------------------+
ubuntu@trove-book:~$ trove show m13
+----------------------+--------------------------------------+
| Property             | Value                                |
+----------------------+--------------------------------------+
| created              | 2015-04-19T23:41:34                  |
| datastore            | mysql                                |
| datastore_version    | 5.6                                  |
| flavor               | 2                                    |
| id                   | c9643f1c-8393-46cd-acb5-6fe85db16f0a |
| ip                   | 172.24.4.6                           |
| name                 | m13                                  |
| replica_of           | 22ac3792-0dd4-4b55-b4b4-b36a8a221ba8 |
| status               | ACTIVE                               |
| updated              | 2015-04-20T00:50:15                  |
| volume               | 2                                    |
| volume_used          | 0.12                                 |
+----------------------+--------------------------------------+
ubuntu@trove-book:~$ trove show m14
+----------------------+--------------------------------------+
| Property             | Value                                |
+----------------------+--------------------------------------+
| created              | 2015-04-19T23:57:33                  |
| datastore            | mysql                                |
| datastore_version    | 5.6                                  |
| flavor               | 2                                    |
| id                   | 22ac3792-0dd4-4b55-b4b4-b36a8a221ba8 |
| ip                   | 172.24.4.7                           |
| name                 | m14                                  |
```

```
| replicas          | 7ac6d15f-75b8-42d7-a3d8-9338743cc9b7, |
|                   | c9643f1c-8393-46cd-acb5-6fe85db16f0a, |
|                   | ed77ec23-6444-427d-bc0c-56a8b202974e |
| status            | ACTIVE                               |
| updated           | 2015-04-20T00:50:15                  |
| volume            | 2                                    |
| volume_used       | 0.12                                 |
+-------------------+--------------------------------------+
```

Another way to break replication between a master and its replica is to detach a replica from its master. This is a nonreversible action. This is something that is used often to generate a copy of a data set at a point in time, and that can subsequently used to generate a new instance from that point in time. This is shown next. The instance m1 is detached from its replication source. Observe that m1 no longer indicates that it is the replica of m14, and m14 no longer lists m1 as a replica.

```
ubuntu@trove-book:~$ trove detach-replica m1
ubuntu@trove-book:~$ trove show m1
+-------------------+--------------------------------------+
| Property          | Value                                |
+-------------------+--------------------------------------+
| created           | 2015-04-09T11:44:42                  |
| datastore         | mysql                                |
| datastore_version | 5.6                                  |
| flavor            | 2                                    |
| id                | ed77ec23-6444-427d-bc0c-56a8b202974e |
| ip                | 172.24.4.3                          |
| name              | m1                                   |
| status            | ACTIVE                               |
| updated           | 2015-04-20T00:56:48                  |
| volume            | 2                                    |
| volume_used       | 0.11                                 |
+-------------------+--------------------------------------+
ubuntu@trove-book:~$ trove show m14
+-------------------+--------------------------------------+
| Property          | Value                                |
+-------------------+--------------------------------------+
| created           | 2015-04-19T23:57:33                  |
| datastore         | mysql                                |
| datastore_version | 5.6                                  |
| flavor            | 2                                    |
| id                | 22ac3792-0dd4-4b55-b4b4-b36a8a221ba8 |
| ip                | 172.24.4.7                          |
| name              | m14                                  |
| replicas          | 7ac6d15f-75b8-42d7-a3d8-9338743cc9b7, |
|                   | c9643f1c-8393-46cd-acb5-6fe85db16f0a |
| status            | ACTIVE                               |
| updated           | 2015-04-20T00:50:15                  |
| volume            | 2                                    |
| volume_used       | 0.12                                 |
+-------------------+--------------------------------------+
```

Failover with a Failed Master

Use the failover command trove eject-replica-source to handle the case of a failed master. When executed against a failed master, this command ejects that master and causes a new master to be elected.

The command has some built-in safeguards. When executed against an instance that is not the replica source, the command produces an error. Since m14 is the current master, we demonstrate this by attempting to eject m13 as the replica source.

```
ubuntu@trove-book: $ trove eject-replica-source m13
ERROR: Instance c9643f1c-8393-46cd-acb5-6fe85db16f0a is not a replica source. (HTTP 400)
```

Also, if we attempt to eject the current master (m14), and the master still has a good heartbeat, the command will fail.

```
ubuntu@trove-book:~$ trove eject-replica-source m14
ERROR: Replica Source 22ac3792-0dd4-4b55-b4b4-b36a8a221ba8 cannot be ejected as it has a
current heartbeat (HTTP 400)
```

We simulate a failed master and then retry the command. In practice a master is said to be failed if a good heartbeat has not been received in a certain amount of time. For the purposes of this simulation, failure was caused by abruptly shutting down the database instance on the guest.

```
ubuntu@trove-book:~$ trove eject-replica-source m14
```

After a brief period we see that m14 has been ejected from the replication (not a replica of anything, nor does it have any replicas) and m12 has been elected to be the master and m13 is the only replica.

```
ubuntu@trove-book:~$ trove show m14
+-------------------+--------------------------------------+
| Property          | Value                                |
+-------------------+--------------------------------------+
| created           | 2015-04-19T23:57:33                  |
| datastore         | mysql                                |
| datastore_version | 5.6                                  |
| flavor            | 2                                    |
| id                | 22ac3792-0dd4-4b55-b4b4-b36a8a221ba8 |
| ip                | 172.24.4.7                           |
| name              | m14                                  |
| status            | ACTIVE                               |
| updated           | 2015-04-20T01:51:27                  |
| volume            | 2                                    |
+-------------------+--------------------------------------+
ubuntu@trove-book:~$ trove show m13
+-------------------+--------------------------------------+
| Property          | Value                                |
+-------------------+--------------------------------------+
| created           | 2015-04-19T23:41:34                  |
| datastore         | mysql                                |
| datastore_version | 5.6                                  |
| flavor            | 2                                    |
| id                | c9643f1c-8393-46cd-acb5-6fe85db16f0a |
| ip                | 172.24.4.6                           |
```

```
| name             | m13                                  |
| replica_of       | 7ac6d15f-75b8-42d7-a3d8-9338743cc9b7 |
| status           | ACTIVE                               |
| updated          | 2015-04-20T01:51:27                  |
| volume           | 2                                    |
| volume_used      | 0.12                                 |
+------------------+--------------------------------------+
ubuntu@trove-book:~$ trove show m12
+------------------+--------------------------------------+
| Property         | Value                                |
+------------------+--------------------------------------+
| created          | 2015-04-10T07:57:07                  |
| datastore        | mysql                                |
| datastore_version| 5.6                                  |
| flavor           | 2                                    |
| id               | 7ac6d15f-75b8-42d7-a3d8-9338743cc9b7 |
| ip               | 172.24.4.4                           |
| name             | m12                                  |
| replicas         | c9643f1c-8393-46cd-acb5-6fe85db16f0a |
| status           | ACTIVE                               |
| updated          | 2015-04-20T01:51:27                  |
| volume           | 2                                    |
| volume_used      | 0.12                                 |
+------------------+--------------------------------------+
```

The check in the eject-replica-source command will not allow you to eject an instance from its role as a master if it has a current heartbeat. What constitutes a current heartbeat?

That check is performed by the task manager in trove/instance/models.py.

```
961     def eject_replica_source(self):

969         service = InstanceServiceStatus.find_by(instance_id=self.id)
970         last_heartbeat_delta = datetime.utcnow() - service.updated_at
971         agent_expiry_interval = timedelta(seconds=CONF.agent_heartbeat_expiry)
972         if last_heartbeat_delta < agent_expiry_interval:
973             raise exception.BadRequest(_("Replica Source %s cannot be ejected"
974                                         " as it has a current heartbeat")
975                                         % self.id)
```

The default value for agent_heartbeat_expiry is 60 seconds as specified in trove/common/cfg.py (shown next) and can be set in trove-taskmanager.conf.

```
151     cfg.IntOpt('agent_heartbeat_expiry', default=60,
152                help='Time (in seconds) after which a guest is considered '
153                     'unreachable'),
```

Therefore, if an instance has a heartbeat that is less than 60 seconds (agent_heartbeat_expiry) old, the preceding check will prevent the command from completing.

Clustering in Trove

Trove provides a framework within which datastores can implement mechanisms to provision and manage multinode configurations called clusters. This framework is based on clustering strategies. For details about how strategies work, refer to the section "Trove Strategies," in Chapter 4. Trove does not itself perform the clustering, instead relying on the strategies that implement database-specific commands that perform clustering in the manner best suited to that database.

The Juno release added support for clustering with MongoDB. The Kilo release also added basic support for clustering for Vertica. In this chapter we demonstrate clustering with MongoDB. We begin by installing the guest image for MongoDB and configuring it for use with Trove.

Installing MongoDB

You install MongoDB from the image found on the OpenStack repository of prebuilt guest images at http://tarballs.openstack.org/trove/images/ubuntu/.

```
ubuntu@trove-book: $ wget http://tarballs.openstack.org/trove/images/ubuntu/mongodb.qcow2
[. . .]
ubuntu@trove-book: $ mv mongodb.qcow2 devstack/files
ubuntu@trove-book: $ cd devstack/files
```

After downloading the image, execute the commands to register the image with Glance and Trove.

```
ubuntu@trove-book:~$ glance image-create --name mongodb --disk-format qcow2 \
> --container-format bare --is-public True < ./devstack/files/mongodb.qcow2
+------------------+--------------------------------------+
| Property         | Value                                |
+------------------+--------------------------------------+
| checksum         | 1e40e81d7579ba305be3bc460db46e13     |
| container_format | bare                                 |
| created_at       | 2015-04-20T20:57:14.000000           |
| deleted          | False                                |
| deleted_at       | None                                 |
| disk_format      | qcow2                                |
| id               | 0a247ab9-4ce5-43eb-902c-d3b040b05284 |
| is_public        | True                                 |
| min_disk         | 0                                    |
| min_ram          | 0                                    |
| name             | mongodb                              |
| owner            | 1ed3e474e68d4cf99a09e0c191aa54bc     |
| protected        | False                                |
| size             | 514719744                            |
| status           | active                               |
| updated_at       | 2015-04-20T20:57:28.000000           |
| virtual_size     | None                                 |
+------------------+--------------------------------------+
```

```
ubuntu@trove-book:~$ trove-manage datastore_update mongodb ''
2015-04-20 16:58:16.853 INFO trove.db.sqlalchemy.session [-] Creating SQLAlchemy engine with
args: {'pool_recycle': 3600, 'echo': False}
Datastore 'mongodb' updated.

ubuntu@trove-book:~$ trove-manage datastore_version_update mongodb 2.4.9 \
> mongodb 0a247ab9-4ce5-43eb-902c-d3b040b05284 mongodb 1
2015-04-20 16:58:54.583 INFO trove.db.sqlalchemy.session [-] Creating SQLAlchemy engine with
args: {'pool_recycle': 3600, 'echo': False}
Datastore version '2.4.9' updated.

ubuntu@trove-book:~$ trove-manage datastore_update mongodb 2.4.9
2015-04-20 16:59:14.723 INFO trove.db.sqlalchemy.session [-] Creating SQLAlchemy engine with
args: {'pool_recycle': 3600, 'echo': False}
Datastore 'mongodb' updated.

ubuntu@trove-book:~$ trove datastore-list
+--------------------------------------+-------------------+
| ID                                   | Name              |
+--------------------------------------+-------------------+
| 41a0c099-38a0-47a0-b348-3a351bfcef55 | mysql             |
| 4518619b-b161-4286-afe3-242137692648 | mongodb           |
+--------------------------------------+-------------------+
```

You are now able to launch an instance using the MongoDB datastore that was just created. Begin by creating a single instance of MongoDB. First, create a custom flavor with values that are suitable for MongoDB.

```
ubuntu@trove-book:~$ nova flavor-create m1.1gb 10 1024 4 1
+----+--------+-----------+------+-----------+------+-------+-------------+-----------+
| ID | Name   | Memory_MB | Disk | Ephemeral | Swap | VCPUs | RXTX_Factor | Is_Public |
+----+--------+-----------+------+-----------+------+-------+-------------+-----------+
| 10 | m1.1gb | 1024      | 4    | 0         |      | 1     | 1.0         | True      |
+----+--------+-----------+------+-----------+------+-------+-------------+-----------+
ubuntu@trove-book $ trove create mongo1 10 --datastore mongodb \
> --datastore_version 2.4.9 --size 4
+-------------------+--------------------------------------+
| Property          | Value                                |
+-------------------+--------------------------------------+
| created           | 2015-04-08T17:02:37                  |
| datastore         | mongodb                              |
| datastore_version | 2.4.9                                |
| flavor            | 10                                   |
| id                | 38af4e34-37c1-4f8d-aa37-36bfb02837fb |
| name              | mongo1                               |
| status            | BUILD                                |
| updated           | 2015-04-08T17:02:37                  |
| volume            | 4                                    |
+-------------------+--------------------------------------+
```

And shortly thereafter

```
ubuntu@trove-book:~$ trove show mongo1
+-------------------+-----------------------------------------+
| Property          | Value                                   |
+-------------------+-----------------------------------------+
| created           | 2015-04-08T17:02:37                     |
| datastore         | mongodb                                 |
| datastore_version | 2.4.9                                   |
| flavor            | 10                                      |
| id                | 38af4e34-37c1-4f8d-aa37-36bfb02837fb    |
| ip                | 10.0.0.3                                |
| name              | mongo1                                  |
| status            | ACTIVE                                  |
| updated           | 2015-04-08T17:02:42                     |
| volume            | 4                                       |
| volume_used       | 3.09                                    |
+-------------------+-----------------------------------------+
```

You can now connect to the Mongo Instance using the Mongo client.

```
ubuntu@trove-book: $ mongo 10.0.0.3
MongoDB shell version: 2.4.9
connecting to: 10.0.0.3/test
Welcome to the MongoDB shell.
For interactive help, type "help".
For more comprehensive documentation, see
        http://docs.mongodb.org/
Questions? Try the support group
        http://groups.google.com/group/mongodb-user
>
Bye
```

You can similarly launch a MongoDB cluster using Trove. This causes the creation of five instances: a MongoDB configuration server, a MongoDB query router, and three nodes representing a single shard with a three-member replica set.

```
trove cluster-create mongo1 mongodb 2.4.9 \
  --instance flavor_id=10,volume=4 \
  --instance flavor_id=10,volume=4 \
  --instance flavor_id=10,volume=4
```

Launching the cluster will launch a number of instances and you can view them and the cluster as a whole with a number of Trove commands. First, use the trove cluster-list command, which lists a currently running cluster.

```
ubuntu@trove-book:~$ trove cluster-list
+--------------------------------------+--------+-----------+-------------------+----------+
| ID                                   | Name   | Datastore | Datastore Version | Task Name|
+--------------------------------------+--------+-----------+-------------------+----------+
| d670484f-88b4-4465-888a-3b8bc0b0bdfc | mongo1 | mongodb   | 2.4.9             | BUILDING |
+--------------------------------------+--------+-----------+-------------------+----------+
```

The trove `cluster-show` command provides more information about the cluster.

```
ubuntu@trove-book:~$ trove cluster-show mongo1
+--------------------+------------------------------------------+
| Property           | Value                                    |
+--------------------+------------------------------------------+
| created            | 2015-04-20T21:12:08                      |
| datastore          | mongodb                                  |
| datastore_version  | 2.4.9                                    |
| id                 | d670484f-88b4-4465-888a-3b8bc0b0bdfc     |
| ip                 | 10.0.0.4                                 |
| name               | mongo1                                   |
| task_description   | Building the initial cluster.            |
| task_name          | BUILDING                                 |
| updated            | 2015-04-20T21:12:08                      |
+--------------------+------------------------------------------+
```

By default, instances that are part of a cluster are not visible in the trove `list` command output unless you also specify the –include-clustered command-line option. To view instances of the cluster you must use the trove `cluster-instances` command.

```
ubuntu@trove-book:~$ trove list
+----+------+-----------+-------------------+--------+-----------+------+
| ID | Name | Datastore | Datastore Version | Status | Flavor ID | Size |
+----+------+-----------+-------------------+--------+-----------+------+
+----+------+-----------+-------------------+--------+-----------+------+
ubuntu@trove-book:~$ trove cluster-instances mongo1
+--------------------------------------+--------------+-----------+------+
| ID                                   | Name         | Flavor ID | Size |
+--------------------------------------+--------------+-----------+------+
| 27097848-a01d-4659-b845-c335a4590fc8 | mongo1-rs1-1 | 10        |    4 |
| bb0b9cfc-6c50-4343-ac42-a3af41cd723a | mongo1-rs1-2 | 10        |    4 |
| ceb3931e-b779-4253-ab93-d0d589949465 | mongo1-rs1-3 | 10        |    4 |
+--------------------------------------+--------------+-----------+------+
```

You can see the underlying Nova instances as the cluster gets built. Observe that there are three replicas of the first shard, a config server, and a query router. The cluster address shown previously in the cluster-show command output is the IP address of the query router.

```
ubuntu@trove-book:~$ nova list
+--------------+-------------------+--------+------------+-------------+------------------+
| ID           | Name              | Status | Task State | Power State | Networks         |
+--------------+-------------------+--------+------------+-------------+------------------+
| 0ca90a73-... | mongo1-configsvr-1 | ACTIVE | -          | Running     | private=10.0.0.3 |
| 4a2fdaf6-... | mongo1-mongos-1   | ACTIVE | -          | Running     | private=10.0.0.4 |
| b1708b87-... | mongo1-rs1-1      | ACTIVE | -          | Running     | private=10.0.0.2 |
| 6f09d1b6-... | mongo1-rs1-2      | ACTIVE | -          | Running     | private=10.0.0.5 |
| 86af57ba-... | mongo1-rs1-3      | ACTIVE | -          | Running     | private=10.0.0.6 |
+--------------+-------------------+--------+------------+-------------+------------------+
```

After a short while the cluster will come online. Next, we examine how the cluster is actually constructed. The indication that the cluster is completely constructed is that the current task name is set to NONE.

```
ubuntu@trove-book:~$ trove cluster-list
+--------------------------------------+--------+-----------+-------------------+----------+
| ID                                   | Name   | Datastore | Datastore Version | Task Name|
+--------------------------------------+--------+-----------+-------------------+----------+
| d670484f-88b4-4465-888a-3b8bc0b0bdfc | mongo1 | mongodb   | 2.4.9             | NONE     |
+--------------------------------------+--------+-----------+-------------------+----------+
ubuntu@trove-book:~$ trove cluster-show mongo1
+-------------------+--------------------------------------+
| Property          | Value                                |
+-------------------+--------------------------------------+
| created           | 2015-04-20T21:12:08                  |
| datastore         | mongodb                              |
| datastore_version | 2.4.9                                |
| id                | d670484f-88b4-4465-888a-3b8bc0b0bdfc |
| ip                | 10.0.0.4                             |
| name              | mongo1                               |
| task_description  | No tasks for the cluster.            |
| task_name         | NONE                                 |
| updated           | 2015-04-20T21:22:13                  |
+-------------------+--------------------------------------+
```

Begin by looking at the configuration file used for launching MongoDB.

Recall that the prepare message sent by the Trove task manager to the guest agent contained config_contents and cluster_config as parameters.

```
53    def prepare(self, context, packages, databases, memory_mb, users,
54                device:path=None, mount_point=None, backup_info=None,
55                config_contents=None, root_password=None, overrides=None,
56                cluster_config=None, snapshot=None):
```

The Trove task manager generates these values using a template. By default, the template chosen is a file called config.template. This file is found in the path pointed to by the configuration setting template_path. By default, template_path is /etc/trove/templates as follows in trove/common/cfg.py:

```
355   cfg.StrOpt('template_path', default='/etc/trove/templates/',
356             help='Path which leads to datastore templates.'),
```

On a system installed with devstack, the file config.template is found in the directory trove/templates/mongodb/. Next, we look at the construct for provisioning the replica set. On the command line, we provided a description of each member of the replica set.

```
trove cluster-create mongo1 mongodb 2.4.9 \
  --instance flavor_id=10,volume=4 \
  --instance flavor_id=10,volume=4 \
  --instance flavor_id=10,volume=4
```

We specified that we want a three-member replica set (by specifying the argument `--instance three` times); we also specified that the three instances are to be of `flavor_id` 10 and with a 4 GB volume attached.

Next, we look at the additional servers that have been provisioned, the configuration server, and the query router. The command (`trove cluster-create`) only specified the three members of the replica set.

The two configuration parameters `num_config_servers_per_cluster` and `num_query_routers_per_cluster` control the number of servers in a MongoDB cluster. The default values are set as shown next (from `trove/common/cfg.py`). A minimum of three cluster members are required, three config servers in each cluster and one query router.

```
709:     cfg.IntOpt('num_config_servers_per_cluster', default=3,
710-              help='The number of config servers to create per cluster.'),
711:     cfg.IntOpt('num_query_routers_per_cluster', default=1,
712-              help='The number of query routers (mongos) to create '
713-                   'per cluster.'),
```

On the system used for the preceding example, we specified that we wanted only one config server per cluster by adding the following lines to the Trove configuration file `trove-taskmanager.conf`:

```
[mongodb]
num_config_servers_per_cluster = 1
num_query_routers_per_cluster = 1
```

The implementation of the MongoDB cluster API is found in the class `MongoDbCluster` in `trove/common/strategies/cluster/experimental/mongodb/api.py`. It uses the preceding settings and validates the request. It verifies that the user quota would allow for the launch of this cluster. This includes verifying that the configuration is valid (at least three servers, as specified by `cluster_member_count`), that the user can launch the requisite number of servers with the specified volumes based on the available quotas, and so on. If that is successful it launches the instances required by the cluster.

```
63   class MongoDbCluster(models.Cluster):
64
65       @classmethod
66       def create(cls, context, name, datastore, datastore_version, instances):
67
72           num_instances = len(instances)
76           flavor_ids = [instance['flavor_id'] for instance in instances]
77           if len(set(flavor_ids)) != 1:
78               raise exception.ClusterFlavorsNotEqual()
```

Note that all flavors have to be the same.

```
79           flavor_id = flavor_ids[0]
```

Save the flavor ID and use it to launch the config server and the query router.

```
80           nova_client = remote.create_nova_client(context)
85           mongo_conf = CONF.get(datastore_version.manager)
86           num_configsvr = mongo_conf.num_config_servers_per_cluster
87           num_mongos = mongo_conf.num_query_routers_per_cluster
```

```
88          delta_instances = num_instances + num_configsvr + num_mongos
89          deltas = {'instances': delta_instances}
90
91          volume_sizes = [instance['volume_size'] for instance in instances
92                          if instance.get('volume_size', None)]

110
111         check_quotas(context.tenant, deltas)
112
113         db_info = models.DBCluster.create(
114             name=name, tenant_id=context.tenant,
115             datastore_version_id=datastore_version.id,
116             task_status=ClusterTasks.BUILDING_INITIAL)
```

This creates the cluster and sets the state to BUILDING_INITIAL.

```
117
118         replica_set_name = "rs1"
119
120         member_config = {"id": db_info.id,
121                          "shard_id": utils.generate_uuid(),
122                          "instance_type": "member",
123                          "replica_set_name": replica_set_name}
124         for i in range(1, num_instances + 1):
125             instance_name = "%s-%s-%s" % (name, replica_set_name, str(i))
126             inst_models.Instance.create(context, instance_name,
127                                         flavor_id,
128                                         datastore_version.image_id,
129                                         [], [], datastore,
130                                         datastore_version,
131                                         volume_size, None,
132                                         availability_zone=None,
133                                         nics=None,
134                                         configuration_id=None,
135                                         cluster_config=member_config)
136
```

That launches the instances requested.

```
137         configsvr_config = {"id": db_info.id,
138                             "instance_type": "config_server"}
139         for i in range(1, num_configsvr + 1):
140             instance_name = "%s-%s-%s" % (name, "configsvr", str(i))
141             inst_models.Instance.create(context, instance_name,
142                                         flavor_id,
143                                         datastore_version.image_id,
144                                         [], [], datastore,
145                                         datastore_version,
146                                         volume_size, None,
147                                         availability_zone=None,
```

```
148                                    nics=None,
149                                    configuration_id=None,
150                                    cluster_config=configsvr_config)
151
```

That launches the configuration server.

```
152             mongos_config = {"id": db_info.id,
153                              "instance_type": "query_router"}
154         for i in range(1, num_mongos + 1):
155             instance_name = "%s-%s-%s" % (name, "mongos", str(i))
156             inst_models.Instance.create(context, instance_name,
157                                         flavor_id,
158                                         datastore_version.image_id,
159                                         [], [], datastore,
160                                         datastore_version,
161                                         volume_size, None,
162                                         availability_zone=None,
163                                         nics=None,
164                                         configuration_id=None,
165                                         cluster_config=mongos_config)
166
```

That launches the query router.

```
167         task_api.load(context, datastore_version.manager).create_cluster(
168             db_info.id)
169
```

Trove next invokes the task manager API create_cluster(), which we describe next. This is the process of converting the instances launched previously into a cluster. We show that the clustering implementation is based on the cluster strategy for MongoDB and the actual commands that perform the MongoDB-specific activities related to clustering are implemented in the MongoDB guest agent.

You can find the Trove task manager create_cluster() method in the cluster strategy for MongoDB. You can find this implementation in the file trove/common/strategies/cluster/experimental/mongodb/taskmanager.py.

After enumerating the instances that are to be part of the cluster, including the configuration servers and the query routers, the process of creating a cluster includes registering the configuration server, creating a replica set, and finally creating a shard.

The code (in _create_cluster()) that attempts to inform the query routers of the config servers is shown next.

```
225         try:
226             for query_router in query_routers:
227                 (self.get_guest(query_router)
228                  .add_config_servers(config_server_ips))
229         except Exception:
230             LOG.exception(_("error adding config servers"))
231             self.update_statuses_on_failure(cluster_id)
232             return
```

Observe that this code invokes the guest agent API on the query router and invokes the add_config_servers() method. This code is in the source file ./trove/common/strategies/cluster/experimental/mongodb/guestagent.py shown next.

```
33   class MongoDbGuestAgentAPI(guest_api.API):

52      def add_config_servers(self, config_servers):
53          LOG.debug("Adding config servers %(config_servers)s for instance"
54                      "%(id)s" % {'config_servers': config_servers,
55                                  'id': self.id})
56          return self._call("add_config_servers", guest_api.AGENT_HIGH_TIMEOUT,
57                              self.version_cap, config_servers=config_servers)
```

Observe that the preceding code invokes the guest API call add_config_servers() using the _call() (blocking) method as described in Chapter 4.

The implementation of add_config_servers() on the guest is in the following code: trove/guestagent/datastore/experimental/mongodb/service.py.

```
218     def add_config_servers(self, config_server_hosts):
219         """
220         This method is used by query router (mongos) instances.
221         """
222         config_contents = self._read_config()
223         configdb_contents = ','.join(['%s:27019' % host
224                                         for host in config_server_hosts])
225         LOG.debug("Config server list %s." % configdb_contents)
226         # remove db path from config and update configdb
227         contents = self._delete_config_parameters(config_contents,
228                                                     ["dbpath", "nojournal",
229                                                      "smallfiles", "journal",
230                                                      "noprealloc", "configdb"])
231         contents = self._add_config_parameter(contents,
232                                                 "configdb", configdb_contents)
233         LOG.info(_("Rewriting configuration."))
234         self.start_db_with_conf_changes(contents)
```

Observe that this code rewrites the configuration file on the query router with the ID of the configuration server, and then restarts the query router.

The code that follows shows the operation of adding a shard. The task manager invokes an API exposed by the MongoDB guest agent (add_shard()).

```
170     def _create_shard(self, query_routers, replica_set_name,
171                         members, cluster_id, shard_id=None):
172         a_query_router = query_routers[0]
173         LOG.debug("calling add_shard on query_router: %s" % a_query_router)
174         member_ip = self.get_ip(members[0])
175         try:
176             self.get_guest(a_query_router).add_shard(replica_set_name,
177                                                         member_ip)
```

The implementation of the add_shard() method on the guest agent, shown next, executes the actual MongoDB command to perform the addition of the shard.

```
261     def add_shard(self, replica_set_name, replica_set_member):
262         """
263         This method is used by query router (mongos) instances.
264         """
265         cmd = 'db.adminCommand({addShard: "%s/%s:27017"})' % (
266             replica_set_name, replica_set_member)
267         self.do_mongo(cmd)
```

As you can see from the preceding examples, clustering strategies implement the actual operations required to convert a group of instances into a MongoDB cluster by performing the low-level operations directly on the guest instance.

You can add additional shards to a running cluster using the add_shard API call. There is currently no command-line interface to add a shard or to reconfigure the replica set. These are planned for inclusion in an upcoming release.

Figure 5-2 shows this. The provisioning of a cluster begins with a request that is received by the Trove API service. The Trove API service forwards the request to the task manager after some validation and then provides the client with a response.

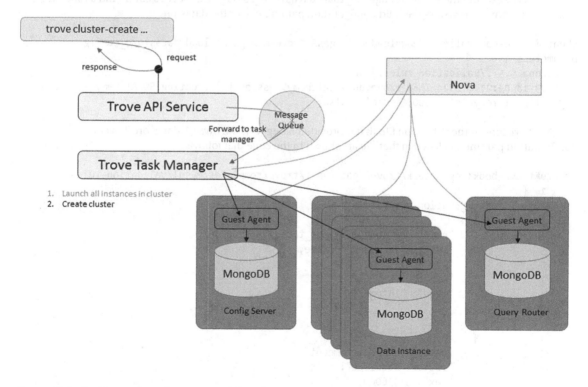

Figure 5-2. *An illustration of MongoDB cluster creation process*

The Trove task manager launches the cluster instances—the data instances, the config server, and the query router—and, when all the instances are running, begins the process of creating a cluster. When that process is complete, the cluster is ready.

The Kilo release also added support for clustering with Vertica. Unlike MongoDB, which requires you to launch query router and configuration server nodes in addition to data nodes, clustering with Vertica only launches data nodes.

The guest agent for Vertica is also experimental and the implementation includes a strategy for the guest agent and the task manager, just like MongoDB. No template is provided for Vertica as part of the current implementation, so the prepare() call sends an empty file to the guest agent. In a manner similar to the MongoDB implementation, the Vertica implementation relies on a Vertica-specific strategy to do the things required to convert a group of instances into a cluster.

Configuration Groups

During the launch of a guest instance, the Trove task manager renders a configuration file for the guest and provides that to the guest via the prepare() call. The previous section ("Clustering with Trove") demonstrated how the configuration file is generated based on a template. Customizing the template is one way to modify the configuration of a guest instance.

Recall also that the during the configuration of a datastore (Chapter 2) the final step in registering a datastore is to execute the trove-manage db_load_datastore_config_parameters command as shown next. This command registers the valid configuration parameters for the datastore.

```
ubuntu@trove-controller:~/downloaded-images$ trove-manage db_load_datastore_config_
parameters \
> percona 5.5 ./validation_rules.json
2015-03-18 09:27:47.524 INFO trove.db.sqlalchemy.session [-] Creating SQLAlchemy engine with
args: {'pool_recycle': 3600, 'echo': False}
```

Next, we look at the validation file that is provided along with the MySQL datastore. Several configuration parameters listed in that file are shown in the code that follows:

```
ubuntu@trove-book:/opt/stack/trove$ cat  -n ./trove/templates/mysql/validation-rules.json
    1  {
    2      "configuration-parameters": [
    3          {
    4              "name": "innodb_file_per_table",
    5              "restart_required": false,
    6              "max": 1,
    7              "min": 0,
    8              "type": "integer"
    9          },

   31          {
   32              "name": "connect_timeout",
   33              "restart_required": false,
   34              "max": 31536000,
   35              "min": 2,
   36              "type": "integer"
   37          },
```

```
73          {
74                  "name": "innodb_open_files",
75                  "restart_required": true,
76                  "max": 4294967295,
77                  "min": 10,
78                  "type": "integer"
79          },
```

Information about each of these MySQL configuration parameters can be found in the MySQL documentation. Once loaded into the database, the values are also exposed through the trove configuration-parameter-list command.

```
ubuntu@trove-book:~$ trove configuration-parameter-list --datastore mysql 5.6
+------------------------------+---------+----------+----------+-------------------+
| Name                         | Type    | Min Size | Max Size | Restart Required  |
+------------------------------+---------+----------+----------+-------------------+
| autocommit                   | integer |          |          |            False  |
| innodb_file_per_table        | integer |          |          |            False  |
| innodb_open_files            | integer |          |          |             True  |
[...]
```

To demonstrate the use of configuration groups, we launch a MySQL 5.6 instance as shown next.

```
ubuntu@trove-book:~$ trove create m2 2 --size 2
+-------------------+---------------------------------------+
| Property          | Value                                 |
+-------------------+---------------------------------------+
| created           | 2015-04-24T11:20:36                   |
| datastore         | mysql                                 |
| datastore_version | 5.6                                   |
| flavor            | 2                                     |
| id                | 53796f4d-b0d8-42f1-b9c6-82260a78150f  |
| name              | m2                                    |
| status            | BUILD                                 |
| updated           | 2015-04-24T11:20:36                   |
| volume            | 2                                     |
+-------------------+---------------------------------------+
```

First, look at the default configuration of the instance using the trove configuration-default command.

```
ubuntu@trove-book:~$ trove configuration-default m2
+------------------------------+----------------------------+
| Property                     | Value                      |
+------------------------------+----------------------------+
| basedir                      | /usr                       |
| connect_timeout              | 15                         |
| datadir                      | /var/lib/mysql             |
| default_storage_engine       | innodb                     |
| innodb_buffer_pool_size      | 600M                       |
| innodb_data_file_path        | ibdata1:10M:autoextend     |
```

```
| innodb_file_per_table    | 1                          |
| innodb_log_buffer_size   | 25M                        |
| innodb_log_file_size     | 50M                        |
| innodb_log_files_in_group| 2                          |
| join_buffer_size         | 1M                         |
| key_buffer_size          | 200M                       |
| local-infile             | 0                          |
| max_allowed_packet       | 4096K                      |
| max_connections          | 400                        |
| max_heap_table_size      | 64M                        |
| max_user_connections     | 400                        |
| myisam-recover           | BACKUP                     |
| open_files_limit         | 2048                       |
| pid_file                 | /var/run/mysqld/mysqld.pid |
| port                     | 3306                       |
| query_cache_limit        | 1M                         |
| query_cache_size         | 32M                        |
| query_cache_type         | 1                          |
| read_buffer_size         | 512K                       |
| read_rnd_buffer_size     | 512K                       |
| server_id                | 334596                     |
| skip-external-locking    | 1                          |
| sort_buffer_size         | 1M                         |
| table_definition_cache   | 1024                       |
| table_open_cache         | 1024                       |
| thread_cache_size        | 16                         |
| thread_stack             | 192K                       |
| tmp_table_size           | 64M                        |
| tmpdir                   | /var/tmp                   |
| user                     | mysql                      |
| wait_timeout             | 120                        |
+--------------------------+----------------------------+
```

As described earlier, the default configuration for an instance is sent down during the prepare() call and the values for this template come from a configuration template if one exists.

```
ubuntu@trove-book:~$ cat -n /opt/stack/trove/trove/templates/mysql/config.template
     1  [client]
     2  port = 3306
     3
     4  [mysqld_safe]
     5  nice = 0
     6
     7  [mysqld]
     8  user = mysql
     9  port = 3306
    10  basedir = /usr
    11  datadir = /var/lib/mysql
    12  ####tmpdir = /tmp
    13  tmpdir = /var/tmp
```

```
14   pid_file = /var/run/mysqld/mysqld.pid
15   skip-external-locking = 1
16   key_buffer_size = {{ (50 * flavor['ram']/512)|int }}M
17   max_allowed_packet = {{ (1024 * flavor['ram']/512)|int }}K
18   thread_stack = 192K
19   thread_cache_size = {{ (4 * flavor['ram']/512)|int }}
20   myisam-recover = BACKUP
21   query_cache_type = 1
22   query_cache_limit = 1M
23   query_cache_size = {{ (8 * flavor['ram']/512)|int }}M
24   innodb_data_file_path = ibdata1:10M:autoextend
25   innodb_buffer_pool_size = {{ (150 * flavor['ram']/512)|int }}M
26   innodb_file_per_table = 1
27   innodb_log_files_in_group = 2
28   innodb_log_file_size=50M
29   innodb_log_buffer_size=25M
30   connect_timeout = 15
31   wait_timeout = 120
32   join_buffer_size = 1M
33   read_buffer_size = 512K
34   read_rnd_buffer_size = 512K
35   sort_buffer_size = 1M
36   tmp_table_size = {{ (16 * flavor['ram']/512)|int }}M
37   max_heap_table_size = {{ (16 * flavor['ram']/512)|int }}M
38   table_open_cache = {{ (256 * flavor['ram']/512)|int }}
39   table_definition_cache = {{ (256 * flavor['ram']/512)|int }}
40   open_files_limit = {{ (512 * flavor['ram']/512)|int }}
41   max_user_connections = {{ (100 * flavor['ram']/512)|int }}
42   max_connections = {{ (100 * flavor['ram']/512)|int }}
43   default_storage_engine = innodb
44   local-infile = 0
45   server_id = {{server_id}}
46
47   [mysqldump]
48   quick = 1
49   quote-names = 1
50   max_allowed_packct = 16M
51
52   [isamchk]
53   key_buffer = 16M
54
55   !includedir /etc/mysql/conf.d/
```

Observe that while some parameters (e.g., connect_timeout) are set to a constant value, others are set to a value that includes variables like 'ram' (e.g., key_buffer_size).

```
key_buffer_size = {{ (50 * flavor['ram']/512)|int }}M
```

The value of the variable 'ram' is evaluated at the time of the creation of the instance. The instance was created with flavor 2, which has 2 GB of RAM (as shown next).

```
ubuntu@trove-book:~$ trove flavor-show 2
+----------+----------+
| Property | Value    |
+----------+----------+
| id       | 2        |
| name     | m1.small |
| ram      | 2048     |
+----------+----------+
```

The computation of 2048 * 50 / 512 results in key_buffer_size being set to 200M on this instance. In the next section we examine how these settings interact with instance resizing operations. We now proceed to demonstrate the use of configuration groups as a mechanism to adjust the configuration on an instance or group of instances.

Assume that there is a group of instances for which you would like to have a wait_timeout of 240s not 120s, and a value of max_connections equal to 200. We can execute the configuration-create command to create a configuration group with those new settings.

```
ubuntu@trove-book:~$ trove configuration-create special-configuration \
> '{ "wait_timeout":240, "max_connections":200}' \
> --description "illustrate a special configuration group" \
> --datastore mysql --datastore_version 5.6
+-----------------------+--------------------------------------------------+
| Property              | Value                                            |
+-----------------------+--------------------------------------------------+
| created               | 2015-04-24T12:04:09                              |
| datastore_name        | mysql                                            |
| datastore_version_id  | b39198b7-6791-4ed2-ab27-e2b9bac3f7b1             |
| datastore_version_name| 5.6                                              |
| description           | illustrate a special configuration group         |
| id                    | dfce6dd7-f4ed-4252-869d-35f20c9a3a8f             |
| instance_count        | 0                                                |
| name                  | special-configuration                            |
| updated               | 2015-04-24T12:04:09                              |
| values                | {u'wait_timeout': 240, u'max_connections': 200}  |
+-----------------------+--------------------------------------------------+
```

You can now attach it to an instance as follows. As a configuration group can be attached to multiple instances at the same time, it makes the configuration of a group of instances significantly easier.

```
ubuntu@trove-book:~$ trove configuration-attach 53796f4d-b0d8-42f1-b9c6-82260a78150f \
> dfce6dd7-f4ed-4252-869d-35f20c9a3a8f
```

This is now reflected on the configuration by an increase in the instance_count, an indication of the number of instances using this configuration group.

```
ubuntu@trove-book:~$ trove configuration-show dfce6dd7-f4ed-4252-869d-35f20c9a3a8f
+------------------------+-------------------------------------------------+
| Property               | Value                                           |
+------------------------+-------------------------------------------------+
| created                | 2015-04-24T12:04:09                             |
| datastore_name         | mysql                                           |
| datastore_version_name | 5.6                                             |
| description            | illustrate a special configuration group        |
| id                     | dfce6dd7-f4ed-4252-869d-35f20c9a3a8f            |
| instance_count         | 1                                               |
| name                   | special-configuration                           |
| updated                | 2015-04-24T12:04:09                             |
| values                 | {"wait_timeout": 240, "max_connections": 200} |
+------------------------+-------------------------------------------------+
```

To get a list of instances using a specified configuration group, you can use the trove configuration-instances command.

```
ubuntu@trove-book:~$ trove configuration-instances dfce6dd7-f4ed-4252-869d-35f20c9a3a8f
+--------------------------------------+------+
| ID                                   | Name |
+--------------------------------------+------+
| 53796f4d-b0d8-42f1-b9c6-82260a78150f | m2   |
+--------------------------------------+------+
```

Finally, you can connect to the instance and interrogate the actual system parameters that were modified and confirm that they did, in fact, change.

```
mysql> select @@global.wait_timeout;
+-----------------------+
| @@global.wait_timeout |
+-----------------------+
|                   240 |
+-----------------------+
1 row in set (0.00 sec)

mysql> select @@global.max_connections;
+--------------------------+
| @@global.max_connections |
+--------------------------+
|                      200 |
+--------------------------+
1 row in set (0.00 sec)
```

The configuration group can be detached from an instance by executing the trove configuration-group-detach command as shown. The instance ID or name is provided as the parameter to the command.

```
ubuntu@trove-book:~$ trove configuration-detach 53796f4d-b0d8-42f1-b9c6-82260a78150f
```

You can now confirm that this did in fact revert the value of max_connections to the default (of 400), and wait_timeout to the default of 120.

```
mysql> select @@global.max_connections;
+---------------------------+
| @@global.max_connections |
+---------------------------+
|                       400 |
+---------------------------+
1 row in set (0.00 sec)

mysql> select @@global.wait_timeout;
+-----------------------+
| @@global.wait_timeout |
+-----------------------+
|                   120 |
+-----------------------+
1 row in set (0.00 sec)
```

In the following example, the configuration group is attached to a single instance. The following steps demonstrate how you attach a configuration group to multiple instances and then manipulate all instances at the same time.

First, a configuration group is attached to three instances; m1, m2, and m3. This configuration group resets two parameters (as earlier): wait_timeout and max_connections.

```
ubuntu@trove-book:~$ trove configuration-attach m1 3226b8e6-fa38-4e23-a4e6-000b639a93d7
ubuntu@trove-book:~$ trove configuration-attach m2 3226b8e6-fa38-4e23-a4e6-000b639a93d7
ubuntu@trove-book:~$ trove configuration-attach m3 3226b8e6-fa38-4e23-a4e6-000b639a93d7

ubuntu@trove-book:~$ trove configuration-show 3226b8e6-fa38-4e23-a4e6-000b639a93d7
+-----------------------+---------------------------------------------+
| Property              | Value                                       |
+-----------------------+---------------------------------------------+
| created               | 2015-04-24T11:22:40                         |
| datastore_name        | mysql                                       |
| datastore_version_name| 5.6                                         |
| description           | illustrate a special configuration group    |
| id                    | 3226b8e6-fa38-4e23-a4e6-000b639a93d7        |
| instance_count        | 3                                           |
| name                  | special-configuration                       |
| updated               | 2015-04-24T11:22:40                         |
| values                | {"wait_timeout": 240, "max_connections": 200} |
+-----------------------+---------------------------------------------+
```

You can verify that the configuration group correctly updated all three instances by querying the value of @@max_connections on all instances.

```
ubuntu@trove-book:~$ mysql -uroot -ppx8F7UuHeHu92BJ6mGzhfQQaGYxMAKKYbzX9 -h 10.0.0.2\
> -e 'select @@global.max_connections, @@global.wait_timeout'
+--------------------------+----------------------+
| @@global.max_connections | @@global.wait_timeout |
+--------------------------+----------------------+
|                      200 |                  240 |
+--------------------------+----------------------+
ubuntu@trove-book:~$ mysql -uroot -pDHueWtKJTXAWHYpJJrNRaNj9gZZzCKcxNk9f -h 10.0.0.3\
> -e 'select  @@global.max_connections, @@global.wait_timeout'
+--------------------------+----------------------+
| @@global.max_connections | @@global.wait_timeout |
+--------------------------+----------------------+
|                      200 |                  240 |
+--------------------------+----------------------+
ubuntu@trove-book:~$ mysql -uroot -pvtcM8cVwAU3bDc9fXMRKqtUbGsAPdpg4UC7x -h 10.0.0.4\
> -e 'select @@global.max_connections, @@global.wait_timeout'
+--------------------------+----------------------+
| @@global.max_connections | @@global.wait_timeout |
+--------------------------+----------------------+
|                      200 |                  240 |
+--------------------------+----------------------+
```

Next, patch the configuration group by changing just one of the two parameters. In this case, you change max_connections from 200 to 100 and immediately verify the value on each of the instances attached with the configuration group.

```
ubuntu@trove-book:~$ trove configuration-patch 3226b8e6-fa38-4e23-a4e6-000b639a93d7 \
> '{ "max_connections": 100 }'

ubuntu@trove-book:~$ mysql -uroot -ppx8F7UuHeHu92BJ6mGzhfQQaGYxMAKKYbzX9 -h 10.0.0.2\
> -e 'select @@global.max_connections, @@global.wait_timeout'
+--------------------------+----------------------+
| @@global.max_connections | @@global.wait_timeout |
+--------------------------+----------------------+
|                      100 |                  240 |
+--------------------------+----------------------+
ubuntu@trove-book:~$ mysql -uroot -pDHueWtKJTXAWHYpJJrNRaNj9gZZzCKcxNk9f -h 10.0.0.3\
> -e 'select  @@global.max_connections, @@global.wait_timeout'
+--------------------------+----------------------+
| @@global.max_connections | @@global.wait_timeout |
+--------------------------+----------------------+
|                      100 |                  240 |
+--------------------------+----------------------+
ubuntu@trove-book:~$ mysql -uroot -pvtcM8cVwAU3bDc9fXMRKqtUbGsAPdpg4UC7x -h 10.0.0.4\
> -e 'select @@global.max_connections, @@global.wait_timeout'
+--------------------------+----------------------+
| @@global.max_connections | @@global.wait_timeout |
+--------------------------+----------------------+
|                      100 |                  240 |
+--------------------------+----------------------+
```

Similar to `trove configuration-patch` which allows you to alter a single parameter in a configuration group, `trove configuration-update` allows you to entirely replace the values being set in a configuration group. Consider the following change.

■ **Note**   The intended effect of the changes in the following example is that `max_connections` and `wait_timeout` are reverted to their defaults and just `connect_timeout` is set to the new value (30).

However, due to a bug (`https://bugs.launchpad.net/trove/+bug/1449238`) this does not quite work as expected.

```
ubuntu@trove-book:~$ trove configuration-show 3226b8e6-fa38-4e23-a4e6-000b639a93d7
+------------------------+--------------------------------------------------+
| Property               | Value                                            |
+------------------------+--------------------------------------------------+
| created                | 2015-04-24T11:22:40                              |
| datastore_name         | mysql                                            |
| datastore_version_name | 5.6                                              |
| description            | illustrate a special configuration group         |
| id                     | 3226b8e6-fa38-4e23-a4e6-000b639a93d7             |
| instance_count         | 3                                                |
| name                   | special-configuration                            |
| updated                | 2015-04-24T11:46:49                              |
| values                 | {"wait_timeout": 240, "max_connections": 100}    |
+------------------------+--------------------------------------------------+
```

As you can see, the `trove configuration-update` command replaces the entire definition of the configuration group (which used to set `wait_timeout` and `max_connections`) to set only `connect_timeout`. The intended behavior of this command is that `wait_timeout` and `max_connections` be restored to their defaults, but this is not being done because of the bug referenced earlier.

```
ubuntu@trove-book:~$ trove configuration-update 3226b8e6-fa38-4e23-a4e6-000b639a93d7 \
> '{ "connect_timeout": 30 }'
ubuntu@trove-book:~$ mysql -uroot -ppx8F7UuHeHu92BJ6mGzhfQQaGYxMAKKYbzX9 -h 10.0.0.2 -e
'select @@global.max_connections, @@global.wait_timeout, @@global.connect_timeout'
+--------------------------+-----------------------+--------------------------+
| @@global.max_connections | @@global.wait_timeout | @@global.connect_timeout |
+--------------------------+-----------------------+--------------------------+
|                      100 |                   240 |                       30 |
+--------------------------+-----------------------+--------------------------+
ubuntu@trove-book:~$ mysql -uroot -pDHueWtKJTXAWHYpJJrNRaNj9gZZzCKcxNk9f -h 10.0.0.3 -e
'select  @@global.max_connections, @@global.wait_timeout, @@global.connect_timeout'
+--------------------------+-----------------------+--------------------------+
| @@global.max_connections | @@global.wait_timeout | @@global.connect_timeout |
+--------------------------+-----------------------+--------------------------+
|                      100 |                   240 |                       30 |
+--------------------------+-----------------------+--------------------------+
```

```
ubuntu@trove-book:~$ mysql -uroot -pvtcM8cVwAU3bDc9fXMRKqtUbGsAPdpg4UC7x -h 10.0.0.4 -e
'select @@global.max_connections, @@global.wait_timeout, @@global.connect_timeout'
+--------------------------+------------------------+-------------------------+
| @@global.max_connections | @@global.wait_timeout  | @@global.connect_timeout |
+--------------------------+------------------------+-------------------------+
|                      100 |                    240 |                      30 |
+--------------------------+------------------------+-------------------------+
ubuntu@trove-book:~$ trove configuration-show 3226b8e6-fa38-4e23-a4e6-000b639a93d7
+-----------------------+---------------------------------------------+
| Property              | Value                                       |
+-----------------------+---------------------------------------------+
| created               | 2015-04-24T11:22:40                         |
| datastore_name        | mysql                                       |
| datastore_version_name| 5.6                                         |
| description           | illustrate a special configuration group    |
| id                    | 3226b8e6-fa38-4e23-a4e6-000b639a93d7        |
| instance_count        | 3                                           |
| name                  | special-configuration                       |
| updated               | 2015-04-24T11:51:33                         |
| values                | {"connect_timeout": 30}                     |
+-----------------------+---------------------------------------------+
```

The intended effect is that `max_connections` and `wait_timeout` are reverted to their defaults and just `connect_timeout` is set to the new value (30).

Instance Resizing

We conclude this chapter with a discussion of instance resizing. For the purposes of this discussion, we consider a running instance of MySQL (m2) as shown next. This instance was created with a flavor of 2 and a disk of 2 GB.

```
ubuntu@trove-book:~$ trove show m2
+--------------------+---------------------------------------+
| Property           | Value                                 |
+--------------------+---------------------------------------+
| created            | 2015-04-24T11:20:36                   |
| datastore          | mysql                                 |
| datastore_version  | 5.6                                   |
| flavor             | 2                                     |
| id                 | 53796f4d-b0d8-42f1-b9c6-82260a78150f  |
| ip                 | 10.0.0.2                              |
| name               | m2                                    |
| status             | ACTIVE                                |
| updated            | 2015-04-24T12:22:50                   |
| volume             | 2                                     |
| volume_used        | 0.11                                  |
+--------------------+---------------------------------------+
```

First, we demonstrate how to increase the size of the volume attached to the instance, in response to the fact that it is expected that there will be more data arriving and that the existing disk space is insufficient. This is easily accomplished by executing the trove resize-volume command.

```
ubuntu@trove-book:~$ trove resize-volume m2 4
```

This briefly places the instance into a state of RESIZE while the operation is performed and upon completion the instance returns to ACTIVE state. Note that the volume size increased from 2 to 4. You can both increase and reduce the size of the volume using this command. If you attempt to reduce the size of the volume, it is up to you to ensure that all your data will fit on the newly resized volume.

```
ubuntu@trove-book:~$ trove show m2
+-------------------+--------------------------------------+
| Property          | Value                                |
+-------------------+--------------------------------------+
| created           | 2015-04-24T11:20:36                  |
| datastore         | mysql                                |
| datastore_version | 5.6                                  |
| flavor            | 2                                    |
| id                | 53796f4d-b0d8-42f1-b9c6-82260a78150f |
| ip                | 10.0.0.2                             |
| name              | m2                                   |
| status            | ACTIVE                               |
| updated           | 2015-04-24T12:29:37                  |
| volume            | 4                                    |
| volume_used       | 0.11                                 |
+-------------------+--------------------------------------+
```

The other operation that is often required is to resize the instance flavor in response to a change in the expected CPU or memory demands on the instance. This can be accomplished by using the trove resize-instance command. But before doing this, we populate some tables and data into the instance. For this example, following is a database (called illustration) and a table (called sample) with one row:

```
mysql> select * from illustration.sample;
+------+------+
| a    | b    |
+------+------+
|   42 |  125 |
+------+------+
1 row in set (0.00 sec)
```

Next, execute the trove resize-instance command and provide it with 3, the proposed new flavor. Recall that the instance m2 was created with flavor 2.

```
ubuntu@trove-book:~$ trove resize-instance m2 3
```

This causes the instance to be placed into the RESIZE state and during this operation a new instance with the target flavor is created and the data volume is reattached to that instance. For this, Trove issues a Nova resize command on the Nova instance underlying the Trove instance.

```
ubuntu@trove-book:~$ trove show m2
+-------------------+-------------------------------------+
| Property          | Value                               |
+-------------------+-------------------------------------+
| created           | 2015-04-24T11:20:36                 |
| datastore         | mysql                               |
| datastore_version | 5.6                                 |
| flavor            | 2                                   |
| id                | 53796f4d-b0d8-42f1-b9c6-82260a78150f |
| ip                | 10.0.0.2                            |
| name              | m2                                  |
| status            | RESIZE                              |
| updated           | 2015-04-24T12:36:25                 |
| volume            | 4                                   |
+-------------------+-------------------------------------+
```

As soon as the resize operation is completed, the instance returns to an ACTIVE state and we now proceed to verify that the data has been retained and that the instance is now of flavor 3. The IP address (10.0.0.2) has also been migrated to the instance of flavor 3.

```
mysql> select * from illustration.sample;
+------+------+
| a    | b    |
+------+------+
|   42 |  125 |
+------+------+
1 row in set (0.08 sec)

ubuntu@trove-book:~$ trove show m2
+-------------------+-------------------------------------+
| Property          | Value                               |
+-------------------+-------------------------------------+
| created           | 2015-04-24T11:20:36                 |
| datastore         | mysql                               |
| datastore_version | 5.6                                 |
| flavor            | 3                                   |
| id                | 53796f4d-b0d8-42f1-b9c6-82260a78150f |
| ip                | 10.0.0.2                            |
| name              | m2                                  |
| status            | ACTIVE                              |
| updated           | 2015-04-24T12:40:09                 |
| volume            | 4                                   |
| volume_used       | 0.11                                |
+-------------------+-------------------------------------+
```

In the section "Configuration Groups," we described two kinds of configuration settings, one that was a constant and one that included variables like the RAM size. We conclude this section by looking at the impact of resizing an instance on a configuration parameter that includes a variable.

On the newly resized instance we find that key_buffer_size is set to 400M as shown next. Recall that on the instance of flavor 2 it was set to 200M and now that instance 3 (with double the memory) is in use, the value has been reset to reflect the higher available RAM.

```
mysql> select @@global.key_buffer_size/(1024*1024);
+---------------------------------------+
| @@global.key_buffer_size/(1024*1024) |
+---------------------------------------+
|                             400.0000 |
+---------------------------------------+
1 row in set (0.00 sec)
```

If a configuration group is attached to an instance and that configuration group provided an override to the default value, then that override would persist. It is important to keep this in mind when using configuration groups and performing instance flavor changes as configuration group overrides do not support a mechanism to specify a formulaic computation of the value (you may only provide a constant).

Terminating Instances

When you no longer need an instance, you can delete it using the `trove delete` command. You can delete clusters using the `trove cluster-delete` command.

The `trove delete` command deletes the database instance and permanently deletes all data stored on that running instance. Backups of the instance are not impacted and can be used at a later time to launch a new instance.

```
ubuntu@trove-book:~$ trove delete m2
ubuntu@trove-book:~$ trove list
+----+------+-----------+-------------------+--------+-----------+------+
| ID | Name | Datastore | Datastore Version | Status | Flavor ID | Size |
+----+------+-----------+-------------------+--------+-----------+------+
+----+------+-----------+-------------------+--------+-----------+------+
```

Similarly, the `trove cluster-delete` command deletes an entire cluster and all instances that form part of the cluster.

Summary

This chapter provided an overview of some advanced operations that can be performed by Trove. It is important to understand that Trove is more than merely a provisioning framework for database instances; it provides capabilities that can be used to manage an instance throughout its life cycle.

In the section "Custom Flavors," we described how you can create custom flavors for use with specific configurations of virtual hardware.

We described how backup and restore are implemented in Trove using datastore-specific strategies. We demonstrated full and incremental backups supported by MySQL, and how you could create a new instance from an existing backup.

Databases offer complex multinode configurations to provide high availability and high performance, and these techniques are usually referred to as replication and clustering. Trove implements both of these capabilities using datastore-specific extensions and strategies.

We demonstrated replication with MySQL. We examined binlog-based replication that was introduced in the Juno release (for MySQL 5.5) and GTID-based replication that was introduced in the Kilo release (for MySQL 5.6). We looked at how to utilize datastore-specific strategies in these implementations and showed the various ways in which you could accomplish a failover.

We demonstrated clustering with MongoDB. We examined in detail the operations involved in creating a cluster and described the implementation of the task manager and guest agent strategies.

In managing large numbers of instances it is cumbersome to establish and manipulate configuration parameters one instance at a time. Configuration groups allow for the creation of a set of parameters that can then be applied to multiple instances at the same time. We examined how configuration groups can be used and how they rely on datastore-specific guest agent implementations to carry out the actual parameter changes.

During the life cycle of an instance it is often required that the resources available to the instance be reconfigured. Sometimes this involves growing or shrinking the storage, and in other cases it involves altering the flavor associated with the instance. We demonstrated both and described how these are implemented.

Finally, when an instance is no longer required, the instance (or cluster) can be deleted to free up all resources that were in use. We examined the commands that you could use to do this.

This chapter does not provide a detailed tutorial about how to use each of the available Trove commands, focusing instead on the more commonly used commands during the life cycle of an instance or a cluster. Appendix B provides a complete list of commands and brief explanations of each.

The next chapter describes the steps involved in debugging and troubleshooting a system when things don't quite go as expected.

CHAPTER 6

■ ■ ■

Debugging and Troubleshooting

In previous chapters we discussed how to install and perform some basic configurations of Trove, as well as how to perform a variety of operations with Trove. We have also looked in detail at the Trove architecture and how the various components of Trove work together.

From time to time you will find that things don't go quite as expected and commands that you execute may encounter difficulties and generate errors. This chapter describes some basic debugging and troubleshooting techniques including

- Accessing the Trove guest instance command line

- Error logs on the Trove controller and guest instance

- Common error scenarios

- Using the OpenStack profiler with Trove

Accessing the Trove Guest Instance Command Line

Sometimes you have a problem setting up the Trove instance and the `trove create` command may fail. Or for some other reason, you may wish to connect to the Trove guest instance and access a command line.

Whether or not you are able to connect to the guest instance depends entirely on the way in which the guest image was constructed and whether you have the appropriate credentials to connect to the guest instance using a shell.

We look at two kinds of guest images in this section.

- guest images from OpenStack which are provided for development and testing at `http://tarballs.openstack.org/trove/images/ubuntu/`

- production-ready guest images distributed by Tesora at `http://www.tesora.com/products/`

To be able to connect to a guest instance and access the command line, all of the following conditions must be satisfied:

- You should have network access to the appropriate port (22 for ssh, 23 for `telnet`)

- A listener should be installed and running on that port

- You need credentials (username and password, or username and private key)

Guest Images from OpenStack

Guest images provided at tarballs.openstack.org (and installed as shown in Chapter 2) have been built in a manner that allows shell access for the user ubuntu using a key pair.

To do this, you need to get the Trove private key, the one that is registered for ssh access on the guest image. This key is available in the trove-integration repository.

The Trove key pair is found in scripts/files/keys. The following code installs the Trove private key (id_rsa) as the private key for the ubuntu user:

```
ubuntu@trove-book:~$ cp -b ~/trove-integration/scripts/files/keys/id_rsa ~/.ssh
ubuntu@trove-book:~$ chmod 400 ~/.ssh/id_rsa
```

Assume that you installed that key, and that you have a Trove instance running, as shown next.

```
ubuntu@trove-book:~$ trove show e7a420c3-578e-4488-bb51-5bd08c4c3cbb
+-------------------+--------------------------------------+
| Property          | Value                                |
+-------------------+--------------------------------------+
| created           | 2015-04-08T16:28:09                  |
| datastore         | mysql                                |
| datastore_version | 5.6                                  |
| flavor            | 2                                    |
| id                | e7a420c3-578e-4488-bb51-5bd08c4c3cbb |
| ip                | 10.0.0.2                             |
| name              | m1                                   |
| status            | BUILD                                |
| updated           | 2015-04-08T16:28:21                  |
| volume            | 1                                    |
+-------------------+--------------------------------------+
```

Now you can connect to the command line on this instance as the user ubuntu using the command ssh ubuntu@10.0.0.2 or simply ssh 10.0.0.2 if you are logged in as the ubuntu user.

```
ubuntu@trove-book:~$ ssh 10.0.0.2
Welcome to Ubuntu 12.04.5 LTS (GNU/Linux 3.2.0-77-virtual x86_64)

 * Documentation:  https://help.ubuntu.com/

  Get cloud support with Ubuntu Advantage Cloud Guest:
    http://www.ubuntu.com/business/services/cloud

The programs included with the Ubuntu system are free software;
the exact distribution terms for each program are described in the
individual files in /usr/share/doc/*/copyright.

Ubuntu comes with ABSOLUTELY NO WARRANTY, to the extent permitted by
applicable law.

ubuntu@m1:~$
```

Now that you are connected to the guest image, you can look around and see what is on that virtual machine (VM).

Guest Images from Tesora

Tesora provides production-ready guest images for download after a registration, at www.tesora.com/ products/. Once you register you receive instructions on how to install these images. Tesora provides these images along with the Community and Enterprise editions of their product.

To install images from Tesora, you execute the add-datastore.sh command, which automatically downloads and configures the image for use by Trove. Once installed, you can use the image to launch a Trove instance using the standard Trove commands.

Images from Tesora use a different mechanism to register the key pair required for ssh access. Tesora images (and Tesora's Community and Enterprise Edition software) rely on the specification of a configuration parameter use_nova_key_name in the Trove task manager configuration file (/etc/trove/ trove-taskmanager.conf).

First, create a key pair and register this key pair with Nova. You can do this by executing the nova keypair-add command. For more information on how to do this, refer to the Nova documentation available at http://docs.openstack.org/user-guide/enduser/cli_nova_configure_access_security_for_ instances.html.

Next, add a line to /etc/trove/trove-taskmanager.conf with the name of that key pair, for example,

```
use_nova_key_name = trove-keypair
```

Then restart the Trove task manager service. All subsequent Trove instances that are created will have the key pair provided and you will be able to connect to those instances using the ssh command.

Reading the Trove Error Logs

The Trove services running on the Trove controller node and the Trove guest agent running on the guest instances generate error logs that provide useful information about the operation of the system. We look at each of these in turn and also describe how to control the information that is sent to the error logs.

Error Logs on Trove Controller Node

When installed with devstack, logging from all services is sent to stdout which is then also sent to a file in /opt/stack/logs/. More precisely, log files are sent to $DEST/logs where $DEST defaults to /opt/stack. The exact location where devstack sends log files is configurable by setting the LOGDIR environment variable before running stack.sh.

When installed from packages, service log files typically are sent to /var/log/ and typically the Trove log files end up in /var/log/trove/. However, this depends on the package set you use, so consult the package documentation for more details.

The Trove API (application programming interface), task manager, and conductor typically log their messages to different files except if you use syslog. You can enable syslog for all logging by setting the --use-syslog command-line option on the launch command for the Trove services.

Error Logs on the Guest Instance

On the guest instance there are two important sets of log files that you need to review from time to time.

- Log files for the system and the guest database
- Log files generated by the Trove guest agent

On an Ubuntu system the system log files of interest are typically the files /var/log/syslog, the files in /var/log/upstart/, and the log files generated by the guest database that are also typically located in /var/log/. For example, MySQL log files are in /var/log/mysql/.

If there are errors before launching the guest agent, they are typically visible in /var/log/upstart/.

The log file generated by the guest agent is in /var/log/trove/ and is called trove-guestagent.log by default.

```
ubuntu@m1:/var/log/trove$ ls -la
total 212
drwxr-xr-x  2 ubuntu root     4096 Mar 17 16:36 .
drwxr-xr-x 11 root   root     4096 Mar 17 16:36 ..
-rw-rw-r--  1 ubuntu ubuntu 205167 Mar 17 16:47 trove-guestagent.log
```

You can change the location of the log file by editing the respective settings in the Trove guest agent. By default, this configuration file is /etc/trove/conf.d/trove-guestagent.conf.

```
ubuntu@m2:/etc/trove/conf.d$ cat -n trove-guestagent.conf

     7  use_syslog = False
     8  debug = True
     9  log_file = trove-guestagent.log
    10  log_dir = /var/log/trove/
    11  ignore_users = os_admin
```

Recall that the guest agent configuration file is stored on the controller (typically in /etc/trove/trove-guestagent.conf), but that too is configurable as shown next (from trove/common/cfg.py).

```
   342      cfg.StrOpt('guest_config',
   343              default='/etc/trove/trove-guestagent.conf',
   344              help='Path to the Guest Agent config file to be injected '
   345                  'during instance creation.'),
```

Some Practical Examples of Looking at Error Logs

The following example demonstrates how to launch a Trove instance on a system configured using devstack, and using the guest images from tarballs.openstack.org. The instance can be launched with a simple trove create command.

```
ubuntu@trove-book:~$ trove create m1 2 --size 2
```

Some minutes later the Nova instance was successfully launched and was assigned IP address 10.0.0.2. This was reflected by Trove but after a few minutes the instance went into an ERROR state. The error messages shown next were logged in the Trove task manager log file (in /opt/stack/logs since the system was launched with devstack).

```
2015-04-25 19:59:59.854 ERROR trove.taskmanager.models [req-0af7d974-9bc8-4233-adc5-
4ad826410b4d radmin trove] Failed to create instance 5065f999-a255-490f-909a-952ec79568bd.
Timeout waiting for instance to become active. No usage create-event was sent.
2015-04-25 19:59:59.870 ERROR trove.taskmanager.models [req-0af7d974-9bc8-4233-adc5-
4ad826410b4d radmin trove] Service status: ERROR
2015-04-25 19:59:59.871 ERROR trove.taskmanager.models [req-0af7d974-9bc8-4233-adc5-
4ad826410b4d radmin trove] Service error description: guestagent error
```

```
ubuntu@trove-book:~$ trove show m1
+-------------------+------------------------------------------+
| Property          | Value                                    |
+-------------------+------------------------------------------+
| created           | 2015-04-25T23:49:49                      |
| datastore         | mysql                                    |
| datastore_version | 5.6                                      |
| flavor            | 2                                        |
| id                | 5065f999-a255-490f-909a-952ec79568bd     |
| name              | m1                                       |
| status            | ERROR                                    |
| updated           | 2015-04-25T23:59:59                      |
| volume            | 2                                        |
+-------------------+------------------------------------------+
```

Looking further at the error log it appears that the task manager launched an instance. Executing the nova list or nova show commands you find that the instance is actually still running and has an IP address of 10.0.0.2. Since shell access to the instance is available, we can get into the instance and look further. The first thing that is apparent is that there is no Trove guest agent log file.

```
ubuntu@trove-book:~$ nova show m1
+-------------------+-----------------------------------------------------------+
| Property          | Value                                                     |
+-------------------+-----------------------------------------------------------+
| flavor            | m1.small (2)                                              |
[. . .]
| id                | 8b920495-5e07-44ae-b9a5-6c0432c12634                      |
| image             | mysql (50b966c1-3c47-4786-859c-77e201d11538)              |
[. . .]
| name              | m1                                                        |
[. . .]
| private network   | 10.0.0.2                                                  |
[. . .]
| status            | ACTIVE                                                    |
[. . .]
+-------------------+-----------------------------------------------------------+
ubuntu@trove-book:~$ ssh 10.0.0.2
[. . .]

ubuntu@m1:~$ ls -l /var/log/trove/
total 0
```

Next, look at the files in /var/log/upstart/ to investigate what happened earlier and locate the trove-guest.log file.

```
ubuntu@m1:~$ sudo cat /var/log/upstart/trove-guest.log
Warning: Permanently added '10.0.0.1' (ECDSA) to the list of known hosts.
Permission denied, please try again.
Permission denied, please try again.
Permission denied (publickey,password).
rsync: connection unexpectedly closed (0 bytes received so far) [Receiver]
rsync error: error in rsync protocol data stream (code 12) at io.c(226) [Receiver=3.1.0]
```

We will describe this further in Chapter 7 on building guest images; for now, note that the issue here is that the devstack guest images are designed for development use, and on first boot they rsync the Trove guest agent code onto the guest instance. To do this, they require the Trove public key be installed in the .ssh/authorized_keys file for the ubuntu user on the devstack host. In this example, this step did not complete.

In Chapter 2, the section "Enable the Default Trove Public Key" describes how to add this key onto your machine. This subject is also described in greater detail in Chapter 7.

Assuming that the trove-guest service was started successfully, you will see the the guest agent log file /var/log/trove/trove-guestagent.log.

If there are errors launching the guest agent, these errors will be logged here. As an example, an attempt to launch a guest failed and the following was found in the guest agent log file:

```
2015-03-03 14:36:24.849 CRITICAL root [-] ImportError: No module named oslo_concurrency
2015-03-03 14:36:24.849 TRACE root Traceback (most recent call last):
2015-03-03 14:36:24.849 TRACE root   File "/home/ubuntu/trove/contrib/trove-guestagent",
line 34, in <module>
2015-03-03 14:36:24.849 TRACE root     sys.exit(main())
2015-03-03 14:36:24.849 TRACE root   File "/home/ubuntu/trove/trove/cmd/guest.py", line 60,
in main
2015-03-03 14:36:24.849 TRACE root     from trove import rpc
2015-03-03 14:36:24.849 TRACE root   File "/home/ubuntu/trove/trove/rpc.py", line 36, in
<module>
2015-03-03 14:36:24.849 TRACE root     import trove.common.exception
2015-03-03 14:36:24.849 TRACE root   File "/home/ubuntu/trove/trove/common/exception.py",
line 20, in <module>
2015-03-03 14:36:24.849 TRACE root     from oslo_concurrency import processutils
2015-03-03 14:36:24.849 TRACE root ImportError: No module named oslo_concurrency
2015-03-03 14:36:24.849 TRACE root
```

This information helps us understand why the trove create call had failed and how it could be remedied (see https://bugs.launchpad.net/trove/+bug/1427699).

By default, devstack configures the system to log debugging messages into the various log files. This can prove useful in troubleshooting problems.

The trove database-list command that follows was executed on the host while also watching the output in the trove-guestagent.log file:

```
ubuntu@trove-book:~$ trove database-list fd124f41-68de-4f51-830b-dbc9ad92a7fa
+--------------------+
| Name               |
+--------------------+
| performance_schema |
| trove-book         |
+--------------------+
```

```
2015-03-17 16:49:13.385 DEBUG trove.guestagent.datastore.mysql.service [-] ---Listing
Databases--- from (pid=918) list_databases /home/ubuntu/trove/trove/guestagent/datastore/
mysql/service.py:423
2015-03-17 16:49:13.512 DEBUG trove.guestagent.datastore.mysql.service [-] database_names =
<sqlalchemy.engine.base.ResultProxy object at 0x360fe90>. from (pid=918) list_databases
/home/ubuntu/trove/trove/guestagent/datastore/mysql/service.py:451
```

```
2015-03-17 16:49:13.516 DEBUG trove.guestagent.datastore.mysql.service [-] database =
('performance_schema', 'utf8', 'utf8_general_ci'). from (pid=918) list_databases
/home/ubuntu/trove/trove/guestagent/datastore/mysql/service.py:455
2015-03-17 16:49:13.519 DEBUG trove.guestagent.datastore.mysql.service [-] database =
('trove-book', 'utf8', 'utf8_general_ci'). from (pid=918) list_databases /home/ubuntu/trove/
trove/guestagent/datastore/mysql/service.py:455
2015-03-17 16:49:13.539 DEBUG trove.guestagent.datastore.mysql.service [-] databases =
[{'_collate': 'utf8_general_ci', '_character_set': 'utf8', '_name': 'performance_schema'},
{'_collate': 'utf8_general_ci', '_character_set': 'utf8', '_name': 'trove-book'}] from
(pid=918) list_databases /home/ubuntu/trove/trove/guestagent/datastore/mysql/service.py:462
```

A great way to understand how Trove works is to enable debugging (described in the next section) and watch the various log files while executing commands. You will be able to follow requests as they work their way through the system and understand the working of the system and what is going wrong. The next section also describes how to change the information being logged.

Understanding the Trove Log Levels

You can categorize diagnostic messages generated by Trove into debug, informational, audit, warn, error, and critical messages. By default, the Trove services and the guest agent are configured to log at the informational level. In addition, back traces are generated in some circumstances.

When configured with devstack, the default is to launch the services with the --debug command-line parameter which enables debug messages as well. You can also enable debugging in the configuration file as shown (from /etc/trove/trove.conf).

```
8  use_syslog = False
9  debug = True
```

Messages in the log file identify the logging level that generated them. Some examples follow, with the identifiers highlighted:

```
2015-04-25 20:20:17.458 DEBUG trove.instance.models [-] Server api_status(NEW). from
(pid=64018) _load_servers_status /opt/stack/trove/trove/instance/models.py:1186
2015-04-25 20:20:17.465 INFO eventlet.wsgi [-] 192.168.117.5 - - [25/Apr/2015 20:20:17] "GET
/v1.0/70195ed77e594c63b33c5403f2e2885c/instances HTTP/1.1" 200 741 0.422295
2015-04-25 20:14:49.889 ERROR trove.guestagent.api [req-0af7d974-9bc8-4233-adc5-4ad826410b4d
radmin trove] Error calling stop_db
2015-04-25 20:14:49.889 TRACE trove.guestagent.api Traceback (most recent call last):
2015-04-25 20:14:49.889 TRACE trove.guestagent.api   File "/opt/stack/trove/trove/
guestagent/api.py", line 62, in _call
```

In addition, you can configure Trove to color code your messages. When viewed on a terminal you would see each class of message in a different color (see Figure 6-1).

```
2015-04-25 20:13:49.507 DEBUG trove.taskmanager.models [req-0af7d974-9bc8-4233-a
n _delete_resources for instance 5065f999-a255-490f-909a-952ec79568bd from (pid=
/trove/trove/taskmanager/models.py:1003
2015-04-25 20:13:49.511 DEBUG urllib3.util.retry [req-0af7d974-9bc8-4233-adc5-4a
retries value: 0 -> Retry(total=0, connect=None, read=None, redirect=0) from (pi
thon2.7/dist-packages/urllib3/util/retry.py:155
2015-04-25 20:13:49.880 DEBUG trove.taskmanager.models [req-0af7d974-9bc8-4233-a
ping datastore on instance 5065f999-a255-490f-909a-952ec79568bd before deleting
lete_resources /opt/stack/trove/trove/taskmanager/models.py:1007
2015-04-25 20:13:49.881 DEBUG trove.guestagent.api [req-0af7d974-9bc8-4233-adc5-
the call to stop MySQL on the Guest. from (pid=64025) stop_db /opt/stack/trove/t
2015-04-25 20:13:49.881 DEBUG trove.guestagent.api [req-0af7d974-9bc8-4233-adc5-
stop_db with timeout 60 from (pid=64025) _call /opt/stack/trove/trove/guestagent
2015-04-25 20:13:49.882 DEBUG oslo_messaging._drivers.amqpdriver [req-0af7d974-9
rove] MSG_ID is e45152d887344910abd23dc79a10ec87 from (pid=64025) _send /usr/loc
_messaging/_drivers/amqpdriver.py:311
2015-04-25 20:14:49.889 ERROR trove.guestagent.api [req-0af7d974-9bc8-4233-adc5-
lling stop_db
2015-04-25 20:14:49.889 TRACE trove.guestagent.api Traceback (most recent call l
2015-04-25 20:14:49.889 TRACE trove.guestagent.api    File "/opt/stack/trove/trov
call
```

Figure 6-1. *Color coding of error messages*

This is done by embedding the ANSI Color Code Escapes into the configuration of the information to be generated on a specific class of message as shown (from /etc/trove/trove.conf).

```
logging_exception_prefix = %(color)s%(asctime)s.%(msecs)03d TRACE %(name)s \
^[[01;35m%(instance)s^[[00m
logging_debug_format_suffix = ^[[00;33mfrom (pid=%(process)d) %(funcName)s \
%(pathname)s:%(lineno)d^[[00m
logging_default_format_string = %(asctime)s.%(msecs)03d %(color)s%(levelname)s \
%(name)s [^[[00;36m-%(color)s] ^[[01;35m%(instance)s%(color)s%(message)s^[[00m
logging_context_format_string = %(asctime)s.%(msecs)03d %(color)s%(levelname)s \
%(name)s [^[[01;36m%(request_id)s ^[[00;36m%(user)s %(tenant)s%(color)s] \
^[[01;35m%(instance)s%(color)s%(message)s^[[00m
```

The token %color is interpreted by the code generating the message and the appropriate escape sequences are introduced for the type of message being generated. The code that follows is from trove/openstack/common/log.py. To further customize these colors, refer to http://en.wikipedia.org/wiki/ANSI_escape_code#Colors.

```
699  class ColorHandler(logging.StreamHandler):
  700      LEVEL_COLORS = {
  701          logging.DEBUG: '\033[00;32m',   # GREEN
  702          logging.INFO: '\033[00;36m',   # CYAN
  703          logging.AUDIT: '\033[01;36m',   # BOLD CYAN
  704          logging.WARN: '\033[01;33m',   # BOLD YELLOW
  705          logging.ERROR: '\033[01;31m',   # BOLD RED
  706          logging.CRITICAL: '\033[01;31m',   # BOLD RED
  707      }
```

Timeouts during instance launch are a common problem that plague beginners with OpenStack. One of the common reasons for this problem is that a virtual machine with insufficient resources (hardware) is being used and the operation of launching a guest instance is taking too long.

By default, when Nova launches an instance for Trove, it does this using a command line like the one that follows; note that it provides the -enable-kvm command-line option and accel=kvm in the -machine option:

```
qemu-system-x86_64 -enable-kvm -name instance-00000003 -S \
-machine pc-i440fx-trusty,accel=kvm,usb=off -m 2048 \
-realtime mlock=off -smp 1,sockets=1,cores=1,threads=1 \
[. . .]
```

In a typical development environment, the user runs Ubuntu in a virtualized environment. OpenStack is installed in that virtualized Ubuntu environment.

If this environment is not set up to enable a kernel-based virtual machine (kvm) sometimes called virtualization technologies, the performance of the nested virtual machine launched by Nova will be very poor and while it will eventually launch, the default timeouts will be insufficient.

To verify whether kernel-based virtualized machines are enabled, execute the kvm-ok command. Following is what you should see if kvm is enabled:

```
ubuntu@trove-book:~$ kvm-ok
INFO: /dev/kvm exists
KVM acceleration can be used
```

Depending on the virtualization software that you are running, the steps for enabling virtualization technologies will be different. Consult the documentation for your software. When running devstack on bare metal, this may be as simple as setting the appropriate option in the BIOS. Not all processors support VT extensions.

Using the OpenStack Profiler with Trove

The OpenStack Profiler (OSProfiler) is a cross-project profiling library. OpenStack consists of a number of projects and each project (like Trove) consists of a number of services. Due to this complexity, it is often hard to understand why something may be running slowly.

The OpenStack profiler helps us understand the performance of a complex OpenStack system by providing a detailed call graph with execution times. The OSProfiler project is available at https://github.com/stackforge/osprofiler.

To enable OSProfiler, you need to perform the following steps. First, add the following lines to localrc before you run OpenStack using devstack:

```
CEILOMETER_BACKEND=mysql
CEILOMETER_NOTIFICATION_TOPICS=notifications,profiler
ENABLED_SERVICES+=,ceilometer-acompute,ceilometer-acentral
ENABLED_SERVICES+=,ceilometer-anotification,ceilometer-collector
ENABLED_SERVICES+=,ceilometer-alarm-evaluator,ceilometer-alarm-notifier
ENABLED_SERVICES+=,ceilometer-api
```

Once devstack is completed, you need to configure Trove to use the profiler by making changes to the Trove configuration files. Edit the trove.conf, trove-taskmanager.conf, trove-conductor.conf, and trove-guestagent.conf files as follows.

```
[profiler]
enabled = true
trace_sqlalchemy = true
```

When you install devstack (running stack.sh), it would have configured the osprofiler filter in the file /etc/trove/api-paste.ini. This includes adding osprofiler in the pipeline, and specifying the filter as follows:

```
[pipeline:troveapi]
pipeline = faultwrapper osprofiler authtoken authorization contextwrapper ratelimit \
extensions troveapp

[filter:osprofiler]
paste.filter_factory = osprofiler.web:WsgiMiddleware.factory
hmac_keys = SECRET_KEY
enabled = yes
```

The preceding configuration requires you to establish a shared secret that must then be provided in order to generate a profiler trace. This example uses the literal string SECRET_KEY, but you can replace it with any string of your own choosing.

Finally, restart the Trove services. This will complete the configuration of the OSProfiler. You can now profile an operation by adding the --profile command-line argument as follows:

```
ubuntu@trove-book:~$ trove --profile SECRET_KEY list
+----+------+-----------+-------------------+--------+-----------+------+
| ID | Name | Datastore | Datastore Version | Status | Flavor ID | Size |
+----+------+-----------+-------------------+--------+-----------+------+
+----+------+-----------+-------------------+--------+-----------+------+
Trace ID: 8bf225b1-0f98-4999-affc-303eb2f74b04
To display the trace, use the following command:
osprofiler trace show --html 8bf225b1-0f98-4999-affc-303eb2f74b04
```

The --profile argument accepts one parameter and that is the value set in the api-paste.ini file as hmac_keys. Since we used the literal string SECRET_KEY, I provide the same on the command line.

Note that once the command is completed, the profiler provides a command that will fetch the profile information. You can now demonstrate the profiler with a more substantial command (like trove create).

```
ubuntu@trove-book:/etc/trove$ trove --profile SECRET_KEY create m2 2 --size 2
+-------------------+--------------------------------------+
| Property          | Value                                |
+-------------------+--------------------------------------+
| created           | 2015-04-28T19:52:23                  |
| datastore         | mysql                                |
| datastore_version | 5.6                                  |
| flavor            | 2                                    |
| id                | 1697d595-7e1d-4173-85e2-664a152d280c |
| name              | m2                                   |
| status            | BUILD                                |
| updated           | 2015-04-28T19:52:23                  |
| volume            | 2                                    |
+-------------------+--------------------------------------+
Trace ID: a9e7c4b6-9e28-48a0-a175-feffd3ed582d
To display the trace, use the following command:
osprofiler trace show --html a9e7c4b6-9e28-48a0-a175-feffd3ed582d
```

By default, the only trace points that you will see are the ones generated from SQL Alchemy (recall that `trace_sqlalchemy` was set to true on all the Trove services). The profile for this `create` call includes a detailed breakdown of all the SQL Alchemy calls that went into the execution of this `create` call. Figure 6-2 shows an example of a profile as viewed in a browser.

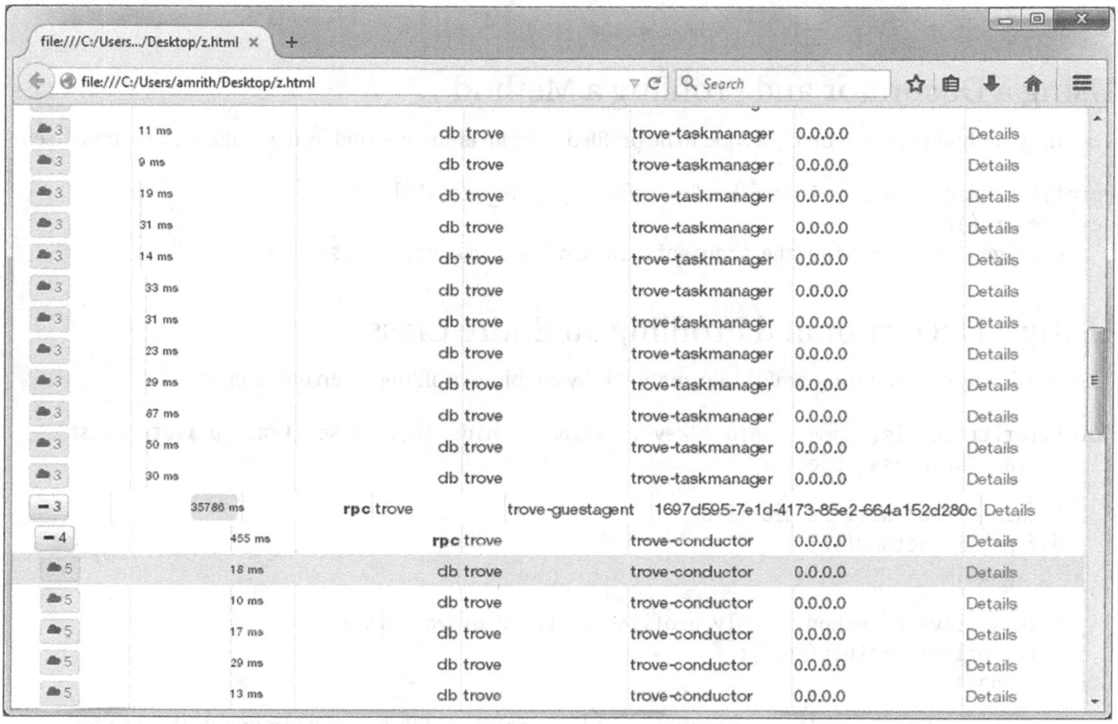

Figure 6-2. *Viewing a profile in a browser*

OSProfiler documents four ways in which code can be instrumented (for details, see https://github.com/stackforge/osprofiler). The following examples summarize each of these and instrument the code involved in the `trove create` command.

Profiling Code between a Start and Stop Location

The first method defines a region of code to be highlighted in the profile by establishing a start and stop location.

```
def prepare():
    profiler.start("name", {"key": "value"})

    # code to be profiled here

    profiler.stop({"information": "dictionary"})
```

Using the Python with Construct to Profile a Block of Code

The second method defines a region of code in a different way, by creating a block of code using the Python with construct.

```
with profiler.Trace("name", info={" key": "value"}):
    # some code here
```

Using a Decorator and Profiling a Method

The third method defines a block of code to be profiled to be an entire method by decorating the method itself.

```
@profiler.trace("name", info={"key": "value"}, hide_args=False)
def prepare():
    # If you need to hide the arguments in profile, use hide_args=True
```

Using a Decorator and Profiling an Entire Class

The fourth way of generating profile information is by enabling profiling on an entire class.

```
@profiler.trace_cls("name", info={"key": "value"}, hide_args=False, trace_private=False)
class TraceThisClass(object):

    # this method will be profiled
    def public_method(self):
        pass

    # this private method is only profiled if trace_private is True
    def _private_method(self):
        pass
```

In the preceding examples, the various methods to enable profiling accept arguments that can be used to augment the profiler information with program state. For example, the profiler.start() method accepts a name and a dictionary. Similarly, profiler.stop() also accepts a dictionary. Other methods accept an info parameter which is an arbitrary dictionary provided by the user, and this information is recorded in the trace for later use.

Before we illustrate how the code in create() and restart() was instrumented to enable profiling we examine the operation of the profiler. Having waited for the instance to come online, the profile was captured using the following command:

```
ubuntu@trove-book:/opt/stack/trove$ trove --profile SECRET_KEY create instance-1 2 --size 2
+-------------------+-------------------------------------+
| Property          | Value                               |
+-------------------+-------------------------------------+
| created           | 2015-04-29T09:05:47                 |
| datastore         | mysql                               |
| datastore_version | 5.6                                 |
| flavor            | 2                                   |
| id                | 31836a32-01b3-4b0f-8bc2-979eb5d5bcb5 |
| name              | instance-1                          |
| status            | BUILD                               |
| updated           | 2015-04-29T09:05:47                 |
| volume            | 2                                   |
+-------------------+-------------------------------------+
```

```
Trace ID: d8d15088-c4e8-4097-af93-19783138392c
To display the trace, use the following command:
osprofiler trace show --html d8d15088-c4e8-4097-af93-19783138392c
```

The output of the osprofiler command can be either --json or --html (the following command shows --html; Figure 6-3 shows the output in a browser).

```
ubuntu@trove-book:/opt/stack/trove$ osprofiler trace show --html \
> d8d15088-c4e8-4097-af93-19783138392c > /tmp/z.html
```

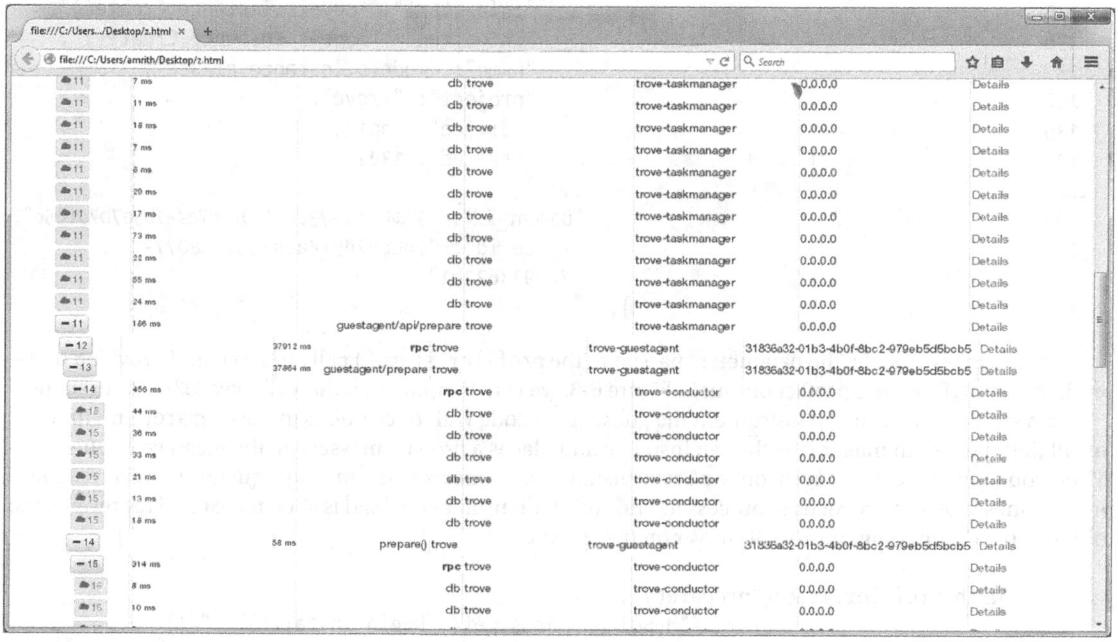

Figure 6-3. *The output of the osprofiler --html command in a browser*

Next, we describe the instrumentation of the create() call that produced the preceding trace. Once you instrument the code, you have to restart all the Trove services.

You can instrument the create() method as shown in the following example to capture the request early in the Trove API service. This change is one of the many changes in the following method (found in trove/instance/service.py):

```
+        profiler.start("models.Instance.create", {"before": "models.Instance.create()"})
         instance = models.Instance.create(context, name, flavor_id,
                                           image_id, databases, users,
                                           datastore, datastore_version,
@@ -244,6 +266,7 @@ class InstanceController(wsgi.Controller):
                                           availability_zone, nics,
                                           configuration, slave_of_id,
                                           replica_count=replica_count)
+        profiler.stop({"after": "models.Instance.create()"})
```

To generate a readable JSON (JavaScript Object Notation) version of the profile, pass the profiler output through a simple JSON formatter.

```
osprofiler trace show --json d8d15088-c4e8-4097-af93-19783138392c | \
> python -m json.tool > /tmp/z.json
```

```
130                                         {
131                                             "children": [],
132                                             "info": {
133                                                 "finished": 1575,
134                                                 "host": "0.0.0.0",
135                                                 "info.start": "models.Instance.Create()",
136                                                 "info.stop": "models.Instance.Create()",
137                                                 "name": "models.Instance.create",
138                                                 "project": "trove",
139                                                 "service": "api",
140                                                 "started": 1322
141                                             },
142                                             "parent_id": "59d4a51c-73cd-4102-b7ed-1b5e7b7df65c",
143                                             "trace_id": "7bccb7d9-4aeb-491e-a077-
                                                a72b923622b1"
144                                         },
```

As shown previously, the parameters passed to the `profiler.start()` call are saved and provided in the profiler output. From the profiler output in Figure 6-3, we can compute that this call took 253ms to execute.

In a similar way, you can instrument the guest agent code with trace points in the `prepare()` method. Recall that the task manager launches an instance and places a prepare message in the message queue. When you launch the guest agent on the Trove instance, it connects to the message queue and receives the prepare message and proceeds to process it. The code with profiler enabled is shown next and represents the initial steps of launching the MySQL server on the instance.

```
+        with profiler.Trace("prepare()",
+                            info={"MySqlAppStatus.get().begin_install()": ""}):
+            MySqlAppStatus.get().begin_install()
+
+        with profiler.Trace("prepare()",
+                            info={"app.install_if_needed": ""}):
+            # status end_mysql_install set with secure()
+            app = MySqlApp(MySqlAppStatus.get())
+            app.install_if_needed(packages)
+
+        with profiler.Trace("prepare()",
+                            info={"device:path": ""}):
+            if device:path:
+                #stop and do not update database
+                app.stop_db()
+                device = volume.VolumeDevice(device:path)
+                # unmount if device is already mounted
+                device.unmount_device(device:path)
+                device.format()
+                if os.path.exists(mount_point):
+                    #rsync exiting data
```

```
+                          device.migrate_data(mount_point)
+                  #mount the volume
+                  device.mount(mount_point)
+                  LOG.debug("Mounted the volume.")
+                  app.start_mysql()
```

Looking at the profiler output we are able to see these were triggered. We can therefore determine the amount of time that each of these blocks of code took to execute and also the service in whose context the code was executed.

```
892              "info": {
893                  "finished": 17909231,
894                  "host": "31836a32-01b3-4b0f-8bc2-979eb5d5bcb5",
895                  "info.MySqlAppStatus:get():begin_install()": "",
896                  "name": "prepare()",
897                  "project": "trove",
898                  "service": "trove-guestagent",
899                  "started": 17909173
900              },
901              "parent_id": "6a1eb340-73e0-48d2-a629-1723733a2036",
902              "trace_id": "71560f39-f83f-410f-ab3e-bcffb1b4cba9"
903          },
904          {
905              "children": [],
906              "info": {
907                  "finished": 17912682,
908                  "host": "31836a32-01b3-4b0f-8bc2-979eb5d5bcb5",
909                  "info.app:install_if_needed": "",
910                  "name": "prepare()",
911                  "project": "trove",
912                  "service": "trove-guestagent",
913                  "started": 17909347
914              },
915              "parent_id": "6a1eb340-73e0-48d2-a629-1723733a2036",
916              "trace_id": "cb16c3c3-164b-4b30-b507-8367c3b792a7"
917          },
918          {
919              "children": [],
920              "info": {
921                  "finished": 17929383,
922                  "host": "31836a32-01b3-4b0f-8bc2-979eb5d5bcb5",
923                  "info.device:path": "",
924                  "name": "prepare()",
925                  "project": "trove",
926                  "service": "trove-guestagent",
927                  "started": 17912744
928              },
929              "parent_id": "6a1eb340-73e0-48d2-a629-1723733a2036",
930              "trace_id": "89bde862-6cae-486d-8476-120602e3ec9a"
931          }
```

Summary

Trove services log diagnostic information. Some log files reside on the Trove controller node, and others reside on the guest instances. This chapter provided an introduction to debugging and troubleshooting by looking at these log files.

To get access to information on the guest instance, you often need to access a command line (shell) on the guest instance. Whether this is possible or not depends on how the guest images were built. This chapter illustrated how to access the shell on guest instances launched with the images that OpenStack provides (on tarballs.openstack.org) for development and testing.

When errors occur, you need to look at the log files generated by the various services. In some cases, you need to look at the log files generated by system services as well. We simulated some common failure scenarios and then illustrated troubleshooting steps.

While this is not, by any means, an exhaustive list of all the troubleshooting steps that one would need to know when operating Trove, we also illustrated a common practice to begin to understand Trove. This involves enabling debugging and executing a set of commands while watching the messages logged in the various log files. With debugging enabled, copious information is logged that will help you understand the processing of messages on a normally operating system and help you spot errors and anomalies when something goes wrong.

A useful debugging tool is the OSProfiler. It helps you understand not only the performance of the system but also the flow of messages through the system. We illustrated how code can be instrumented for use with the OSProfiler tool, and how profiler traces can be extracted from the system.

CHAPTER 7

■ ■ ■

Building Guest Images for Trove

In previous chapters we examined the steps involved in downloading, configuring, and operating Trove. We described the architecture of Trove in detail and illustrated how the various components of the Trove architecture work together.

Throughout these descriptions, we mentioned that you can create Trove guest instances by launching guest images that are registered with Glance, but we did not delve into what it took to construct one of these images.

As described in Chapter 2, Trove does not provide guest images for all the databases that it supports; it provides a framework within which a Database as a Service (DBaaS) can be operated. In order to operate a DBaaS, you need to create or obtain guest images for the required databases.

Some guest images are available from OpenStack at http://tarballs.openstack.org/trove/images/ubuntu/. The Trove continuous integration (CI) system uses these images, and you can use them for development and testing, but they are not suitable for production use. Tesora (www.tesora.com) also offers for download production-ready guest images for a number of databases.

This chapter describes guest images in more detail and provides detailed instructions on how you can build your own guest images. It describes the reference *elements* provided by Trove (in the trove-integration project) and shows how you can adapt them to build your own customized guest images.

Using Prebuilt Trove Guest Images

A Trove guest image is an image that

- Is registered with Glance

- Is bootable by Nova

- Contains components that are part of the delivery of the DBaaS capability offered by Trove

Components of a Trove Guest Image

A Trove guest image should at the very minimum contain a Trove guest agent (or the ability to obtain and launch a Trove guest agent) for the database that is to be provided.

As we have described earlier, Trove exposes a public API that represents an abstraction of a variety of database operations, including provisioning and management. The implementation within Trove often requires database-specific code to be implemented on a guest instance, and this is done by the Trove guest agent.

Recall that guest images provided by `tarballs.openstack.org` do not contain the guest agent code on them; instead, they copy the code from the host system at launch time. This is the reason the Trove `ssh` key must be added to the `authorized_keys` file for the ubuntu user. A failure to do that leads to an error that was illustrated in the chapter on debugging and troubleshooting. The presence of this well-known key on the instance is another thing that makes these images ideal for testing and not suitable for production use.

Registering a Trove Guest Image

Once you build a guest image, you need to register it with Glance and Trove. In Chapter 2 we listed these steps in brief as we demonstrated how to install the Percona 5.5 datastore, and in Chapter 5 we listed the steps as we registered a MongoDB 2.4.9 guest image. In this section we will explore these steps in more detail.

First, register a guest image with Glance as shown in the following example (which is the same one we used in Chapter 2). This causes Glance to store the image for later use. The image receives a Glance ID, which you use later.

```
ubuntu@trove-controller:~$ glance image-create --name percona \
> --disk-format qcow2 \
> --container-format bare --is-public True --file ~/downloaded-images/percona.qcow2
+------------------+--------------------------------------+
| Property         | Value                                |
+------------------+--------------------------------------+
| checksum         | 963677491f25a1ce448a6c11bee67066     |
| container_format | bare                                 |
| created_at       | 2015-03-18T13:19:18                  |
| deleted          | False                                |
| deleted_at       | None                                 |
| disk_format      | qcow2                                |
| id               | 80137e59-f2d6-4570-874c-4e9576624950 |
| is_public        | True                                 |
| min_disk         | 0                                    |
| min_ram          | 0                                    |
| name             | percona                              |
| owner            | 979bd3efad6f42448ffa55185a122f3b     |
| protected        | False                                |
| size             | 513343488                            |
| status           | active                               |
| updated_at       | 2015-03-18T13:19:30                  |
| virtual_size     | None                                 |
+------------------+--------------------------------------+
```

This is sufficient information for you to be able to boot the image using Nova; however, in order to boot it using Trove, some additional steps are required. Registration with Trove maps the Glance image ID shown previously to the name of the datastore and its version. In this case, the datastore was Percona version 5.5.

First, register a datastore for percona, using the following command.

```
ubuntu@trove-controller:~ $ trove-manage datastore_update percona ''
```

The second parameter (here, an empty string) indicates that you are merely registering the datastore percona and you will provide additional information about it later.

Next, you associate a specific datastore and version to a Glance image and provide some additional information about the guest image.

```
ubuntu@trove-controller:~ $ trove-manage datastore_version_update percona 5.5 \
> percona 80137e59-f2d6-4570-874c-4e9576624950 \
> "percona-server-server-5.5" 1
```

The following list describes the various arguments:

- `trove-manage datastore_version_update` is the command; `percona` is the datastore; 5.5 is the version number.

- `percona` is the manager that will administer this datastore. The manager name provides a link to the datastore-specific extension in the Trove guest agent; for Percona this is 'trove.guestagent.datastore.mysql.manager.Manager'. Each database type supported by Trove has a specific Manager class that is looked up based on the manager name. The manager name is also used to select the appropriate set of configuration parameters (called a section) provided in the various Trove configuration files.

- `80137e59-f2d6-4570-874c-4e9576624950` is the ID of the Glance image. This id is provided in the output of the `glance image-create` command as shown previously.

- `"percona-server-server-5.5"` is a list of package names that are passed to the guest agent in the `prepare()` message. This is typically used by the guest agent to install or update packages to the latest versions.

- 1, the last parameter, indicates that the datastore version should be marked active.

You can get all of this information by executing the command `trove-manage datastore_version_update -h`.

Next, you specify the default version of the datastore that you want to use.

```
ubuntu@trove-controller:~$ trove-manage datastore_update percona 5.5
```

Consider a system where you have the datastore `percona` and guest images for both versions 5.5 and 5.6. This command specifies which version of the datastore should be launched if the datastore version is not specified as part of the `trove-create` command. In the event that a system were configured with both Percona 5.5 and 5.6, the preceding command would set version 5.5 to be the default.

On this system, the command `trove create m2 2 --datastore percona --size 3` would launch an instance of Percona 5.5. To launch an instance of Percona 5.6 you would have to specify the `--datastore_version 5.6` command-line argument to the `trove create` command.

Trove configuration groups let you specify a number of configuration settings and then apply those settings to one or more database instances. Trove needs a list of validation rules that it can use to make sure the settings in a configuration group are valid for a particular database. You need to provide these rules before you can define a configuration group and attach it to an instance. A guest image should provide a user with a set of validation rules if the default rules for the datastore (which are provided with Trove) are not sufficient.

Next, you register the validation rules for the Percona 5.5 guest image by executing the following command:

```
ubuntu@trove-controller:~ $ trove-manage db_load_datastore_config_parameters \
> percona 5.5 ./validation_rules.json
```

Finally, on a system with multiple datastores installed, what datastore should be launched if the user does not provide one to the trove create command? This can be specified by using the default_datastore parameter in /etc/trove.conf. To force the system to launch Percona instead of MySQL, Chapter 2 provided the change shown next.

```
ubuntu@trove-controller:~ $ sed -i \
> 's/default_datastore = mysql/default_datastore = percona/' \
> ./trove.conf
ubuntu@trove-controller:~ $ diff ./trove.conf.original ./trove.conf
10c10
< default_datastore = mysql
---
> default_datastore = percona
```

Before making this change, the command trove create would attempt to launch a MySQL datastore if you did not specify the --datastore option. After this change the same command would attempt to launch a Percona datastore if you did not specify the --datastore option.

Building Guest Images with Disk Image Builder

If you do not wish to use the prebuilt images that are available for download at http://tarballs. openstack.org/trove/images/ubuntu/ (which are intended for development and testing purposes) or the images distributed by Tesora, then you have to build your own images.

You can use any mechanism that generates an image that can be launched with Nova but for the purposes of this example, we focus on building guest images using the popular Disk Image Builder (DIB) tool. (DIB was originally written by the Hewlett-Packard Development Company and NTT Docomo, Inc.) The online documentation about building an image with DIB can be found at https://git.openstack.org/cgit/openstack/diskimage-builder/tree/doc/source/user_guide.

Installing Disk Image Builder

Begin by installing DIB on the machine on which you will be building images. DIB is I/O and CPU intensive. DIB requires at least 4 GB of memory, but more is highly recommended.

DIB is run directly out of the source repository. Installation of DIB is as simple as cloning the source repository.

```
ubuntu@trove-book:/opt/stack$ git clone https://git.openstack.org/openstack/diskimage-
builder
Cloning into 'diskimage-builder'...
remote: Counting objects: 10617, done.
remote: Compressing objects: 100% (5445/5445), done.
remote: Total 10617 (delta 5965), reused 8516 (delta 4300)
Receiving objects: 100% (10617/10617), 1.75 MiB | 1006.00 KiB/s, done.
Resolving deltas: 100% (5965/5965), done.
Checking connectivity... done.
```

You also need to ensure that you have qemu-img and kpartx installed on your machine. If they are not available, you need to install them as well. You can install them using the following command:

```
ubuntu@trove-book:/opt/stack$ sudo apt-get install qemu-utils kpartx
```

Disk Image Builder Elements

DIB functions by executing a sequence of commands provided to it. The sequence of commands, when executed completely, will result in the production of a guest image. The commands are provided on the command line and each command is a DIB element.

A DIB element in turn consists of a collection of scripts that must be executed in a specified sequence. In effect, DIB is a framework within which these scripts are executed, in the specified sequence, and with each script executed in its own appropriate context. We will describe contexts further in the section "Phases Within an Element"

Disk Image Builder Elements

DIB ships with a number of elements. You are free to use these elements in constructing your own images.

Note some of the highlighted elements that follow, including apt-conf, rhel, rhel7, yum, centos, fedora, opensuse, ubuntu, and debian. DIB itself is a tool that you can run on a number of operating systems and you can use it to generate guest images that contain many different operating systems. DIB elements are provided in diskimage-builder/elements.

```
ubuntu@trove-book:/opt/stack/diskimage-builder/elements$ ls
apt-conf                          dib-run-parts              pypi
apt-preferences                   disable-selinux            ramdisk
apt-sources                       dkms                       ramdisk-base
architecture-emulation-binaries   dpkg                       rax-nova-agent
baremetal                         dracut-network             redhat-common
base                              dracut-ramdisk             rhel
cache-url                         element-manifest           rhel7
centos                            enable-serial-console      rhel-common
centos7                           epel                       rpm-distro
centos-minimal                    fedora                     select-boot-kernel-initrd
cleanup-kernel-initrd             fedora-minimal             selinux-permissive
cloud-init-datasources            hwburnin                   serial-console
cloud-init-nocloud                hwdiscovery                simple-init
debian                            ilo                        source-repositories
debian-minimal                    install-static             stable-interface-names
debian-systemd                    install-types              svc-map
debian-upstart                    ironic-agent               uboot
debootstrap                       ironic-discoverd-ramdisk   ubuntu
deploy                            iso                        ubuntu-core
deploy-baremetal                  local-config               ubuntu-minimal
deploy-ironic                     manifests                  ubuntu-signed
deploy-kexec                      mellanox                   vm
deploy-targetcli                  modprobe-blacklist         yum
deploy-tgtadm                     opensuse                   yum-minimal
devuser                           package-installs           zypper
dhcp-all-interfaces               pip-cache
dib-init-system                   pkg-map
```

Trove Reference Elements

In addition to the elements provided by DIB, Trove provides a number of reference elements for databases that are supported by Trove and you can use these in constructing your own images. The Trove reference elements are found in the trove-integration repository in trove-integration/scripts/files/elements.

```
ubuntu@trove-book:/opt/stack/trove-integration/scripts/files/elements$ ls -l
total 68
drwxrwxr-x 5 ubuntu ubuntu 4096 Apr 23 19:48 fedora-guest
drwxrwxr-x 3 ubuntu ubuntu 4096 Apr 23 19:48 fedora-mongodb
drwxrwxr-x 3 ubuntu ubuntu 4096 Apr 23 19:48 fedora-mysql
drwxrwxr-x 3 ubuntu ubuntu 4096 Apr 23 19:48 fedora-percona
drwxrwxr-x 3 ubuntu ubuntu 4096 Apr 23 19:48 fedora-postgresql
drwxrwxr-x 3 ubuntu ubuntu 4096 Apr 23 19:48 fedora-redis
drwxrwxr-x 3 ubuntu ubuntu 4096 Apr 23 19:48 ubuntu-cassandra
drwxrwxr-x 3 ubuntu ubuntu 4096 Apr 23 19:48 ubuntu-couchbase
drwxrwxr-x 3 ubuntu ubuntu 4096 Apr 23 19:48 ubuntu-couchdb
drwxrwxr-x 4 ubuntu ubuntu 4096 Apr 23 19:48 ubuntu-db2
drwxrwxr-x 6 ubuntu ubuntu 4096 Apr 23 19:48 ubuntu-guest
drwxrwxr-x 3 ubuntu ubuntu 4096 Apr 23 19:48 ubuntu-mongodb
drwxrwxr-x 4 ubuntu ubuntu 4096 Apr 23 19:48 ubuntu-mysql
drwxrwxr-x 4 ubuntu ubuntu 4096 Apr 23 19:48 ubuntu-percona
drwxrwxr-x 3 ubuntu ubuntu 4096 Apr 23 19:48 ubuntu-postgresql
drwxrwxr-x 3 ubuntu ubuntu 4096 Apr 23 19:48 ubuntu-redis
drwxrwxr-x 4 ubuntu ubuntu 4096 Apr 23 19:48 ubuntu-vertica
```

Building a Guest Image from Trove Reference Elements

One way to build your own guest image is to use the reference elements provided with Trove. As previously mentioned, these elements are available in the trove-integration repository in trove-integration/scripts/files/elements.

The command-line help for the disk-image-create command provides very detailed information about the various options available with the system. The command is located in disk-image-builder/bin.

```
ubuntu@trove-book:/opt/stack/diskimage-builder$ bin/disk-image-create --help
Usage: disk-image-create [OPTION]... [ELEMENT]...

Options:
    -a i386|amd64|armhf -- set the architecture of the image(default amd64)
    -o imagename -- set the imagename of the output image file(default image)
    -t qcow2,tar,vhd,raw -- set the image types of the output image files (default qcow2)
        File types should be comma separated. VHD outputting requires the vhd-util
        executable be in your PATH.
    -x -- turn on tracing
    -u -- uncompressed; do not compress the image - larger but faster
    -c -- clear environment before starting work
    --image-size size -- image size in GB for the created image
    --image-cache directory -- location for cached images(default ~/.cache/image-create)
    --max-online-resize size -- max number of filesystem blocks to support when resizing.
        Useful if you want a really large root partition when the image is deployed.
        Using a very large value may run into a known bug in resize2fs.
```

```
        Setting the value to 274877906944 will get you a 1PB root file system.
        Making this value unnecessarily large will consume extra disk space
        on the root partition with extra file system inodes.
  --min-tmpfs size -- minimum size in GB needed in tmpfs to build the image
  --mkfs-options -- option flags to be passed directly to mkfs.
        Options should be passed as a single string value.
  --no-tmpfs -- do not use tmpfs to speed image build
  --offline -- do not update cached resources
  --qemu-img-options -- option flags to be passed directly to qemu-img.
        Options need to be comma separated, and follow the key=value pattern.
  --root-label label -- label for the root filesystem.  Defaults to 'cloudimg-rootfs'.
  --ramdisk-element -- specify the main element to be used for building ramdisks.
        Defaults to 'ramdisk'.  Should be set to 'dracut-ramdisk' for platforms such
        as RHEL and CentOS that do not package busybox.
  --install-type -- specify the default installation type. Defaults to 'source'. Set to
'package' to use package based installations by default.
  -n skip the default inclusion of the 'base' element
  -p package[,package,package] -- list of packages to install in the image
  -h|--help -- display this help and exit


ELEMENTS_PATH will allow you to specify multiple locations for the elements.

NOTE: At least one distribution root element must be specified.

NOTE: If using the VHD output format you need to have a patched version of vhd-util
installed for the image
        to be bootable. The patch is available here: https://github.com/emonty/vhd-util/blob/
master/debian/patches/citrix
        and a PPA with the patched tool is available here: https://launchpad.net/~openstack-
ci-core/+archive/ubuntu/vhd-util

Examples:
    disk-image-create -a amd64 -o ubuntu-amd64 vm ubuntu
    export ELEMENTS_PATH=~/source/tripleo-image-elements/elements
    disk-image-create -a amd64 -o fedora-amd64-heat-cfntools vm fedora heat-cfntools
```

The example command provided earlier would create perfectly usable Nova images, the first one of an Ubuntu system and the second one of a Fedora system.

The reference elements provided by Trove require a variety of configuration options to be set. You must therefore set several environment variables to appropriate values for your setup. A failure to set some of these variables will result in an error. The following output lists and explains these variables. The values shown in the settings that follow reflect the values that were set on a default devstack-based installation as described in Chapter 2.

```
# HOST_USERNAME is the name of the user on the Trove host machine.
# It is used to identify the location of the authorized_keys, id_rsa, and
# id_rsa.pub files that are to be used in guest image creation.
export HOST_USERNAME=ubuntu

# HOST_SCP_USERNAME is the name of the user on the Trove host machine
# used to connect from the guest while copying the guest agent code
```

```
# during the upstart process.
export HOST_SCP_USERNAME=ubuntu

# GUEST_USERNAME is the name of the user on the Trove guest who will
# run the guest agent and perform a number of other jobs. This user
# is created during the image build process if it does not exist.
export GUEST_USERNAME=ubuntu

# NETWORK_GATEWAY is set to the IP address of the Trove host machine and used
# during the rsync process to copy the guest agent code during the upstart
# process
export NETWORK_GATEWAY=10.0.0.1

# REDSTACK_SCRIPTS is a pointer to files in the trove-integration project.
# redstack is the old name for trove-integration, at the time when Trove was
# called red dwarf.
export REDSTACK_SCRIPTS=/opt/stack/trove-integration/scripts

# PATH_TROVE is the path to the Trove source code and this is used
# in the rsync of code to the guest.
export PATH_TROVE=/opt/stack/trove

# ESCAPED_PATH_TROVE is the escaped version of PATH_TROVE and is used
# for much the same purpose as PATH_TROVE.
export ESCAPED_PATH_TROVE='\/opt\/stack\/trove'

# SSH_DIR is a path to the .ssh directory for the user on the host
# and is used in the image creation process to obtain the the
# authorized_keys, id_rsa and id_rsa.pub files.
export SSH_DIR=/home/ubuntu/.ssh

# GUEST_LOGDIR is the location on the guest where the Trove log
# file is to be stored.
export GUEST_LOGDIR=/var/log/trove/

# ESCAPED_GUEST_LOGDIR is the escaped version of GUEST_LOGDIR.
export ESCAPED_GUEST_LOGDIR='\/var\/log\/trove\/'

# the DIB element cloud-init-datasources uses this value to determine
# the data sources that must be queried during first boot to obtain
# instance metadata.
export DIB_CLOUD_INIT_DATASOURCES='ConfigDrive'

# DATASTORE_PKG_LOCATION is not used in the creation of the MySQL instance
# but is used by some databases (currently DB2 and Vertica) to identify the
# location of a downloaded package containing the database. Other databases
# merely obtain this using apt-get or the appropriate package management
# command. This variable is used for databases that do not allow this, and
# for example, require the user to click on a license agreement in order to
# obtain the database software.
export DATASTORE_PKG_LOCATION=""
```

Once you have set the previous variables to the appropriate values for your configuration you can create a Trove guest image for the MySQL database using the following command:

```
/opt/stack/diskimage-builder/bin/disk-image-create -a amd64 \
-o /home/ubuntu/images/ubuntu_mysql/ubuntu_mysql -x \
--qemu-img-options compat=0.10 ubuntu vm heat-cfntools cloud-init-datasources \
ubuntu-guest ubuntu-mysql
```

This will generate the default qcow2 (QEMU copy on write) image which will be stored in /home/ubuntu/images/ubuntu_mysql/ubuntu_mysql.qcow2.

Building a Guest Image Using 'redstack'

In addition to providing reference elements for many databases, Trove also provides a utility called redstack that can perform many useful operations in Trove. One of them is to build a guest image.

You can easily build a guest image using the Trove reference elements with a single redstack command as shown in the following example:

```
ubuntu@trove-book:/opt/stack/trove-integration/scripts$ ./redstack build-image mysql
[. . .]
Converting image using qemu-img convert
+ qemu-img convert -c -f raw /tmp/image.mQWg8TpZ/image.raw -O qcow2 -o compat=0.10 /home/
ubuntu/images/ubuntu_mysql/ubuntu_mysql.qcow2-new
+ OUT_IMAGE_PATH=/home/ubuntu/images/ubuntu_mysql/ubuntu_mysql.qcow2-new
+ finish_image /home/ubuntu/images/ubuntu_mysql/ubuntu_mysql.qcow2
+ '[' -f /home/ubuntu/images/ubuntu_mysql/ubuntu_mysql.qcow2 -a 0 -eq 0 ']'
+ mv /home/ubuntu/images/ubuntu_mysql/ubuntu_mysql.qcow2-new /home/ubuntu/images/ubuntu_
mysql/ubuntu_mysql.qcow2
+ echo 'Image file /home/ubuntu/images/ubuntu_mysql/ubuntu_mysql.qcow2 created...'
Image file /home/ubuntu/images/ubuntu_mysql/ubuntu_mysql.qcow2 created...

ubuntu@trove-book:/opt/stack/trove-integration/scripts$ cd /home/ubuntu/images/ubuntu_mysql

ubuntu@trove-book:~/images/ubuntu_mysql$ ls -l
total 484572
drwxrwxr-x 3 ubuntu ubuntu      4096 May  1 07:30 ubuntu_mysql.d
-rw-r--r-- 1 ubuntu ubuntu 497549312 May  1 07:33 ubuntu_mysql.qcow2
```

The preceding command has generated a mysql image (ubuntu_mysql.qcow2). You can replace mysql on the command line with percona, mongodb, redis, cassandra, couchbase, postgresql, couchdb, vertica, or db2, and redstack will build you a guest image for those databases. When running this command to generate either a Vertica or a DB2 guest image, make sure you download the database software (using the web-based process with a click-through) and place it at a location identified by the environment variable DATASTORE_PKG_LOCATION.

For example, assume that you wanted to build the DB2 Express-C guest image for Ubuntu. You would download DB2 Express-C (Linux 64 bit) software from IBM from www-01.ibm.com/software/data/db2/express-c/download.html and then complete a registration process, and review and accept a license agreement. You will then be able to download the package as a .tar.gz file.

Now you place the .tar.gz file that you have downloaded in a place accessible from the machine where you will run the disk-image-create or redstack build-image command. This location could either be on an accessible filesystem or on a location accessible using wget. You then set the environment variable

DATASTORE_PKG_LOCATION. Assuming that the file is stored in /home/ubuntu/db2/<filename>.tar.gz, you should set DATASTORE_PKG_LOCATION to that path name. Assuming that the file is stored on some private web-accessible repository at www.somewhere.com/db2/db2-linux-64-bit.tar.gz, you would set DATASTORE_PKG_LOCATION to that URL (uniform resource locator).

■ **Note**   Using redstack or the DIB tool to create a guest image of a database that requires explicit permissions to download does not automatically provide you with the right to redistribute the resulting image. Ensure that whatever you do with the guest images you create remains consistent with your obligations under the software licensing agreements you accepted when you downloaded the software.

Understanding How Disk Image Builder Works

The previous sections have described how to run DIB with reference elements and generate a disk image for Trove. In this section we examine the operation of DIB in more detail.

The command line to disk-image-create provides a list of elements to execute in the construction of a guest image. Images are constructed in a chroot environment and DIB has the ability to execute some commands within the chroot environment and some commands outside the chroot environment. This makes it possible for DIB to copy files from outside the chroot environment into the chroot environment, and then execute a command within the chroot environment.

DIB constructs a filesystem with the image contents, creates a file (as a loopback device), and copies the entire filesystem into that file. The loopback device is an ext4 filesystem that is large enough to hold all of the required contents.

DIB begins with a base distribution element, which provides a base distribution image that is used as the starting point for the filesystem. It then executes the other elements in a specified and deterministic order. Each element consists of a set of commands that modify the contents of the filesystem that is being constructed.

We will explore some simple elements and describe the components of an element in general. We begin with the ubuntu-mysql reference element provided by Trove.

```
ubuntu@trove-book:/opt/stack/trove-integration/scripts/files/elements$ find ubuntu-mysql
ubuntu-mysql
ubuntu-mysql/install.d
ubuntu-mysql/install.d/30-mysql
ubuntu-mysql/pre-install.d
ubuntu-mysql/pre-install.d/20-apparmor-mysql-local
ubuntu-mysql/pre-install.d/10-percona-apt-key
ubuntu-mysql/README.md
```

The element ubuntu-mysql is a directory and within it is a README.md file. It is recommended (but unfortunately not enforced) that all elements contain a README file.

In addition, the directory can contain other files and directories, and some directories have a special meaning to DIB. These directories are called phase directories.

Within each phase directory (install.d, pre-install.d in the previous example) are executable files, which are named with a two-digit numeric prefix.

Phases Within an Element

Table 7-1 provides an overview of the various phases.

Table 7-1. Phases Within an Element

Phase Name	Where this runs	Description
root.d	Outside chroot	The root.d phase is the first phase to run, and it is used to adapt the initial filesystem and make it suitable for subsequent phases within the element. Typically this is used to adapt alternative distributions or customizations.
extra-data.d	Outside chroot	The extra-data.d phase is used to copy data from the host environment into the chroot environment for use in later phases of the element.
		As this phase runs outside chroot, it has full access to the host and should copy files into a location specified by $TMP_HOOKS_PATH. A later phase (which runs in the chroot environment) can pick it up there and move it to the final location.
pre-install.d	Inside chroot	This is the first phase to execute within the chroot environment and is typically used to customize the environment before actual package installation. This makes it the ideal place to register repositories, keys, and other information that will be used in subsequent phases.
install.d	Inside chroot	This phase runs immediately after pre-install.d and within the chroot environment and is traditionally used to install packages and perform other operations that are image specific.
		All install.d steps are run before the next step (post-install.d) runs.
		So if there are operations that you need to do after, for example, all packages are installed and before the post-install.d step for any element is run, then do these operations here.
post-install.d	Inside chroot	This step is run after all install.d commands are executed and is traditionally used to handle all tasks that must be performed (during the image creation) before the first boot of the image.
		For example, suppose a package installed in install.d does not register itself for auto-launch on instance startup; this is a good place to run chkconfig.
block-device.d	Outside chroot	This phase is used to customize the image that will be made, by doing things such as adding partitions or performing any cleanup of partitions.
finalise.d	Inside chroot	This phase runs after block-device.d has had a chance to perform any operations to adjust the partitions and the filesystem, and is executed after the root file system has been copied onto the mounted (loopback) filesystem.
		This phase is executed in the final phase, so it is executed after all earlier phases in all elements have been executed.
cleanup.d	Inside chroot	This is the final opportunity to clean up the root filesystem content and remove any temporary settings that were required during the build process.

Execution Sequence

Recall that DIB executes commands in a specified and deterministic order. Next, we describe how to construct this order.

First, DIB identifies all the elements referenced. Since elements can have dependencies, the list of elements provided on the command line may be expanded to include other elements that must also be executed.

Once the final list of elements is constructed, DIB begins with the first phase, root.d, and identifies all commands, in all elements, intended for execution in the root.d phase. It constructs an ordered list of these elements, first sorting on the numeric two-digit prefix and then sorting within a numeric prefix in alphabetical order. It then proceeds to execute those commands in order.

When it has executed all commands in a phase, DIB moves on to the next phase and repeats the same process.

To illustrate this, we created two fictitious elements, 1st-element and 2nd-element. All phases were populated in these elements with commands numbered 10-<phase>-f, and 20-<phase>-f in 1st-element, and 10-<phase>-s and 20-<phase>-s in 2nd-element. Then we ran the following disk-image-create command.

```
ubuntu@trove-book:~/elements$ /opt/stack/diskimage-builder/bin/disk-image-create -n \
> -a amd64 -o /tmp/test centos 1st-element 2nd-element
```

The following output results from the execution of the root.d and pre-install.d phases; we have highlighted the commands in the fictitious elements.

```
Target: root.d
```

Script	Seconds
10-centos6-cloud-image	11.384
10-root-f	**0.007**
10-root-s	**0.011**
20-root-f	**0.009**
20-root-s	**0.009**
50-yum-cache	0.068
90-base-dib-run-parts	0.037

```
Target: pre-install.d
```

Script	Seconds
00-fix-requiretty	0.022
00-usr-local-bin-secure-path	0.010
01-override-yum-arch	0.010
01-yum-install-bin	0.022
01-yum-keepcache	0.015
02-package-installs	36.148
02-yum-repos	0.015
10-pre-install-f	**0.017**
10-pre-install-s	**0.008**

15-remove-grub	0.033
20-pre-install-f	**0.010**
20-pre-install-s	**0.008**
99-package-uninstalls	0.157

As you can see, all commands in a phase are executed together and DIB moves from phase to phase. Within a phase, all commands for that phase (for all candidate elements) are sorted and executed in a deterministic order.

Understanding the Trove Reference Elements

In the previous section, we showed how DIB uses elements and executes commands that help to create an image. In this section we look in detail at the Trove reference elements and explain how they function.

For this example, we use the MySQL elements. We also look at unique aspects of some of the other elements, including the use of DATASTORE_PKG_LOCATION by the DB2 element.

To build a MySQL guest image, use the ubuntu-guest and ubuntu-mysql reference elements. These are located in scripts/files/elements/ubuntu-guest and scripts/files/elements/ubuntu-mysql in the trove-integration repository.

The ubuntu-mysql element is quite simple.

```
ubuntu@trove-book:/opt/stack/trove-integration/scripts/files/elements/ubuntu-mysql$ find.
.
./install.d
./install.d/30-mysql
./pre-install.d
./pre-install.d/20-apparmor-mysql-local
./pre-install.d/10-percona-apt-key
./README.md
```

From the description of the layout of an element, it is apparent that this element defines just three commands.

```
pre-install.d/20-apparmor-mysql-local
pre-install.d/10-percona-apt-key

install.d/30-mysql
```

The ubuntu-guest element is a little bit more involved and defines the following commands:

```
./pre-install.d/60-loopback-host        ./extra-data.d/20-guest-upstart
./pre-install.d/04-baseline-tools       ./extra-data.d/62-ssh-key
./pre-install.d/01-trim-pkgs            ./extra-data.d/15-reddwarf-dep

./install.d/05-base-apps
./install.d/98-ssh
./install.d/62-ssh-key                  ./post-install.d/10-ntp
./install.d/50-user                     ./post-install.d/05-ipforwarding
./install.d/20-etc                      ./post-install.d/90-apt-get-update
./install.d/15-reddwarf-dep             ./post-install.d/62-trove-guest-sudoers
./install.d/99-clean-apt
```

We begin by examining the extra-data.d phase which is the first one for which we have any commands. These commands will be executed in the following order:

```
./extra-data.d/15-reddwarf-dep
./extra-data.d/20-guest-upstart
./extra-data.d/62-ssh-key
```

```
ubuntu@trove-book:/opt/stack/trove-integration/scripts/files/elements/ubuntu-guest$ cat -n
./extra-data.d/15-reddwarf-dep
    1  #!/bin/bash
    2
    3  set -e
    4  set -o xtrace
    5
    6  # CONTEXT: HOST prior to IMAGE BUILD as SCRIPT USER
    7  # PURPOSE: Setup the requirements file for use by 15-reddwarf-dep
    8
    9  source $_LIB/die
   10
   11  REQUIREMENTS_FILE=${REDSTACK_SCRIPTS}/files/requirements/ubuntu-requirements.txt
   12
   13  [ -n "$TMP_HOOKS_PATH" ] || die "Temp hook path not set"
   14  [ -e ${REQUIREMENTS_FILE} ] || die "Requirements not found"
   15
   16  sudo -Hiu ${HOST_USERNAME} dd if=${REQUIREMENTS_FILE} of=${TMP_HOOKS_PATH}/
requirements.txt
```

Recall that the extra-data.d phase is run outside the chroot environment and is used to copy files from outside the chroot environment into a place on the chroot environment ($TMP_HOOKS_PATH) and a subsequent step will take the files to their final location.

The purpose of this file is to copy a requirements.txt file, which is part of the trove-integration repository, into the guest. This file defines the python libraries that are required to be installed on the guest.

The other two commands in this phase are 20-guest-upstart and 62-ssh-key, which copy the configuration for the guest instance and the ssh-related files (private key, public key, authorized_keys) for the user identified by $HOST_USERNAME user into $TMP_HOOKS_PATH.

Once the extra-data.d phase is complete, DIB moves on to the pre-install.d phase. Recall that pre-install.d executes inside the chroot environment. We observe that both elements have some commands for this phase and the order in which they will be executed is

```
pre-install.d/01-trim-pkgs
pre-install.d/04-baseline-tools
pre-install.d/10-percona-apt-key
pre-install.d/20-apparmor-mysql-local
pre-install.d/60-loopback-host
```

Each of these commands performs a part of the process of preparing a guest image. 01-trim-pkgs removes a number of packages from the base image and helps reduce the size of the Trove guest image. 04-baseline-tools installs some basic tools on the guest instance. 10-percona-apt-key registers the Percona APT (Advanced Packaging Tool) key and registers Percona in the sources.list file used by apt to allow a later command to install software from the Percona repository. 20-apparmor-mysql-local configures AppArmor on the guest instance and allows the database to write to /tmp. Finally 60-loopback-host adds the hostname into the /etc/hosts file with an IP address of 127.0.0.1 (the loopback address). This allows the guest instance to resolve its own name.

Once the pre-install.d phase is complete DIB moves to the install.d phase. Recall that install.d executes inside the chroot environment. We observe that both elements have some commands for this phase and the order of execution is

```
install.d/05-base-apps
install.d/15-reddwarf-dep
install.d/20-etc
install.d/30-mysql
install.d/50-user
install.d/62-ssh-key
install.d/98-ssh
install.d/99-clean-apt
```

The commands in 05-base-apps install the packages ntp and apparmor-utils. 15-reddwarf-dep picks up where the extra-data.d command with the same name left off, and performs a pip install using the requirements.txt file as shown next.

```
20   TMP_HOOKS_DIR="/tmp/in_target.d"
21
22   pip install -q --upgrade -r ${TMP_HOOKS_DIR}/requirements.txt
```

Recall that extra-data.d/20-guest-upstart dropped trove-guest.conf into $TMP_HOOKS_PATH. The command 20-etc copies this file into /etc/trove/ on the guest instance filesystem.

The command 30-mysql performs the actual installation of the MySQL server onto the guest image as shown next.

```
ubuntu@trove-book:/opt/stack/trove-integration/scripts/files/elements$ cat -n ./ubuntu-
mysql/install.d/30-mysql
     1   #!/bin/sh
     2
     3   # CONTEXT: GUEST during CONSTRUCTION as ROOT
     4   # PURPOSE: Install controller base required packages
     5
     6   set -e
     7   set -o xtrace
     8
     9   export DEBIAN_FRONTEND=noninteractive
    10   apt-get -y install libmysqlclient18 mysql-server-5.6 percona-xtrabackup
    11
    12   cat >/etc/mysql/conf.d/no_perf_schema.cnf <<_EOF_
    13   [mysqld]
    14   performance:schema = off
    15   _EOF_
```

The command 50-user adds the user $GUEST_USERNAME on the guest instance. The command 62-ssh-key completes the work started by extra-data.d/62-ssh-key and installs the private key, the public key, and the authorized_keys files in the right place on the guest instance. The command 98-ssh configures the openssh-server package and the command 99-clean-apt cleans up the aptitude repository.

After all commands in the `install.d` phase are complete, DIB moves on to `post-install.d` and executes the following commands inside the chroot environment:

```
./post-install.d/05-ipforwarding
./post-install.d/10-ntp
./post-install.d/62-trove-guest-sudoers
./post-install.d/90-apt-get-update
```

The command `05-ipforwarding` enables IP forwarding in `/etc/sysctl.conf`, `10-ntp` configures NTP. `62-trove-guest-sudoers` adds the user `$GUEST_USERNAME` to the sudoers list on the guest (makes `$GUEST_USERNAME` able to sudo with no password). `90-apt-get-update` just runs an `apt-get update` to bring the aptitude repository metadata up to date. This completes the commands provided by the `ubuntu-guest` and `ubuntu-mysql` elements. DIB handles the rest of the image creation process.

Next, we examine `extra-data.d/20-copy-db2-pkgs` in the `ubuntu-db2` element. This element is used to generate a DB2 Express-C guest image. Recall that DB2 is a database that is licensed and is not installable from an apt repository (the way MySQL was installed earlier in `install.d/30-mysql`).

```
14  # First check if the package is available on the local filesystem.
15  if [ -f "${DATASTORE_PKG_LOCATION}" ]; then
16      echo "Found the DB2 Express-C packages in ${DATASTORE_PKG_LOCATION}."
17      dd if="${DATASTORE_PKG_LOCATION}" of=${TMP_HOOKS_PATH}/db2.tar.gz
18  # else, check if the package is available for download in a private repository.
19  elif wget ${DATASTORE_DOWNLOAD_OPTS} "${DATASTORE_PKG_LOCATION}" -O ${TMP_HOOKS_
PATH}/db2.tar.gz; then
20      echo "Downloaded the DB2 Express-C package from the private repository"
21  else
22      echo "Unable to find the DB2 package at ${DATASTORE_PKG_LOCATION}"
23      echo "Please register and download the DB2 Express-C packages to a private
repository or local filesystem."
24      exit -1
25  fi
```

Note that this command copies an installable file from the location specified in `${DATASTORE_PKG_LOCATION}` and places it in `${TMP_HOOKS_PATH}/db2.tar.gz`. The code shown previously also attempts to handle the case where the location provided is a local file or accessible via a URL. Since this is part of the `extra-data.d` phase, it is executed outside the chroot environment. The process of installing DB2 is completed by `install.d/10-db2`, which uses the file saved in the earlier `extra-data.d` phase.

From the preceding discussion, it should be apparent that the steps performed by the elements are the same commands that would be performed manually to set up a machine as a guest instance. DIB provides a framework within which to express these commands and have them executed in the appropriate context (inside chroot, outside chroot) and in the right order to produce the desired image.

Using the Guest Agent Code

A Trove guest instance is a virtual machine launched in response to a `trove create` request from a user. This instance has the following installed on it:

- A database chosen by the user

- A Trove guest agent for that database

The preceding section showed (`install.d/30-mysql`) how to install the guest database into the image, but it did not describe how to copy the actual guest agent code into the image.

There are two ways in which the guest agent code can get onto the guest instance.

- It can be installed at runtime

- It can be installed into the guest image at image creation time

The Trove reference elements (DIB elements) from trove-integration use the former approach, which we examine in more detail now.

Guest Agent Code Installed at Runtime

In the preceding example of the steps involved in creating a guest image with the Trove reference elements, we highlighted three steps: `install.d/30-mysql`, `extra-data.d/20-guest-upstart`, and `install.d/20-etc`. While the first of these takes care of the installation of the guest database (MySQL in this case), the other two handle the creation of an upstart configuration file that will be executed on the guest instance.

Ubuntu uses `upstart` (a replacement of the `init` daemon) to handle the creation of tasks and services during system boot.

The command `20-guest-upstart` renders the upstart configuration file based on a template and places it in `$TMP_HOOKS_PATH` and `20-etc` installs this configuration file. Recall that the `extra-data.d` phase runs outside the chroot environment and the `install.d` phase runs inside the chroot environment.

The result of these two phases is that the guest instance has a `trove-guest.conf` file installed in `/etc/init` which is shown next.

```
ubuntu@m1:/$ cat -n /etc/init/trove-guest.conf
     1  description "Trove Guest"
     2  author "Auto-Gen"
     3
     4  start on (filesystem and net-device-up IFACE!=lo)
     5  stop on runlevel [016]
     6  chdir /var/run
     7  pre-start script
     8      mkdir -p /var/run/trove
     9      chown ubuntu:root /var/run/trove/
    10
    11      mkdir -p /var/lock/trove
    12      chown ubuntu:root /var/lock/trove/
    13
    14      mkdir -p /var/log/trove/
    15      chown ubuntu:root /var/log/trove/
    16
    17      # Copy the trove source from the user's development environment
    18      if [ ! -d /home/ubuntu/trove ]; then
```

```
19          sudo -u ubuntu rsync -e 'ssh -o UserKnownHostsFile=/dev/null -o
            StrictHostKeyChecking=no' -avz --exclude='.*' ubuntu@10.0.0.1:/opt/stack/trove/
            /home/ubuntu/trove
20      fi
21
22      # Ensure conf dir exists and is readable
23      mkdir -p /etc/trove/conf.d
24      chmod -R +r /etc/trove
25
26  end script
27
28  script

39
40          exec su -c "/home/ubuntu/trove/contrib/trove-guestagent $TROVE_CONFIG" ubuntu
41  end script
```

The highlighted section of code is executed each time the `trove-guest` service is started including on the first boot of the guest instance. It verifies whether a directory (`/home/ubuntu/trove`) exists and if it does not, it copies the source code for Trove from the host machine using `rsync`.

This causes the Trove guest agent code to be populated onto the guest instance and later launched (line 40).

We already have described the process for registering the Trove public key on the host machine. That was to facilitate this `rsync` operation which uses `ssh` to get the Trove code from the host machine.

The Trove reference elements are intended for development and testing purposes and not production operation. This mechanism of copying the guest agent onto the guest at launch time has some distinct benefits for a developer.

For example, suppose that you want to modify Trove such that it involves changes to the code that is part of the guest agent. To test this code, all you have to do is launch a new guest instance and your new code will be instantly available on the guest instance.

Contrast this with a scheme that installs the guest agent code into the guest image. Any changes that you make to the guest agent code would require you to generate a new guest image, register it with Glance and Trove, and only then be in a position to test it out.

While ideal from a development perspective, rsync'ing code from the host machine has some distinct disadvantages for one wishing to build a production-ready guest image. First, this scheme requires the guest to have access to source code at runtime, which implies that different instances could potentially be running different versions of the guest agent code. It is also a potential vector that could be used to compromise the guest instance. As well, this rsync operation takes time that delays the launch of the guest instance, which is undesirable.

For these reasons, production-ready guest images should be built slightly differently as explained in the following section.

Guest Agent Code Installed at Build Time

Production-ready guest images will typically have guest agent code installed into the guest image. In this section, we describe how you can accomplish this.

The guest agent code is available during the guest image creation process. This may either be on the local filesystem of the machine generating the guest image or in some web-based repository. In either case, an `extra-data.d` command can be used to copy the desired guest agent code into `$TMP_HOOKS_PATH`. A subsequent command run in the `install.d` phase can install the guest agent code into its final location on the guest image.

On instance launch, the guest agent code is available on the guest instance and can be launched directly. This approach has some benefits but also introduces a complication.

In cases where there is a dependency between Trove host code and guest agent code, this method introduces a version dependency between the Trove host and the vintage of the guest image. It is important to highlight that this does not introduce any additional risks over the scheme of installing guest agent code at runtime. In either instance the objective is to have consistent code running on the host and the guest agent. The complications that this introduces relate solely to the convenience of being able to launch a new instance and having the right code installed and executed on the guest. Contrast this with being required to build (or procure) a new guest image, registering that with Glance and Trove, and then being able to launch a new instance.

In production environments, however, this approach is much preferred.

Guest Images on Different Operating Systems

DIB can be run on a variety of operating systems, including Ubuntu, RHEL, Fedora, Centos, and openSUSE. In addition DIB distributes reference elements for all of these base operating systems.

Trove also provides reference elements for some databases on the Fedora operating system.

```
ubuntu@trove-book:/opt/stack/trove-integration/scripts/files/elements$ ls -1 fedora* -d
fedora-guest
fedora-mongodb
fedora-mysql
fedora-percona
fedora-postgresql
fedora-redis
```

We now examine these elements and highlight the key differences between these elements and the ubuntu elements described earlier.

```
ubuntu@trove-book:/opt/stack/trove-integration/scripts/files/elements$ find fedora-mysql/
fedora-mysql/
fedora-mysql/install.d
fedora-mysql/install.d/10-mysql
fedora-mysql/README.md
```

As with the ubuntu command install.d/30-mysql, the fedora command 10-mysql installs the MySQL server and Percona XtraBackup.

```
ubuntu@trove-book:/opt/stack/trove-integration/scripts/files/elements$ cat -n fedora-mysql/
install.d/10-mysql
     1  #!/bin/sh
     2
     3  # CONTEXT: GUEST during CONSTRUCTION as ROOT
     4  # PURPOSE: Install controller base required packages
     5
     6  set -e
     7  set -o xtrace
     8
     9  yum -y install mysql mysql-server-5.6 percona-xtrabackup
```

The `fedora-guest` element is very similar to the `ubuntu-guest` element and provides the commands listed next. These commands perform the same functions as their `ubuntu` counterparts.

```
./install.d/62-ssh-key
./install.d/50-user
./install.d/20-etc
./install.d/15-reddwarf-dep

./post-install.d/60-loopback-host
./post-install.d/05-ipforwarding
./post-install.d/90-yum-update
./post-install.d/62-trove-guest-sudoers

./extra-data.d/20-guest-upstart
./extra-data.d/62-ssh-key
./extra-data.d/15-reddwarf-dep
```

Additional information about generating Trove-compatible images for RedHat Enterprise Linux is available at

`www.rdoproject.org/forum/discussion/1010/creation-of-trove-compatible-images-for-rdo/p1`

Summary

Trove instances are Nova instances launched from guest images created specifically for use with Trove. These images will cause the creation of an instance that will have a running database server and a Trove guest agent for the database.

This chapter described the structure of a Trove guest image and the process for registering a Trove guest image with Glance and Trove. It examined the concepts of the default Trove datastore and the default version of a Trove datastore and how these are configured.

The chapter also took a close look at the Disk Image Builder tool, including how DIB is installed and how DIB and Trove provide DIB elements and reference elements. We described how a guest image can be built using Trove reference elements and using the Trove `redstack` command.

The chapter also examined how DIB works and how it constructs a guest image from a base operating system image and applies transformations based on elements that provide commands that are executed in a deterministic order. We described the phases in which DIB executes commands and the structure of an element and examined the Trove reference elements in detail.

This chapter also described two ways in which Trove guest agent code can be installed on a guest instance: the first being to install the guest agent code at instance runtime and the second being to install the guest agent code into the image at image build time. We described the advantages and disadvantages of these two approaches. Guest images for development and testing are simpler to use if they copy the guest agent code at runtime. This approach facilitates rapid iteration during the development cycle at the small expense of launch time and the configuration requirements. Guest images that install the guest agent code at build time are better for production use cases.

This chapter and the preceding chapters have provided you with an overview of DBaaS, a quick-start on installing and operating Trove, a detailed understanding of the architecture and components of Trove, advanced configurations and operations, how to debug and troubleshoot Trove, and how to build guest images for Trove.

The appendices will provide reference material, including a detailed look at the Trove configuration files, the Trove API, and the Trove command-line interface.

CHAPTER 8

■ ■ ■

Operating Trove in Production

In previous chapters we examined the steps involved in downloading, configuring, and operating Trove, the architecture of Trove, and the way the various components of the Trove architecture work together. We showed how to build guest images for use with Trove.

Throughout these descriptions, we focused on illustrating concepts that helped explain how Trove worked, and how the various components worked together in order to deliver the functionality of a Database as a Service (DBaaS). In the previous chapters, we did not focus specifically on operational aspects of running such a service. That is the focus of this chapter.

In this chapter we describe how you would architect and operate a Trove deployment. It describes some best practices and considerations for operating Trove at scale.

Many of the things that you must do to operate Trove in production and at scale have to do with the setup of the underlying environment. We do not attempt to document all of these in detail. Rather, we illustrate some of the best practices in these areas, and where possible we provide one or more references that you can consult for the relevant implementation details.

Configuring the Trove Infrastructure

A properly functioning Trove instance has several infrastructural components, including the Trove controller(s), the infrastructure database, and the transport mechanism used by the Trove message bus.

Figure 8-1 illustrates the architecture of an OpenStack system and where Trove fits into this.

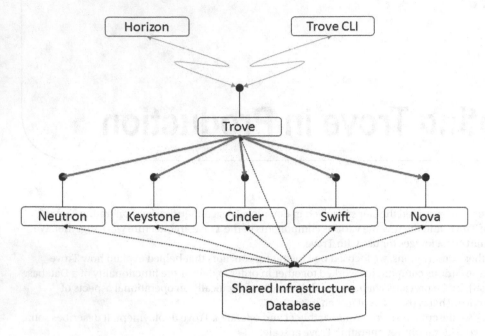

***Figure 8-1.** A simple OpenStack deployment with Trove*

Figure 8-1 shows a simple OpenStack system. Trove is a consumer of services provided by Neutron, Keystone, Cinder, Swift, and Nova. When a user requests an instance from Trove, this results in a number of requests to the underlying services.

It is important to understand that the individual services communicate with each other only over their public APIs. Therefore, one could equally create a configuration that looked like Figure 8-2.

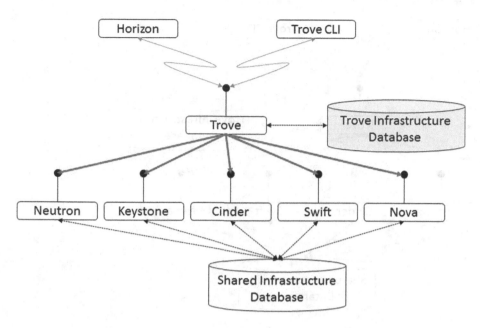

Figure 8-2. *A deployment with a dedicated Trove infrastructure database*

Configuring Trove to Use Dedicated Infrastructure

Trove does not need to share the infrastructure database with the rest of the services. In fact, each service could be configured to have its own private infrastructure database.

In a similar vein, while most of the OpenStack services use a message bus of some kind (Trove uses a message bus provided with the Oslo messaging library [oslo.messaging]), there is nothing that requires Trove to share the same message bus infrastructure as the rest of OpenStack. In fact, it is highly advisable that Trove have its own message bus. This is shown next.

Figure 8-2 shows the core OpenStack services using a shared message queue and a shared infrastructure database, while Trove has a dedicated message queue and infrastructure database.

The core OpenStack services can also have dedicated message queues and infrastructure databases.

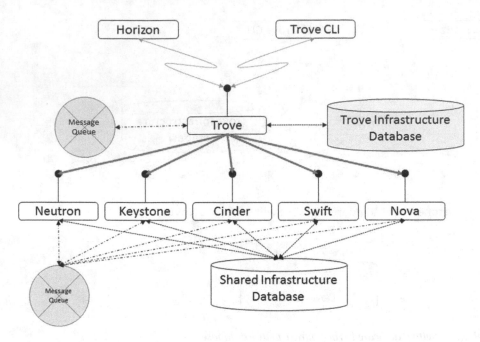

Figure 8-3. *Trove with a dedicated message queue and infrastructure database*

When operated at scale, the individual OpenStack service components may require additional scalability and resiliency. To this end, a deployment may adopt the horizontally scaled architecture shown in Figure 8-4.

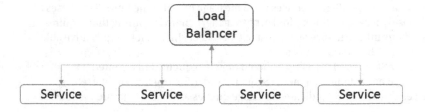

Figure 8-4. *Showing a horizontally scaled OpenStack service and load balancer*

In this depiction, the load balancer may be merely a round-robin DNS (Domain Name System) or a more sophisticated load balancer that routes traffic to each of the individual service instances based on rules.

In either situation, the service instances would all share the same message queue and infrastructure database.

In Figure 8-4, the IP address of the service would be the outward-facing IP address of the load balancer.

In the specific case of Trove, which has three major controller side components (Trove API, Trove task manager, and Trove conductor), one could further scale out these services—as shown in Figure 8-5.

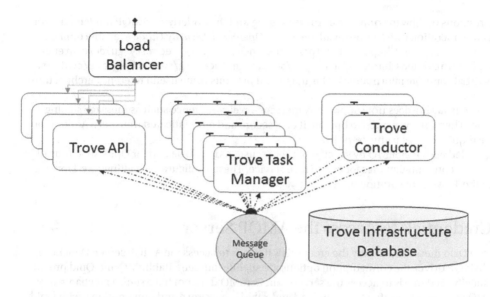

Figure 8-5. *Illustrating the scaling of different Trove components*

Each component of Trove could be scaled independently.

- If you think there will be a large number of concurrent connections to the API, then you should scale the API service.

- The heavy lifting in Trove is done by the task manager, so you should scale that along with the API service.

- If you think a large number of instances will be running, then scale the Trove conductor service.

All these individual service components would reference the same underlying infrastructure database and message queue. A load balancer would be used to send incoming requests to one of a number of Trove API service instances. The task manager and conductor do not directly expose public interfaces and receive work and communicate with the rest of the system through the shared message queue.

Trove and the rest of OpenStack are architected to be loosely coupled systems and the benefit of this loose coupling is the ability to scale individual components based on workload.

Another benefit of scaling components is to improve service reliability through redundancy.

In a similar way, the underlying infrastructure database and message queue could also be scaled according to the best practices for those technologies. The infrastructure database is typically a MySQL database and this can be scaled with Galera (Percona XtraDB) Cluster.

Configuring Security on the AMQP Server

Trove uses `oslo.messaging` as its underlying RPC mechanism. AMQP-based solutions like RabbitMQ, Qpid, and ZeroMQ are often used as the underlying transport, but RabbitMQ tends to be the most common choice.

RabbitMQ and Qpid support transport-level security (TLS) and ZeroMQ does not currently support TLS. TLS with ZeroMQ can, however, be achieved using IPsec or other mechanisms.

Especially in the context of Trove, we strongly recommend that the AMQP server and the communications on the message queue be secured not just through not just the use of TLS but also through the physical isolation of the networks over which message queue traffic is sent.

Detailed instructions on how to configure oslo.messaging and the underlying AMQP implementation for proper and secure operation with SSL are available in the *OpenStack Security Guide* available online at http://docs.openstack.org (see Chapter 4 at http://docs.openstack.org/security-guide/content/secure_communication.html and Chapter 12 at http://docs.openstack.org/security-guide/content/message_queuing.html for more information). This document presents some useful reference architectures and case studies.

Currently oslo.messaging does not support any message-level confidence such as message signing or sender validation. Therefore, you need to operate it on a secure and authenticated transport. Additional considerations are required when using ZeroMQ.

TLS can be enabled with RabbitMQ by specifying rabbit_use_ssl = True and for Qpid, specify qpid_protocol = ssl in the configuration files for each Trove service. These configuration settings are Trove specific and set in the Trove configuration files.

Providing Credentials to Access the AMQP Server

You need to give the Oslo messaging library the credentials it needs to access the AMQP server. Depending on your choice of AMQP driver, the configuration options are slightly different. RabbitMQ and Qpid provide a mechanism to specify credentials to access the servers, but ZeroMQ does not have such a mechanism.

With RabbitMQ you would specify rabbit_userid and rabbit_password and other options, with Qpid you would specify qpid_username and qpid_password, as well as other service specific parameters.

As described in Chapter 4, by default the Trove API service reads its configuration from /etc/trove/trove.conf (specified on the command line). Similarly the Trove task manager is typically instructed to read configuration from /etc/trove/trove-taskmanager.conf and the Trove conductor from /etc/trove/trove-conductor.conf.

Guest instances are provided a configuration file on launch, and this is rendered at launch time by the task manager based on the template whose location is specified in the configuration option guest_config.

The simplest configuration is to have all of these files provide the same credentials. However, this is neither required nor advisable. It is advantageous to use different credentials for the services. Following is a simple setup where the controller node services share a set of credentials and the guests all use a different set of credentials:

```
ubuntu@trove-book:~$ grep 'rabbit_' /etc/trove/trove.conf
rabbit_password = trovepassword
rabbit_userid = troverabbit
ubuntu@trove-book:~$ grep 'rabbit_' /etc/trove/trove-taskmanager.conf
rabbit_password = trovepassword
rabbit_userid = troverabbit
ubuntu@trove-book:~$ grep 'rabbit_' /etc/trove/trove-conductor.conf
rabbit_password = trovepassword
rabbit_userid = troverabbit
ubuntu@trove-book:~$ grep 'rabbit_' /etc/trove/trove-guestagent.conf
rabbit_password = guestpassword
rabbit_host = 10.0.0.1
rabbit_userid = troveguest
```

In addition, you can restrict the permissions to these users with access control at the RabbitMQ level. Following is one such set of restricted permissions with which a system can be operated:

```
root@trove-book:~# rabbitmqctl list_permissions
Listing permissions in vhost "/" ...
[. . .]
troveguest      (trove.*|guestagent)      (trove.*|guestagent)      (guestagent.*|trove.*)
troverabbit     .*      .*      .*
...done.
```

For more information on how to do this, see the documentation for your respective AMQP service.

Securing the Guest

The guest instance contains the database server that the user requested, along with the Trove guest agent. In the interest of data security for the data on the server, and for proper operation of the database and the service, it is important to secure the guest and prevent unauthorized activities on it.

Using SSH on Guest Instances

End users of the databases provisioned with Trove do not need shell access to the instance(s) on which the databases are running. All operations that users can perform on the database instances can be performed through the command-line interface or the user interface.

Operators may wish to retain the ability to access the shell on an instance to debug some specific problems or take some infrequent maintenance activity. In environments where the guest instance has multiple interfaces, one connected to a private management network and another to a public network, it is advisable to configure the ssh daemon (sshd) to listen only on the private management interface. You can configure this in the sshd configuration file (sshd_config). The sample text that follows is from an Ubuntu guest instance:

```
# Use these options to restrict which interfaces/protocols sshd will bind to
#ListenAddress ::
ListenAddress 10.0.0.3
```

You can do this only once the instance boots (and it knows its own IP address).

Disable root login on the instances and require SSH with a certificate. This considerably increases the security on the instance. These are set in sshd_config.

```
PermitRootLogin no
PasswordAuthentication no
```

Place a public key (authorized_keys) on the images used to boot guest instances and protect the private key. Only users with the private key will be able to log in. Further configure the authorized_keys file and specify from restrictions which control the IP address(es) from which ssh clients can connect to the machine. You can achieve the same thing by configuring /etc/hosts.allow and it is advisable to do both. For more information about this, refer to man ssh and man hosts.allow.

It is strongly advised that you adopt these and a variety of other general hygiene steps around the proper configuration of SSH on guest instances. In addition, configuring AppArmor, SE Linux, or some equivalent mandatory access control system on guest instances is advised.

Should you need to configure a system where end users have shell access to the system, here are some suggestions on the proper configuration of such a system.

Having placed all users who need shell access to the guest instance in a single group, configure sshd to permit key-based authentication to the system for all users in that group. Move the authorized_keys file from the default location of ~/.ssh/authorized_keys to a secure location where the user has no write permission (AuthorizedKeysFile in sshd_config). Configure sshd to then place users into a chroot jail upon login and disable X11 and port forwarding. The chroot jail would contain the files that the user should have access to, and nothing more.

However, doing this would require you to have sshd listen on the public interface as well and this is not advisable. However, should this be required, consider also restricting source addresses from where ssh would be allowed.

Using Security Groups and Network Security

It is always advisable to attach a security group that allows traffic only to the designated database port for the specified database(s). For example, on a MySQL instance that would be to restrict access to only port 3306 and the TCP protocol.

Security groups are configured through Nova Networking or Neutron and should be used whenever possible. It is advantageous to manipulate security groups through Nova. In addition, if you set the tcp_ports and udp_ports parameter for a datastore in the trove-taskmanager.conf file, those ports are passed to Nova Networking or Neutron for the creation of a security group. These definitions (from common/cfg.py are shown next).

```
422  # Mysql
423  mysql_group = cfg.OptGroup(
424      'mysql', title='MySQL options',
425      help="Oslo option group designed for MySQL datastore")
426  mysql_opts = [
427      cfg.ListOpt('tcp_ports', default=["3306"],
428                  help='List of TCP ports and/or port ranges to open '
429                       'in the security group (only applicable '
430                       'if trove_security_groups_support is True).'),
431      cfg.ListOpt('udp_ports', default=[],
432                  help='List of UDP ports and/or port ranges to open '
433                       'in the security group (only applicable '
434                       'if trove_security_groups_support is True).'),
```

Here is what these settings would look like in the trove-taskmanager.conf file.

```
[mysql]
tcp_ports = 3306
```

Trove as a Client of Other OpenStack Services

Trove is a client of the other OpenStack services, and when provisioning resources, it does so by contacting those services. For example, to provision a compute instance, it contacts Nova, and to provision block storage, it contacts Cinder.

Consuming Services from a Private OpenStack Setup

The service end point that it uses can be tailored and this is often a configuration option that operators use. Figure 8-6 shows this configuration.

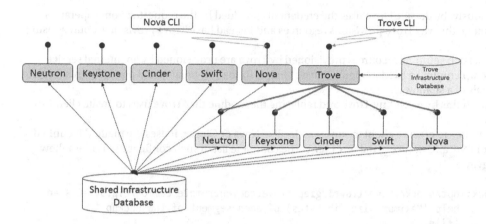

Figure 8-6. *A production deployment of Trove showing public and private OpenStack services*

Trove is one of the services offered by this OpenStack system. This system exposes a number of services (Trove, Nova, Swift, Cinder, Keystone, and Neutron) at the top, and all of these expose their public APIs to end users.

Internally, a private OpenStack setup is operated and Trove is configured to point to these internal services. Operators have done this for several reasons, including in some cases the fact that the hardware that is used to operate Trove is different from the hardware used for the Nova compute service and the storage is often configured differently.

When configured in this way, the Nova instances provisioned by Trove would be provisioned through the internal OpenStack setup used by Trove and the user would not have access to the Nova end point to the internal OpenStack system to directly manipulate the instance.

To do this the operator sets the appropriate configuration parameters to Trove (from common/cfg.py) to identify the services that are being overridden. Trove uses the specified end points when creating a client to request resources from those services.

```
50      cfg.StrOpt('nova_compute_url', help='URL without the tenant segment.'),

55      cfg.StrOpt('neutron_url', help='URL without the tenant segment.'),

60      cfg.StrOpt('cinder_url', help='URL without the tenant segment.'),

70      cfg.StrOpt('swift_url', help='URL ending in AUTH_.'),

75      cfg.StrOpt('trove_auth_url', default='http://0.0.0.0:5000/v2.0',
76                 help='Trove authentication URL.'),
```

These are pointed to the end points exposed by the private OpenStack setup. In the absence of these overrides, Trove looks to Keystone and queries the public URLs to use.

When contacting the private OpenStack end points, Trove still uses the credentials provided by the requestor. In other words, when Trove provisions resources, it does so with the end user's credentials.

Using Shadow Tenants and Service Tenants

As described previously, by default Trove uses the credentials provided by the requestor. Some operators have chosen to change the way Trove provisions resources and instead have Trove provision resources using a different tenant.

In the simplest such setup, all resources provisioned by Trove are provisioned by an internal service tenant. Another setup employs a fixed mapping of user tenants to shadow tenants and provisions resources using the credentials of a shadow tenant.

They accomplish this by extending Trove and replacing the module that Trove uses to create clients to the other services.

When Trove wishes to create a client to some service like Nova or Cinder, it uses the method identified by remote_nova_client and remote_cinder_client. The complete list of such configurations is as follows (from common/cfg.py):

```
ubuntu@trove-book:/opt/stack/trove/trove$ grep trove.common.remote common/cfg.py -C 3 -n
285-                  help='Maximum size (in bytes) of each segment of the backup '
286-                  'file.'),
287-      cfg.StrOpt('remote_dns_client',
288:                  default='trove.common.remote.dns_client',
289-                  help='Client to send DNS calls to.'),
290-      cfg.StrOpt('remote_guest_client',
291:                  default='trove.common.remote.guest_client',
292-                  help='Client to send Guest Agent calls to.'),
293-      cfg.StrOpt('remote_nova_client',
294:                  default='trove.common.remote.nova_client',
295-                  help='Client to send Nova calls to.'),
296-      cfg.StrOpt('remote_neutron_client',
297:                  default='trove.common.remote.neutron_client',
298-                  help='Client to send Neutron calls to.'),
299-      cfg.StrOpt('remote_cinder_client',
300:                  default='trove.common.remote.cinder_client',
301-                  help='Client to send Cinder calls to.'),
302-      cfg.StrOpt('remote_heat_client',
303:                  default='trove.common.remote.heat_client',
304-                  help='Client to send Heat calls to.'),
305-      cfg.StrOpt('remote_swift_client',
306:                  default='trove.common.remote.swift_client',
307-                  help='Client to send Swift calls to.'),
308-      cfg.StrOpt('exists_notification_transformer',
309-                  help='Transformer for exists notifications.'),
```

The module remote.py (common/remote.py) contains the following initializations:

```
188   create_dns_client = import_class(CONF.remote_dns_client)
189   create_guest_client = import_class(CONF.remote_guest_client)
190   create_nova_client = import_class(CONF.remote_nova_client)
```

```
191  create_swift_client = import_class(CONF.remote_swift_client)
192  create_cinder_client = import_class(CONF.remote_cinder_client)
193  create_heat_client = import_class(CONF.remote_heat_client)
194  create_neutron_client = import_class(CONF.remote_neutron_client)
```

When a new instance is being created, for example, the task manager executes the create() method (instances/models.py) as shown in the following example:

```
665-  @classmethod
666-  def create(cls, context, name, flavor_id, image_id, databases, users,
667-            datastore, datastore_version, volume_size, backup_id,
668-            availability_zone=None, nics=None, configuration_id=None,
669-            slave_of_id=None, cluster_config=None, replica_count=None):
670-
671-      datastore_cfg = CONF.get(datastore_version.manager)
672:      client = create_nova_client(context)
673-      try:
674-          flavor = client.flavors.get(flavor_id)
675-      except nova_exceptions.NotFound:
676-          raise exception.FlavorNotFound(uuid=flavor_id)
677-
678-      deltas = {'instances': 1}
679-      volume_support = datastore_cfg.volume_support
680-      if volume_support:
681-          validate_volume_size(volume_size)
682-          deltas['volumes'] = volume_size
```

The important aspect here is on line 672, which creates the Nova client. By setting CONF.remote_nova_client and providing an alternate implementation, the operator can specify how the underlying instance is provisioned. We illustrate this for the Nova client, but the same is the case for other clients as well.

By default, the Nova client is created by the code shown in the following example, from common/remote.py. Observe that the credentials from the context are used to create the Nova client.

```
89   def nova_client(context):
90       if CONF.nova_compute_url:
91           url = '%(nova_url)s%(tenant)s' % {
92               'nova_url': normalize_url(CONF.nova_compute_url),
93               'tenant': context.tenant}
94       else:
95           url = get_endpoint(context.service:catalog,
96                      service:type=CONF.nova_compute_service:type,
97                      endpoint_region=CONF.os_region_name,
98                      endpoint_type=CONF.nova_compute_endpoint_type)
99
100      client = Client(context.user, context.auth_token,
101                  bypass_url=url, project_id=context.tenant,
102                  auth_url=PROXY_AUTH_URL)
103      client.client.auth_token = context.auth_token
104      client.client.management_url = url
105      return client
```

An alternate implementation of this code would specify the credentials of the service tenant or shadow tenant, as shown in the following example.

Recall that when code in Trove launches a Nova instance, it relies on the code identified by the remote_nova_client configuration parameter, which (by default) is set to trove.common.remote.nova_client.

An alternate implementation of the nova_client could be something like the following code (from https://review.openstack.org/#/c/193010).

```
from oslo.config import cfg as oslo_cfg
from trove.common import cfg
from trove.common.remote import normalize_url
import trove.openstack.common.log as logging
from novaclient.v1_1.client import Client as NovaClient


CONF = cfg.CONF
PROXY_AUTH_URL = CONF.trove_auth_url
LOG = logging.getLogger(__name__)

def nova_client_trove_admin(context=None):
    """

    Returns a nova client object with the trove admin credentials
    :param context: original context from user request
    :type context: trove.common.context.TroveContext
    :return novaclient: novaclient with trove admin credentials
    :rtype: novaclient.v1_1.client.Client

    """

    client = NovaClient(CONF.nova_proxy_admin_user,
                        CONF.nova_proxy_admin_pass,
                        CONF.nova_proxy_admin_tenant_name,
                        auth_url=PROXY_AUTH_URL,
                        service:type=CONF.nova_compute_service:type,
                        region_name=CONF.os_region_name)

    if CONF.nova_compute_url and CONF.nova_proxy_admin_tenant_id:
        client.client.management_url = "%s/%s/" % (
            normalize_url(CONF.nova_compute_url),
            CONF.nova_proxy_admin_tenant_id)

    return client
```

According to this implementation, the Nova instance is launched using a set of credentials other than the context of the user requesting the Trove instance, and further, it could request the Nova instance from a Nova service other than the default compute service.

In practice, having multiple Nova services and reserving a private Nova service for specific clients (like Trove) has several benefits. This private Nova service could provision instances on specialized hardware, and in a specific environment that an end user could not directly access.

Summary

Trove is deployed and in production at scale at a number of sites. In this chapter, we have reviewed some practices used by these operators. This list is by no means exhaustive, and users must also follow best practices for operating any large production deployment.

These include techniques used to properly configure the underlying infrastructure that Trove relies on. We provide some descriptions of how Trove and other services can be scaled to handle large deployments with many users and instances.

Security of the message queue is very important and we describe some important techniques for enabling transport-level security on the AMQP service.

You must secure the guest instance because inadvertent actions by a user who is allowed to connect to a guest instance's shell could cause a failure of the database and potentially a loss of data and an interruption of service. We provide some techniques for securing the guest instance, including how to configure SSH on the instance. We show how this can be done by making changes in the `trove-taskmanager.conf` file.

Trove is a client of other OpenStack services and some operators choose to operate a private OpenStack setup for Trove. This is sometimes done because the hardware used for databases is different from the hardware that is provisioned directly through the publicly available compute service.

Some operators configure Trove to provision resources for Trove using a shadow tenant or a service tenant. We describe the various ways in which one can make these customizations, including the various configuration parameters that are available for this purpose.

APPENDIX A

■ ■ ■

Trove Configuration Options

This appendix describes the Trove configuration options in more detail, and documents numerous important settings that you can use to customize the operation of Trove.

Trove has a large number of configuration options and each of the three Trove services (API, task manager, and conductor) has its own configuration files, as does the Trove guest agent.

Trove Configuration Files

The Trove services (trove-conductor, trove-taskmanager, trove-api) and the Trove guest agent accept a number of command-line options that specify the configuration options to use.

Consider for example, the trove-conductor service whose command line provides the following three options: --config-dir, --config-file and --log-config.

--config-dir DIR   Path to a config directory to pull *.conf files from.
                      This file set is sorted, so as to provide a
                      predictable parse order if individual options are
                      over-ridden. The set is parsed after the file(s)
                      specified via previous --config-file, arguments hence
                      over-ridden options in the directory take precedence.

--config-file PATH   Path to a config file to use. Multiple config files
                      can be specified, with values in later files taking
                      precedence. The default files used are: None.

--log-config-append PATH, --log_config PATH
                      The name of a logging configuration file. This file is
                      appended to any existing logging configuration files.
                      For details about logging configuration files, see the
                      Python logging module documentation.

Except for the ordering and precedence, --config-dir and --config-file are used to specify general configuration options and --log-config is used to specify logging configuration information.

On a system launched using devstack, the invocation of the Trove services (on an Ubuntu system) on the Trove controller is

```
/usr/local/bin/trove-api --config-file=/etc/trove/trove.conf
/usr/local/bin/trove-taskmanager --config-file=/etc/trove/trove-taskmanager.conf
/usr/local/bin/trove-conductor --config-file=/etc/trove/trove-conductor.conf
```

Each Trove service on the Trove controller host has its own configuration file. The Trove API service uses the file /etc/trove/trove.conf while the Trove task manager and the Trove conductor use the files /etc/trove/trove-taskmanager.conf and /etc/trove/trove-conductor.conf, respectively.

The typical invocation of the Trove guest agent is

```
/home/ubuntu/trove/contrib/trove-guestagent --config-dir=/etc/trove/conf.d
```

```
ubuntu@m1:/etc/trove/conf.d$ ls -l
total 8
-rw-rw-r-- 1 root root 123 Apr 24 11:06 guest_info.conf
-rw-rw-r-- 1 root root 937 Apr 24 11:06 trove-guestagent.conf
```

The Trove guest agent uses the --config-dir option and there are typically two configuration files in that directory. We look now at the configuration options and the structure of a configuration file.

Trove configuration options are defined in a number of places but the majority of the options are defined in trove/common/cfg.py. Trove uses oslo.config to parse and manage configuration files. Detailed documentation about oslo.config is available at http://docs.openstack.org/developer/oslo.config/.

Configuration files are plain text files with multiple sections. Each section contains name value pairs. A section is a word enclosed within '[' and ']' like [mysql] or [mongodb]. A setting is a line like the following:

```
bind_port = 9000
```

Configuration files typically begin with a [DEFAULT] section. In the absence of an explicit [DEFAULT] section, if you do not specify any other section name, [DEFAULT] is assumed.

The configuration file system works along with the command-line parsing mechanism. Consider the following configuration file specification:

```
[DEFAULT]
    bind_port = 9000

[mysql]
    port = 3306
    volume_support = True
```

These same options are accessible in code as shown here.

```
ubuntu@trove-book:/opt/stack/trove$ cat -n opts.py
     1  from oslo_config import cfg
     2
     3  opts = [
     4      cfg.IntOpt('bind_port', default=9000),
     5  ]
     6
     7  mysql_opts = [
     8      cfg.IntOpt('port', default=3306),
     9      cfg.BoolOpt('volume_support', default=True),
    10  ]
    11
    12  CONF = cfg.CONF
    13
    14  CONF.register_opts(mysql_opts, group='mysql')
```

```
15  CONF.register_opts(opts)
16
17
18  print CONF.bind_port
19  print CONF.mysql.port
20  print CONF.mysql.volume_support
21
```

```
ubuntu@trove-book:/opt/stack/trove$ python opts.py
9000
3306
True
```

Trove Configuration Options

This section provides a brief description of several of Trove's configuration options including the default value. Since each Trove service uses its own configuration file, we also list the configuration files in which these values should be specified in the "Service" column: API refers to the Trove API service and the trove.conf configuration file; TM refers to the Trove task manager service and the trove-taskmanager.conf file; CO refers to the Trove conductor service and the trove-conductor.conf; and GA refers to the guest agent; values for the guest agent are specified in the template file on the Trove controller instance and are provided to the guest instance on boot. The default values for each parameter reflect the values that would be set if no values were provided in any configuration file or on the command line.

Table A-1. *General Configuration Options*

Option	Description	Service	Default Value
admin_roles	Specifies the roles to add to the admin user.	API	['admin']
agent_call_high_timeout	The maximum amount of time to wait for the guest agent to perform long-running operations.	API TM	60 seconds
agent_call_low_timeout	The maximum amount of time to wait for the guest agent to perform short-running operations.	API TM	5 seconds
agent_heartbeat_expiry	Some operations (such as failover) are not allowed on an instance that has an "active" heartbeat. If the last heartbeat message from an instance is older than this amount of time, the instance is considered to have an expired heartbeat.	TM	60 seconds
agent_heartbeat_time	The amount of time that the guest has to respond to a heartbeat request.	TM	10 seconds
agent_replication_snapshot_timeout	Maximum amount of time for a replication snapshot to complete.	TM	36000 seconds
api_paste_config	File name of the paste.deploy configuration file for the API Service.	API	api-paste.ini
backlog	WSGI Socket backlog.	API	4069

(continued)

Table A-1. (*continued*)

Option	Description	Service	Default Value
backup_aes_cbc_key	The default password used to encrypt and decrypt backups. This string is passed directly to the openssl command if encryption is enabled (see backup_use_openssl_encryption).	GA	"default_aes_cbc_key"
backup_chunk_size	Block size for reads and writes of backups.	GA	65536
backup_segment_max_size	Maximum size of each segment of a backup on Swift.	GA	2147483648
backups_page_size	Number of lines per page for listing backups.	TM	20
backup_swift_container	Name of the Swift container to use for backups.	GA	database_backups
backup_use_gzip_compression	Indicate whether backups should be compressed using gzip.	GA	True
backup_use_openssl_encryption	Indicate whether backups should be encrypted using ssl. The password used for encryption is the value of the backup_aes_cbc_key option.	GA	True
backup_use_snet	Whether to use internal network in transferring data to Swift.	GA	False
bind_host	Interface on which API service will listen.	API	0.0.0.0 (all interfaces)
bind_port	Port on which API service will listen.	API	8779
black_list_regex	IP addresses to be excluded from a listing of host IP addresses. This is used to suppress any internal networks.	TM API	None
block_device:mapping	The name of the device to use for mapping the Cinder volume on the Nova instance.	TM API	vdb
cinder_endpoint_type	The Cinder end point type to use.	TM API	publicURL
cinder_service:type	Some OpenStack implementations may have multiple Cinder end points and the service type is used to determine which end point to use.	TM API	volumev2
cinder_url	The Cinder service URL (without the tenant qualification).	TM API	None
cinder_volume_type	Cinder volume type to use.	TM	None
cloudinit_location	Path to folder with cloudinit scripts.	TM	/etc/trove/cloudinit
cluster_delete_time_out	Maximum time to wait for a cluster delete.	TM	180 seconds

(continued)

Table A-1. (*continued*)

Option	Description	Service	Default Value
clusters_page_size	Number of lines per page when listing clusters.	TM API	20
cluster_usage_timeout	Maximum time to wait for a cluster to become active.	TM API	675 seconds
conductor_manager	Qualified class name to use for conductor manager.	CO	trove.conductor.manager.Manager
conductor_queue	Message queue name the conductor will listen on.	CO	trove-conductor
config_dir	Only specified on the command line of the guest agent (by default) to point to the directory with configuration files.	GA	/etc/trove/conf.d
config_file	Command-line parameter to API, task manager and conductor (by default) to identify their respective configuration files.	API TM CO	API:'/etc/trove/trove.conf' Task Manager: '/etc/trove/trove-taskmanager.conf' Conductor: '/etc/trove/trove-conductor.conf'
configurations_page_size	Number of lines per page when listing configuration groups.	TM API	20
databases_page_size	Number of lines per page when listing configuration groups.	TM API	20
datastore_manager	Used on the guest agent to identify the datastore manager to be used. This is the name of the datastore. This value is rendered on instance creation and placed in guest_info.conf.	GA	
datastore_registry_ext	Extension for default datastore managers to allow the use of custom managers.	GA	{}
debug	Whether debug messages should be logged or not. Typically specified on the command line, may also be placed in the configuration file.	API TM CO GA	False
default_datastore	The datastore to launch by default if one is not specified in the create call. If this value is not specified, a datastore must be specified in the create call.	API	None
default_neutron_networks	When Neutron is used for networking, this is the list of network ID's of neutron networks that must be attached to the guest instance irrespective of the other interfaces that may be specified as part of a create call.	TM API	None

(*continued*)

Table A-1. (*continued*)

Option	Description	Service	Default Value
default_password_length	Default length of generated passwords (such as on root-enable). This is passed directly to passlib.utils.generate_password() as the size parameter.	GA	36
device_path	The data volume path for a MySQL instance.	TM API	/dev/vdb
dns_account_id	Credentials to connect with Designate.	TM API	" "
dns_auth_url	Authorization URL for Designate.	TM API	" "
dns_domain_id	DNS domain ID.	TM API	" "
dns_domain_name	DNS domain name.	TM API	" "
dns_driver	The DNS driver that Trove will use.	TM API	trove.dns.driver. DnsDriver
dns_endpoint_url	End point for Designate.	TM API	0.0.0.0
dns_hostname	Hostname used when adding DNS entries.	TM API	" "
dns_instance_entry_factory	Factory for adding DNS entries.	TM API	trove.dns.driver. DnsInstanceEntryFactory
dns_management_base_url	Management URL for Designate service.	TM API	" "
dns_passkey	The password for Designate access.	TM API	" "
dns_region	The region name for Designate.	TM API	" "
dns_service_type	Service type for DNS (if configured).	TM API	" "
dns_time_out	Timeout when making DNS requests.	TM API	120 seconds
dns_ttl	Time to live on DNS entries.	TM API	300 seconds
dns_username	The user name for Designate access.	TM API	" "
format_options	Options to use when formatting a volume. This option is passed along with volume_fstype to the mkfs command.	GA	-m 5

(*continued*)

Table A-1. (*continued*)

Option	Description	Service	Default Value
guest_config	The name of the template to use when rendering the guest agent configuration.	TM	/etc/trove/trove-guestagent.conf
guest_id	Specified in guest_info.conf, the configuration file rendered by the task manager and installed on the guest instance before launching the guest agent.	GA	
guest_info	The name of the file to be rendered with guest configuration information. This file will be placed along with the config file rendered based on the template specified by the guest_config parameter.	TM	guest_info.conf
heat_endpoint_type	The Heat end point type to use.	TM API	publicURL
heat_service_type	The name of the Heat service, used to query Keystone.	TM API	orchestration
heat_time_out	Timeout when interacting with the Heat service.	TM API	60 seconds
heat_url	The URL for the Heat service (without tenant qualification).	TM API	None
host	Interface on which listen for RPC messages.	API TM CO GA	0.0.0.0
hostname_require_valid_ip	Used in validating the host name specified along with a MySQL username. By default, the MySQL wildcard character of '%' is allowed. This option defines whether other values are verified to be valid.	GA	True
http_delete_rate	Rate limit on API delete requests.	API	200 a minute
http_get_rate	Rate limit on API GET requests.	API	200 a minute
http_mgmt_post_rate	Rate limit on management API POST requests.	API	200 a minute
http_post_rate	Rate limit on API POST requests.	API	200 a minute
http_put_rate	Rate limit on API PUT requests.	API	200 a minute
ignore_dbs	The list of MySQL databases to ignore when listing databases.	GA API	'lost+found', '#mysql50#lost+found', 'mysql', 'information_schema']

(*continued*)

Table A-1. (*continued*)

Option	Description	Service	Default Value
ignore_users	List of MySQL users that should be ignored when listing users (these are internal user IDs used by the database and should not be exposed via Trove).	GA API	'os_admin', 'root'. Note that the default guest agent template created by devstack (/etc/trove/trove-guestagent.conf) only specifies os_admin.
injected_config_location	The name of the directory where configuration files are injected onto the guest.	TM	/etc/trove/conf.d
instances_page_size	Number of lines per page when listing instances.	TM API	20
ip_regex	The regular expression containing the IP addresses to be included in a listing of host IP addresses. This "white list" filter is applied in conjunction with the "black list" filter specified by black_list_regex.	TM API	None.
log_config_append	Determines whether or not to append to existing log files. The default (if unspecified) is True.	API TM CO GA	True
log_date_format	The format in which to log the date and time in a message.	API TM CO GA	%Y-%m-%d %H:%M:%S
log_dir	The location in which to place the logging output. The default template for the guest agent specifies this as /var/log/trove.	API TM CO GA	None.
log_file	The name of the file in which to place the logging output. The default template for the guest agent specifies this as trove-guestagent.log.	API TM CO GA	None
max_accepted_volume_size	The maximum size for a Trove guest instance data volume in gigabytes.	API	5 (gigabytes)
max_backups_per_user	The maximum number of backups allowed per tenant.	API	50
max_header_line	The maximum length of the header in a WSGI message in bytes. This value may have to be generated if using Keystone v3.	API	16384 (bytes)
max_instances_per_user	The maximum number of instances per tenant.	API	5

(*continued*)

Table A-1. (*continued*)

Option	Description	Service	Default Value
max_volumes_per_user	The maximum number of volumes per tenant.	API	20
mount_options	Options passed to the mount command when mounting the data volume.	GA	defaults,noatime
network_driver	The name of the driver to use for networking. Change this to trove.network.neutron. NeutronDriver when using Neutron.	TM API	trove.network.nova .NovaNetwork
network_label_regex	The regular expression to match the name of the Trove private network. Change this to ".*" when using Neutron.	TM	^private$
neutron_endpoint_type	The Neutron end point type to use.	API TM	publicURL
neutron_service_type	The name of the Neutron service, used to query Keystone.	TM API	network
neutron_url	The URL for the Neutron service (without tenant qualification).	TM API	None
notification_driver	The name of the driver to use for notifications.	TM API	[]
nova_compute_endpoint_type	The Nova end point type to use.	API TM	publicURL
nova_compute_service_type	The name of the Nova service, used to query Keystone.	TM API	Compute
nova_compute_url	The URL for the Nova service (without tenant qualification).	TM API	None
nova_proxy_admin_pass	Proxy administration user password to use when connecting to Nova.	TM	''
nova_proxy_admin_tenant_name	Proxy administration tenant name to use when connecting to Nova.	TM	''
nova_proxy_admin_user	Proxy administration username to use when connecting to Nova.	TM	''
num_tries	The number of times to check to see if a volume exists.	GA	3
os_region_name	The name of the OpenStack region for this Trove instance. Used in searching the service catalog.	GA TM API CO	RegionOne
profiler.enabled	Enable the OpenStack profiler.	TM API CO GA	False

(*continued*)

Table A-1. (*continued*)

Option	Description	Service	Default Value
profiler.trace_ sqlalchemy	Enable tracing of the sqlalchemy driver using OpenStack profiler. When enabled, SQL queries executed by Trove services are logged in the profile output.	TM API CO GA	True
quota_driver	Driver to use for managing Trove quotas.	TM API	trove.quota.quota .DbQuotaDriver
reboot_time_out	Time to wait for an instance to return to ACTIVE after a reboot.	API	120 seconds
region	The region where this service is located.	GA TM API	LOCAL_DEV
remote_cinder_ client	Implementation of the Cinder client.	GA API TM	trove.common.remote .cinder_client
remote_dns_ client	Implementation of the Designate client.	GA API TM	trove.common.remote .dns_client
remote_guest_ client	Implementation of the guest agent client.	API TM	trove.common.remote .guest_client
remote_heat_ client	Implementation of the Heat client.	GA API TM	trove.common.remote .heat_client
remote_neutron_ client	Implementation of the Neutron client.	GA API TM	trove.common.remote .neutron_client
remote_nova_client	Implementation of the Nova client.	GA API TM	trove.common.remote .nova_client
remote_swift_ client	Implementation of the Swift client.	GA API TM	trove.common.remote .swift_client
report_interval	Periodic task run interval.	GA TM	10 seconds
resize_time_out	Maximum amount of time to wait for a resize to complete.	TM	600 seconds
restore_usage_ timeout	Maximum amount of time to wait for a restore operation to complete.	TM	36000 seconds
revert_time_out	Maximum amount of time to wait for a Nova instance to come back ACTIVE after a revert operation.	TM	600 seconds
root_grant	Permissions to grant to the MySQL root user.	GA	ALL
root_grant_option	Grant the user the GRANT permission.	GA	True

(*continued*)

Table A-1. (*continued*)

Option	Description	Service	Default Value
rpc_backend	RPC back end to use.	GA TM CO API	Rabbit
server_delete_ time_out	Maximum amount of time to wait for a server delete operation.	TM	60 seconds
sql_query_ logging	Allow insecure query logging through SQL Alchemy on the guest instance.	GA	False
state_change_ wait_time	Maximum amount of time to wait for an instance state change.	GA	180 seconds
storage_ namespace	The storage namespace (object storage for backup).	GA	strove.guestagent. strategies. storage.swift
storage_strategy	The storage strategy (object storage for backup).	GA	SwiftStorage
swift_endpoint_ type	Endpoint type for the object storage service.	GA API TM	publicURL
swift_service_ type	Service type for the object storage service, used to look up in Keystone.	GA API TM	object-store
swift_url	Service URL for object storage service.	GA API TM	None
taskmanager_ manager	Implementation of the task manager.	TM	trove.taskmanager. manager.Manager
taskmanager_ queue	Name of the task manager queue used by the API to message the task manager.	API	Taskmanager
tcp_keepidle	TCP Keep Idle timeout for WSGI.	API	600 seconds
template_path	Location of Trove template files.	TM	/etc/trove/templates/
trove_api_ workers	Number of API worker threads.	API	Number of cores available.
trove_auth_url	Trove authentication URL.	TM CO GA	http://0.0.0.0:5000/ v2.0
trove_conductor_ workers	Number of conductor worker threads.	CO	Number of CPU's available
trove_dns_ support	Enable Trove DNS support.	TM API	False
trove_security_ group_name_prefix	Prefix for Trove security group name; used to prefix the instance ID.	TM	SecGroup

(*continued*)

Table A-1. (*continued*)

Option	Description	Service	Default Value
trove_security_group_rule_cidr	CIDR to use when creating Trove security rules.	TM	0.0.0.0/0
trove_security_groups_support	Enable Trove security groups.	TM	True
trove_volume_support	Enable persistent volume (Cinder) support.	TM API	True
update_status_on_fail	Set the service and instance task statuses to ERROR when an instance fails to become active within the configured usage_timeout.	TM	True
upgrade_levels.conductor	Current software level of conductor service.	CO	icehouse
upgrade_levels.guestagent	Current software level of guest agent service.	GA	icehouse
upgrade_levels.taskmanager	Current software level of the task manager service.	TM	icehouse
usage_sleep_time	Time to sleep during check for status on an active guest.	TM	5 seconds
usage_timeout	Time in seconds to wait for a guest to become active.	TM	600 seconds
use_heat	Use Heat for instance provisioning.	TM	False
use_nova_server_config_drive	Use Config Drive for file injection into Nova instances.	TM	False
use_nova_server_volume	Provision a Cinder volume for the Nova instance. If False, the volume and the instance are created independently.	TM	False
users_page_size	Maximum number of lines per page when listing users.	GA API	20
verbose	Enable verbose error logging.	TM API GA CO	False
verify_swift_checksum_on_restore	Verify the checksum of the Swift object during restore operations.	GA	True
volume_format_timeout	Maximum amount of time to wait during volume format operation.	GA	120 seconds
volume_fstype	Volume type during format operation.	GA	Ext3
volume_time_out	Maximum amount of time to wait during volume attach operation.	TM API	60 seconds

Datastore-Specific Configuration Options

Table A-2. *Cassandra-Specific Configuration Options*

Option	Description	Service	Default Value
cassandra .backup_incremental_strategy	Incremental backup runner. Currently not implemented.	GA	{}
cassandra .backup_namespace	Backup namespace. Currently not implemented.	GA	None
cassandra .backup_strategy	Backup strategy. Currently not implemented.	GA	None
cassandra .device_path	Data volume path for instance.	TM API	/dev/vdb
cassandra .mount_point	Location where data volume (device:path) should be mounted on the instance.	TM GA	/var/lib/cassandra
cassandra .replication_strategy	Replication strategy. Currently not implemented.	GA	None
cassandra .restore_namespace	Restore namespace. Currently not implemented.	GA	None
cassandra .tcp_ports	List of TCP ports or port ranges to open on the guest instance if security group support is enabled.	TM API	7000, 7001, 9042, 9160
cassandra .udp_ports	List of UDP ports or port ranges to open on the guest instance if security group support is enabled.	TM API	None
cassandra .volume_support	Whether to store data on a Cinder volume (use ephemeral volume if False).	TM API	True

Table A-3. *Couchbase-Specific Configuration Options*

Option	Description	Service	Default Value
couchbase. backup_incremental_ strategy	Incremental backup runner. Currently not implemented.	GA	{}
couchbase. backup_namespace	Backup namespace for Couchbase.	GA	trove.guestagent .strategies. backup.experimental .couchbase_impl
couchbase. backup_strategy	Backup strategy for Couchbase.	GA	CbBackup
couchbase. device_path	Data volume path for Couchbase instance.	TM API	/dev/vdb

(continued)

211

Table A-3. (*continued*)

Option	Description	Service	Default Value
couchbase. mount_point	Location where data volume (device_path) should be mounted on the instance.	TM GA	/var/lib/couchbase
couchbase. replication_strategy	Replication strategy. Currently not implemented.	GA	None
couchbase. restore_namespace	Restore namespace for Couchbase.	GA	trove.guestagent .strategies. restore.experimental .couchbase_impl
couchbase. root_on_create	Whether a root user should be enabled by default on Couchbase instances.	API	True
couchbase. tcp_ports	List of TCP ports or port ranges to open on the guest instance if security group support is enabled.	TM API	8091, 8092, 4369, 11209-11211, 21100-21199
couchbase. udp_ports	List of UDP ports or port ranges to open on the guest instance if security group support is enabled.	TM API	None
couchbase. volume_support	Whether to store data on a Cinder volume (use ephemeral volume if False).	TM API	True

Table A-4. *Couchdb-Specific Configuration Options*

Option	Description	Service	Default Value
couchdb. backup_incremental_ strategy	Incremental backup runner. Currently not implemented.	GA	{}
couchdb. backup_namespace	Backup namespace for Couchdb. Current not implemented.	GA	None
couchdb. backup_strategy	Backup strategy for Couchdb. Currently not implemented.	GA	None
couchdb. device_path	Data volume path for Couchbase instance.	TM API	/dev/vdb
couchdb. mount_point	Location where data volume (device_path) should be mounted on the instance.	TM GA	/var/lib/ couchdb
couchdb. replication_ strategy	Replication strategy. Currently not implemented.	GA	None
couchdb. restore_namespace	Restore namespace for Couchbase.	GA	None

(*continued*)

Table A-4. (*continued*)

Option	Description	Service	Default Value
couchdb.root_on_create	Whether a root user should be enabled by default on Couchdb instances.	API	False
couchdb.tcp_ports	List of TCP ports or port ranges to open on the guest instance if security group support is enabled.	TM API	['5984']
couchdb.udp_ports	List of UDP ports or port ranges to open on the guest instance if security group support is enabled.	TM API	[]
couchdb.volume_support	Whether to store data on a Cinder volume (use ephemeral volume if False).	TM API	True

Table A-5. *DB2-Specific Configuration Options*

Option	Description	Service	Default Value
db2.backup_incremental_strategy	Incremental backup runner. Currently not implemented.	GA	{}
db2.backup_namespace	Backup namespace for DB2.	GA	None
db2.backup_strategy	Backup strategy for DB2.	GA	None
db2.device_path	Data volume path for DB2 instance.	TM API	/dev/vdb
db2.ignore_users	List of DB2 database users that should be ignored when listing users (these are internal user IDs used by the database and should not be exposed via Trove).	GA	['PUBLIC', 'DB2INST1']
db2.mount_point	Location where data volume (device_path) should be mounted on the instance.	TM GA	/home/db2inst1/db2inst1
db2.replication_strategy	Replication strategy. Currently not implemented.	GA	None
db2.restore_namespace	Restore namespace for DB2.	GA	None
db2.root_on_create	Whether a root user should be enabled by default on DB2 instances.	API	False
db2.tcp_ports	List of TCP ports or port ranges to open on the guest instance if security group support is enabled.	TM API	50000
db2.udp_ports	List of UDP ports or port ranges to open on the guest instance if security group support is enabled.	TM API	None
db2.volume_support	Whether to store data on a Cinder volume. (Use ephemeral volume if False).	TM API	True

Table A-6. *MongoDB-Specific Options*

Option	Description	Service	Default Value
mongodb.api_strategy	The name of the implementation of the MongoDB specific API extensions.	API	trove.common.strategies .cluster.experimental .mongodb.api .MongoDbAPIStrategy
mongodb. backup_incremental_strategy	Backup incremental strategy for MongoDB. Currently not implemented.	GA	{}
mongodb.backup_namespace	Backup namespace. Currently not implemented.	GA	None
mongodb.backup_strategy	Backup strategy. Currently not implemented.	GA	None
mongodb.cluster_support	Is MongoDB cluster support enabled?	API	True
mongodb.device_path	Data volume for MongoDB instance.	TM API	/dev/vdb
mongodb.guestagent_strategy	Guest agent strategy implementation for MongoDB.	GA	trove.common.strategies .cluster.experimental .mongodb.guestagent .MongoDbGuestAgentStrategy
mongodb.mount_point	Location where data volume (device_path) should be mounted on the instance.	TM GA	/var/lib/mongodb
mongodb. num_config_servers_per_ cluster	The number of configuration servers to launch in a newly created cluster.	API	3
mongodb. num_query_routers_per_ cluster	The number of query routers to launch in a newly created cluster.	API	1
mongodb.replication_ strategy	Replication strategy for MongoDB. Currently not implemented.	GA	None
mongodb.restore_namespace	Restore namespace for MongoDB. Currently not implemented.	GA	None
mongodb.taskmanager_strategy	Task manager strategy extensions for MongoDB clustering.	TM	trove.common.strategies .cluster.experimental .mongodb.taskmanager .MongoDbTaskManagerStrategy

(continued)

Table A-6. (*continued*)

Option	Description	Service	Default Value
mongodb.tcp_ports	List of TCP ports or port ranges to open on the guest instance if security group support is enabled.	TM API	2500, 27017
mongodb.udp_ports	List of UDP ports or port ranges to open on the guest instance if security group support is enabled.	TM API	None
mongodb.volume_support	Whether to store data on a Cinder volume (use ephemeral volume if False).	TM API	True

Table A-7. *MySQL-Specific Configuration Option*

Option	Description	Service	Default Value
mysql.backup_incremental_strategy	Incremental backup runner for MySQL.	GA	{'InnoBackupEx': 'InnoBackupExIncremental'}
mysql.backup_namespace	Backup namespace for MySQL backup implementation.	GA	trove.guestagent .strategies .backup.mysql_impl
mysql.backup_strategy	Backup strategy for MySQL.	GA	InnoBackupEx
mysql.device_path	Data volume path for instance.	TM API	/dev/vdb
mysql.mount_point	Location where data volume (device_path) should be mounted on the instance.	TM GA	/var/lib/mysql
mysql.replication_namespace	Replication namespace for MySQL. Note that the default changed in the Kilo release.	GA	trove.guestagent .strategies .replication.mysql_gtid
mysql.replication_strategy	Replication strategy for MySQL. Note that the default changed in the Kilo release.	GA	MysqlGTIDReplication
mysql.restore_namespace	Restore namespace for MySQL.	GA	trove.guestagent .strategies .restore.mysql_impl
mysql.root_on_create	Whether a root user should be enabled by default on MySQL instances.	API	False

(*continued*)

Table A-7. (*continued*)

Option	Description	Service	Default Value
`mysql.tcp_ports`	List of TCP ports or port ranges to open on the guest instance if security group support is enabled.	TM API	3306
`mysql.udp_ports`	List of UDP ports or port ranges to open on the guest instance if security group support is enabled.	TM API	None
`mysql.usage_timeout`	Maximum amount of time to wait for the guest to come active.	TM	400 seconds
`mysql.volume_support`	Whether to store data on a Cinder volume (use ephemeral volume if False).	TM API	True

Table A-8. *Percona-Specific Configuration Options*

Option	Description	Service	Default Value
`percona.` `backup_incremental` `_strategy`	Incremental backup runner.	GA	`{'InnoBackupEx':` `'InnoBackupExIncremental'}`
`percona.` `backup_namespace`	Backup namespace.	GA	`trove.guestagent.strategies` `.backup.mysql_impl`
`percona.` `backup_strategy`	Backup strategy.	GA	`InnoBackupEx`
`percona.` `device_path`	Data volume path for instance.	TM API	`/dev/vdb`
`percona.` `mount_point`	Location where data volume (device_path) should be mounted on the instance.	GA TM	`/var/lib/mysql`
`percona.` `replication_namespace`	Replication namespace.	GA	`trove.guestagent` `.strategies` `replication.mysql_gtid`
`percona.` `replication_password`	Password for the Trove replication user.	GA	`NETOU7897NNLOU`
`percona.` `replication_strategy`	Replication strategy.	GA	`MysqlGTIDReplication`
`percona.` `replication_user`	Replication user for Percona.	GA	`slave_user`
`percona.` `restore_namespace`	Restore namespace.	GA	`trove.guestagent` `.strategies.restore` `.mysql_impl`

(*continued*)

Table A-8. (*continued*)

Option	Description	Service	Default Value
percona. root_on_create	Enable root user by default when creating a new instance.	API	False
percona. tcp_ports	List of TCP ports or port ranges to open on the guest instance if security group support is enabled.	TM API	3306
percona. udp_ports	List of UDP ports or port ranges to open on the guest instance if security group support is enabled.	TM API	None
percona. usage_timeout	Amount of time to wait for a new instance to come ACTIVE.	TM	450 seconds
percona. volume_support	Whether to store data on a Cinder volume (use ephemeral volume if False).	TM	True

Table A-9. *PostgreSQL-Specific Configuration Options*

Option	Description	Service	Default Value
postgresql. backup_incremental_strategy	Incremental backup runner. Not currently implemented.	GA	{}
postgresql. backup_namespace	Backup namespace for PostgreSQL.	GA	trove.guestagent .strategies .backup.experimental .postgresql_impl
postgresql. backup_strategy	Backup strategy for PostgreSQL.	GA	PgDump
postgresql. device_path	Data volume path for instance.	TM API	/dev/vdb
postgresql. ignore_dbs	The list of PostgreSQL databases to ignore when listing databases.	GA API	['postgres']
postgresql. ignore_users	List of PostgreSQL users that should be ignored when listing users (these are internal user IDs used by the database and should not be exposed via Trove).	GA API	['os_admin', 'postgres', 'root']
postgresql. mount_point	Location where data volume (device_path) should be mounted on the instance.	GA TM	/var/lib/postgresql

(*continued*)

Table A-9. (*continued*)

Option	Description	Service	Default Value
postgresql. restore_namespace	Restore namespace for PostgreSQL.	GA	trove.guestagent .strategies. restore.experimental .postgresql_impl
postgresql. root_on_create	Enable root user by default when creating a new instance.	API	False
postgresql. tcp_ports	List of TCP ports or port ranges to open on the guest instance if security group support is enabled.	TM API	5432
postgresql. udp_ports	List of UDP ports or port ranges to open on the guest instance if security group support is enabled.	TM API	None
postgresql. volume_support	Whether to store data on a Cinder volume (use ephemeral volume if False).	TM API	True

Table A-10. *Redis-Specific Options*

Option	Description	Service	Default Value
redis. backup_incremental_strategy	Backup incremental strategy. Not currently implemented.	GA	{}
redis. backup_namespace	Backup namespace. Not currently implemented.	GA	None
redis. backup_strategy	Backup strategy. Not currently implemented.	GA	None
redis. device:path	Data volume path for instance. Redis does not support volumes so this is defaulted to None.	TM API	None
redis. mount_point	Location where data volume (device_path) should be mounted on the instance.	GA TM	/var/lib/ redis
redis. replication_strategy	Replication strategy. Not currently implemented.	GA	None
redis. restore_namespace	Restore namespace. Not currently implemented.	GA	None
redis. tcp_ports	List of TCP ports or port ranges to open on the guest instance if security group support is enabled.	TM API	6379
redis. udp_ports	List of UDP ports or port ranges to open on the guest instance if security group support is enabled.	TM API	None
redis. volume_support	Whether to store data on a Cinder volume (use ephemeral volume if False).	TM API	False

Table A-11. *Vertica-Specific Configuration Options*

Option	Description	Service	Default Value
vertica. api_strategy	Vertica-specific extensions to the API service.	API	trove.common.strategies .cluster.experimental .vertica.api .VerticaAPIStrategy
vertica. backup_incremental _strategy	Backup incremental strategy. Currently not implemented.	GA	{}
vertica. backup_namespace	Backup namespace. Currently not implemented.	GA	None
vertica. backup_strategy	Backup strategy. Currently not implemented.	GA	None
vertica. cluster_member_count	Minimum number of cluster members in a Vertica cluster.	API	3
vertica. cluster_support	Is support for Vertica clusters enabled?	API	True
vertica. device:path	Data volume path for instance. Vertica does not support volumes so this is defaulted to None.	TM API	/dev/vdb
vertica. guestagent_strategy	Vertica guest agent strategy implementation.	GA	trove.common.strategies .cluster.experimental .vertica.guestagent .VerticaGuestAgentStrategy
vertica. mount_point	Location where data volume (device_path) should be mounted on the instance.	GA TM	/var/lib/vertica
vertica. readahead_size	Vertica read-ahead size parameter (Vertica specific).	GA	2048
vertica. replication_strategy	Replication strategy. Not currently implemented.	GA	None
vertica. restore_namespace	Restore namespace. Not currently implemented.	GA	None
vertica. taskmanager_strategy	Vertica-specific task manager extensions.	TM	trove.common.strategies .cluster.experimental .vertica.taskmanager .VerticaTaskManagerStrategy

Summary

In this appendix we described the various configuration options that you can use to alter the behavior of Trove. We provided a description of how each Trove service determines its own configuration, the default files used to configure each of the services, and the default values for each of the many configuration options listed.

We have provided Tables A-1 through A-11 as references and to help a user or an administrator of a Trove system to configure the deployment to best suit his or her needs.

Take care when changing these options. Changing some of these options can lead to permanent data loss and/or interruption of service.

APPENDIX B

■ ■ ■

The Trove Command-Line Interface

This appendix describes the Trove command-line interface (CLI) in detail and documents the various commands and options that are available on the command line.

The Command-Line Interface

To an operator or administrator of Trove, the CLI consists of two commands, trove and trove-manage.

The trove command is a Python program that interacts entirely with the Trove RESTful API.

The trove-manage command is a Python program that uses SQLAlchemy and the Trove models to make changes to the Trove infrastructure database. We look at each in turn.

The trove Command

The trove command provides a list of all the subcommands that it supports as well as the various optional arguments that are applicable to all subcommands. This information can be accessed by issuing the command trove --help.

Table B-1 provides an overview of the subcommands the trove command provides (grouped by the type of functionality they provide).

Table B-1. *trove Subcommands*

Function	Subcommand	Description
Backup	backup-copy	(Not implemented in the Kilo release.) Creates a backup from another backup.
	backup-create	Creates a backup of an instance.
	backup-delete	Deletes a backup.
	backup-list	Lists available backups.
	backup-list-instance	Lists available backups for an instance.
	backup-show	Shows details of a backup.
Cluster	cluster-create	Creates a new cluster.
	cluster-delete	Deletes a cluster.
	cluster-instances	Lists all instances of a cluster.
	cluster-list	Lists all the clusters.
	cluster-show	Shows details of a cluster.

(continued)

Table B-1. (*continued*)

Function	Subcommand	Description
Configuration	configuration-attach	Attaches a configuration group to an instance.
	configuration-create	Creates a configuration group.
	configuration-default	Shows the default configuration of an instance.
	configuration-delete	Deletes a configuration group.
	configuration-detach	Detaches a configuration group from an instance.
	configuration-instances	Lists all instances associated with a configuration group.
	configuration-list	Lists all configuration groups.
	configuration-parameter-list	Lists available parameters for a configuration group.
	configuration-parameter-show	Shows details of a configuration parameter.
	configuration-patch	Patches a configuration group.
	configuration-show	Shows details of a configuration group.
	configuration-update	Updates a configuration group.
Database Instance	create	Creates a new instance.
	list	Lists all the instances.
	restart	Restarts an instance.
	show	Shows details of an instance.
	update	Updates an instance: edits name, configuration, or replica source.
	delete	Deletes an instance.
Database and User Extensions	database-create	Creates a database on an instance.
	database-delete	Deletes a database from an instance.
	database-list	Lists available databases on an instance.
	user-create	Creates a user on an instance.
	user-delete	Deletes a user from an instance.
	user-grant-access	Grants access to a database(s) for a user.
	user-list	Lists the users for an instance.
	user-revoke-access	Revokes access to a database for a user.
	user-show	Shows details of a user of an instance.
	user-show-access	Shows access details of a user of an instance.
	user-update-attributes	Updates a user's attributes on an instance.
	root-enable	Enables root for an instance and resets if already exists.

(*continued*)

Table B-1. (*continued*)

Function	Subcommand	Description
	root-show	Gets status if root was ever enabled for an instance.
Datastore	datastore-list	Lists available datastores.
	datastore-show	Shows details of a datastore.
	datastore-version-list	Lists available versions for a datastore.
	datastore-version-show	Shows details of a datastore version.
Database Replication	detach-replica	Detaches a replica instance from its replication source.
	eject-replica-source	Ejects a replica source from its set.
	promote-to-replica-source	Promotes a replica to be the new replica source of its set.
Flavor	flavor-list	Lists available flavors.
	flavor-show	Shows details of a flavor.
Limit	limit-list	Lists the limits for a tenant.
Metadata	metadata-create	(Not implemented in the Kilo release.) Creates metadata in the database for instance <id>.
	metadata-delete	(Not implemented in the Kilo release.) Deletes metadata for instance <id>.
	metadata-edit	(Not implemented in the Kilo release.) Replaces metadata value with a new one, this is nondestructive.
	metadata-list	(Not implemented in the Kilo release.) Shows all metadata for instance <id>.
	metadata-show	(Not implemented in the Kilo release.) Shows metadata entry for key <key> and instance <id>.
	metadata-update	(Not implemented in the Kilo release.) Updates metadata, this is destructive.
Resize	resize-instance	Resizes an instance with a new flavor.
	resize-volume	Resizes the volume size of an instance.
Security	secgroup-add-rule	Creates a security group rule.
	secgroup-delete-rule	Deletes a security group rule.
	secgroup-list	Lists all security groups.
	secgroup-list-rules	Lists all rules for a security group.
	secgroup-show	Shows details of a security group.

You can display detailed help for each command by executing the `help` subcommand. For example, to get help about the `backup-create` subcommand, you can type the following:

```
ubuntu@trove-book:~$ trove help backup-create
usage: trove backup-create <instance> <name>
                           [--description <description>] [--parent <parent>]
Creates a backup of an instance.
Positional arguments:
  <instance>               ID or name of the instance.
  <name>                   Name of the backup.
Optional arguments:
  --description <description>  An optional description for the backup.
  --parent <parent>        Optional ID of the parent backup to perform an
                           incremental backup from.
```

Each subcommand may have additional positional and optional arguments. As shown previously, the `backup-create` subcommand requires an instance ID or name as the first positional parameter and a backup name as a second positional parameter. Optional parameters are also supported. You could generate the backup of an instance by issuing the following command:

```
ubuntu@trove-book:~$ trove backup-create m3 'backup of m3' \
> --description 'this is a backup of m3'
+-------------+--------------------------------------+
| Property    | Value                                |
+-------------+--------------------------------------+
| created     | 2015-04-24T11:39:03                  |
| description | this is a backup of m3               |
| id          | 109daea8-fa84-4b76-afd5-830e2fae3853 |
| instance_id | c399c99a-ee17-4048-bf8b-0ea5c36bb1cb |
| locationRef | None                                 |
| name        | backup of m3                         |
| parent_id   | None                                 |
| size        | None                                 |
| status      | NEW                                  |
| updated     | 2015-04-24T11:39:03                  |
+-------------+--------------------------------------+
```

Backup Subcommands

backup-copy

```
usage: trove backup-copy <name> <backup>
                         [--region <region>] [--description <description>]
Creates a backup from another backup.
Positional arguments:
  <name>                   Name of the backup.
  <backup>                 Backup ID of the source backup.
Optional arguments:
  --region <region>        Region where the source backup resides.
  --description <description>  An optional description for the backup.
```

■ **Note**   The `backup-copy` subcommand is not implemented in the Kilo release on the back end.

When launching an instance, you can provide the `create` subcommand with a previously generated backup as a source. When doing this, it is necessary that the backup be in the same region where you are launching the instance. The `backup-copy` command allows you to copy a backup from one region to another.

backup-create

```
usage: trove backup-create <instance> <name>
                           [--description <description>] [--parent <parent>]
Creates a backup of an instance.
Positional arguments:
  <instance>                 ID or name of the instance.
  <name>                     Name of the backup.
Optional arguments:
  --description <description>  An optional description for the backup.
  --parent <parent>          Optional ID of the parent backup to perform an
                             incremental backup from.
```

The `backup-create` subcommand is used to create a backup of an instance. The instance identification and a name for the backup are mandatory arguments. The name of the backup need not be unique.

When the `--parent` argument is provided, an incremental backup is generated with the provided parent being the starting point. A common operational practice is to create a full backup periodically and to create an incremental backup on a more frequent basis. To generate such a chain of backups of some instance (m3 in the example that follows), one would use the following sequence of commands:

```
ubuntu@trove-book:~$ trove backup-create m3 'full backup 2'
+-------------+------------------------------------------+
| Property    | Value                                    |
+-------------+------------------------------------------+
| description | full backup 2                            |
| id          | 109daea8-fa84-4b76-afd5-830e2fae3853     |
| instance_id | c399c99a-ee17-4048-bf8b-0ea5c36bb1cb     |
| parent_id   | None                                     |
[...]
ubuntu@trove-book:~$ trove backup-create m3 'incremental 1' \
> --parent 109daea8-fa84-4b76-afd5-830e2fae3853
+-------------+------------------------------------------+
| Property    | Value                                    |
+-------------+------------------------------------------+
| description | full backup 2                            |
| id          | 8be95576-fe62-494b-a23f-cf47929a8b39     |
| instance_id | c399c99a-ee17-4048-bf8b-0ea5c36bb1cb     |
| parent_id   | 109daea8-fa84-4b76-afd5-830e2fae3853     |
[...]
```

```
ubuntu@trove-book:~$ trove backup-create m3 'incremental 2' \
> --parent 8be95576-fe62-494b-a23f-cf47929a8b39
+-------------+----------------------------------------+
| Property    | Value                                  |
+-------------+----------------------------------------+
| description | full backup 2                          |
| id          | 7f683ada-3870-40e5-8ec6-7abb0fb75e5b   |
| instance_id | c399c99a-ee17-4048-bf8b-0ea5c36bb1cb   |
| parent_id   | 8be95576-fe62-494b-a23f-cf47929a8b39   |
[...]
```

The first backup is a full backup, the second is an incremental backup identifying the full backup as the parent. The third is an incremental backup identifying the second (i.e., incremental 1) as the parent.

Another common operational practice is to create a full backup periodically and to create an incremental backup on a more frequent basis, with each incremental backup being based on the full backup. This means that the system can be fully recovered based on the full backup and the one incremental backup rather than a chain of backups.

backup-delete

```
usage: trove backup-delete <backup>
Deletes a backup.
Positional arguments:
  <backup>  ID of the backup.
```

When you wish to delete a backup you need merely provide the ID of the backup. Consider however, this chain of backups created using the --parent option to the backup-create subcommand.

```
ubuntu@trove-book:~$ trove backup-show 8be95576-fe62-494b-a23f-cf47929a8b39 | grep parent_id
| parent_id   | 7f683ada-3870-40e5-8ec6-7abb0fb75e5b   |
ubuntu@trove-book:~$ trove backup-show 7f683ada-3870-40e5-8ec6-7abb0fb75e5b | grep parent_id
| parent_id   | 109daea8-fa84-4b76-afd5-830e2fae3853   |
ubuntu@trove-book:~$ trove backup-show 109daea8-fa84-4b76-afd5-830e2fae3853 | grep parent_id
| parent_id   | None                                   |
```

Attempting to delete the full backup at the head of this chain (109daea8-fa84-4b76-afd5-830e2fae3853) causes that backup and all of its incremental backups to be deleted.

```
ubuntu@trove-book:~$ trove backup-delete 109daea8-fa84-4b76-afd5-830e2fae3853
ubuntu@trove-book:~$ trove backup-list
+----+-------------+------+--------+-----------+---------+
| ID | Instance ID | Name | Status | Parent ID | Updated |
+----+-------------+------+--------+-----------+---------+
+----+-------------+------+--------+-----------+---------+
```

backup-list

```
usage: trove backup-list [--limit <limit>] [--datastore <datastore>]
Lists available backups.
Optional arguments:
  --limit <limit>            Return up to N number of the most recent backups.
  --datastore <datastore>    Name or ID of the datastore to list backups for.
```

Generates a list of backups available to the user. To list backups for a specific instance use the backup-list-instance subcommand.

backup-list-instance

```
usage: trove backup-list-instance [--limit <limit>] <instance>
Lists available backups for an instance.
Positional arguments:
  <instance>         ID or name of the instance.
Optional arguments:
  --limit <limit>  Return up to N number of the most recent backups.
```

To generate a list of all backups available to the user, use the backup-list subcommand.

backup-show

```
usage: trove backup-show <backup>
Shows details of a backup.
Positional arguments:
  <backup>  ID of the backup.
```

Shows all available information about a specified backup.

Cluster Subcommands

cluster-create

```
usage: trove cluster-create <name> <datastore> <datastore_version>
                            [--instance <flavor_id=flavor_id,volume=volume>]
Creates a new cluster.
Positional arguments:
  <name>                      Name of the cluster.
  <datastore>                 A datastore name or UUID.
  <datastore_version>         A datastore version name or UUID.
Optional arguments:
  --instance <flavor_id=flavor_id,volume=volume>
                              Create an instance for the cluster. Specify
                              multiple times to create multiple instances.
```

The cluster-create subcommand launches a cluster of instances. The mandatory arguments are the name of the cluster, the datastore, and the datastore version.

The format of the --instance argument is dependent on the datastore: for MongoDB, specify information about the first shard that will be created at cluster creation time. In addition, query routers and configuration servers will also be created. The number(s) of query routers and configuration servers are determined by the Trove configuration options (in trove-taskmanager.conf) mongodb.num_query_routers_per_cluster and mongodb.num_config_servers_per_cluster.

```
ubuntu@trove-book:~$ trove cluster-create c1 mongodb 2.4.9 \
> --instance flavor_id=2,volume=1 \
> --instance flavor_id=2,volume=1 \
> --instance flavor_id=2,volume=1
```

For Vertica, specify information about the cluster instances to be created. No additional instances are created for a Vertica cluster.

cluster-delete

```
usage: trove cluster-delete <cluster>
Deletes a cluster.
Positional arguments:
  <cluster>  ID of the cluster.
```

The cluster-delete subcommand deletes all instances and resources that were created for the cluster, including (in the case of MongoDB) query routers and configuration servers.

cluster-instances

```
usage: trove cluster-instances <cluster>
Lists all instances of a cluster.
Positional arguments:
  <cluster>  ID or name of the cluster.
```

The cluster-instances subcommand lists the instances that are part of a cluster, including (in the case of MongoDB) any query routers and configuration servers that form part of the cluster.

cluster-list

```
usage: trove cluster-list [--limit <limit>] [--marker <ID>]
Lists all the clusters.
Optional arguments:
  --limit <limit>  Limit the number of results displayed.
  --marker <ID>    Begin displaying the results for IDs greater than the
                   specified marker. When used with --limit, set this to the
                   last ID displayed in the previous run.
```

The cluster-list subcommand lists all clusters on the system.

cluster-show

```
usage: trove cluster-show <cluster>
Shows details of a cluster.
Positional arguments:
  <cluster>  ID or name of the cluster.
```

Given a cluster, the cluster-show subcommand shows details about the cluster.

Configuration Subcommands

configuration-attach

```
usage: trove configuration-attach <instance> <configuration>
Attaches a configuration group to an instance.
Positional arguments:
  <instance>       ID or name of the instance.
  <configuration>  ID of the configuration group to attach to the instance.
```

For details about the configuration commands see in Chapter 5.

configuration-create

```
usage: trove configuration-create <name> <values>
                                  [--datastore <datastore>]
                                  [--datastore_version <datastore_version>]
                                  [--description <description>]
Creates a configuration group.
Positional arguments:
  <name>                         Name of the configuration group.
  <values>                       Dictionary of the values to set.
Optional arguments:
  --datastore <datastore>        Datastore assigned to the configuration
                                 group. Required if default datastore is not
                                 configured.
  --datastore_version <datastore_version>
                                 Datastore version ID assigned to the
                                 configuration group.
  --description <description>    An optional description for the
                                 configuration group.
```

For details about the configuration commands see in Chapter 5.

configuration-default

```
usage: trove configuration-default <instance>
Shows the default configuration of an instance.
Positional arguments:
  <instance>  ID or name of the instance.
```

For details about the configuration commands see in Chapter 5.

configuration-delete

```
usage: trove configuration-delete <configuration_group>
Deletes a configuration group.
Positional arguments:
  <configuration_group>  ID of the configuration group.
```

For details about the configuration commands see in Chapter 5.

configuration-detach

```
usage: trove configuration-detach <instance>
Detaches a configuration group from an instance.
Positional arguments:
  <instance>  ID or name of the instance.
```

For details about the configuration commands see in Chapter 5.

configuration-instances

```
usage: trove configuration-instances <configuration_group>
Lists all instances associated with a configuration group.
Positional arguments:
  <configuration_group>  ID of the configuration group.
```

For details about the configuration commands see in Chapter 5.

configuration-list

```
usage: trove configuration-list
Lists all configuration groups.
```

For details about the configuration commands see in Chapter 5.

configuration-parameter-list

```
usage: trove configuration-parameter-list <datastore_version>
                                [--datastore <datastore>]
Lists available parameters for a configuration group.
Positional arguments:
  <datastore_version>     Datastore version name or ID assigned to the
                          configuration group.
Optional arguments:
  --datastore <datastore> ID or name of the datastore to list configuration
                          parameters for. Optional if the ID of the
                          datastore_version is provided.
```

For details about the configuration commands see in Chapter 5.

configuration-parameter-show

```
usage: trove configuration-parameter-show <datastore_version> <parameter>
                                   [--datastore <datastore>]
```
Shows details of a configuration parameter.
Positional arguments:
  <datastore_version>   Datastore version name or ID assigned to the
                             configuration group.
                 Name of the configuration parameter.
Optional arguments:
  --datastore <datastore>   ID or name of the datastore to list configuration
                             parameters for. Optional if the ID of the
                             datastore_version is provided.

For details about the configuration commands see in Chapter 5.

configuration-patch

```
usage: trove configuration-patch <configuration_group> <values>
```
Patches a configuration group.
Positional arguments:
  <configuration_group> ID of the configuration group.
  <values>   Dictionary of the values to set.

For details about the configuration commands see in Chapter 5.

configuration-show

```
usage: trove configuration-show <configuration_group>
```
Shows details of a configuration group.
Positional arguments:
  <configuration_group> ID of the configuration group.

For details about the configuration commands see in Chapter 5.

configuration-update

```
usage: trove configuration-update <configuration_group> <values>
                                  [--name <name>]
                                  [--description <description>]
```
Updates a configuration group.
Positional arguments:
  <configuration_group>   ID of the configuration group.
  <values>   Dictionary of the values to set.
Optional arguments:
  --name <name>   Name of the configuration group.
  --description <description> An optional description for the configuration
                               group.

For details about the configuration commands see in Chapter 5.

Database Instance Subcommands

create

```
usage: trove create <name> <flavor_id>
                    [--size <size>]
                    [--databases <databases> [<databases> ...]]
                    [--users <users> [<users> ...]] [--backup <backup>]
                    [--availability_zone <availability_zone>]
                    [--datastore <datastore>]
                    [--datastore_version <datastore_version>]
                    [--nic <net-id=net-uuid,v4-fixed-ip=ip-addr,port-id=port-uuid>]
                    [--configuration <configuration>]
                    [--replica_of <source:instance>] [--replica_count <count>]
```

Creates a new instance.
Positional arguments:
```
  <name>                        Name of the instance.
  <flavor_id>                   Flavor of the instance.
```
Optional arguments:
```
  --size <size>                 Size of the instance disk volume in GB used for database
                                data directory.
                                Required when volume support is enabled.
  --databases <databases> [<databases> ...]
                                Optional list of databases to create on instance.
  --users <users> [<users> ...] Optional list of users to create on the instance in the form
                                user:password.
  --backup <backup>             A backup ID which will be loaded into the instance.
  --availability_zone <availability_zone>
                                The Zone hint to give to nova.
  --datastore <datastore>       A datastore name or ID.
  --datastore_version <datastore_version>
                                A datastore version name or ID.
  --nic <net-id=net-uuid,v4-fixed-ip=ip-addr,port-id=port-uuid>
                                Create a NIC on the instance. Specify option
                                multiple times to create multiple NICs. net-
                                id: attach NIC to network with this ID
                                (either port-id or net-id must be
                                specified), v4-fixed-ip: IPv4 fixed address
                                for NIC (optional), port-id: attach NIC to
                                port with this ID (either port-id or net-id
                                must be specified).
  --configuration <configuration>
                                ID of the configuration group to attach to
                                the instance.
  --replica_of <source:instance> ID or name of an existing instance to
                                replicate from.
  --replica_count <count>       Number of replicas to create (defaults to 1).
```

The trove create command is used to create a new instance. The name and instance flavor are the only required parameters to this command. If the datastore requires a Cinder volume as a persistent location to store data, the --size parameter is also required.

```
ubuntu@trove-book:~$ trove create m2 2
ERROR: Volume size was not specified. (HTTP 400)
```

We describe some of the other commonly used options next: for datastores that support the databases and users extensions, you can create a set of users and databases on the newly created instance by specifying the --databases and --users parameters. Launch a database instance from an existing backup using the --backup parameter. The --configuration parameter allows you to associate a configuration group with the instance on launch.

list

```
usage: trove list [--limit <limit>] [--marker <ID>] [--include-clustered]
Lists all the instances.
Optional arguments:
  --limit <limit>      Limit the number of results displayed.
  --marker <ID>        Begin displaying the results for IDs greater than the
                       specified marker. When used with --limit, set this to
                       the last ID displayed in the previous run.
  --include-clustered  Include instances that are part of a cluster (default
                       false).
```

The list subcommand provides a list of all instances launched by the tenant. If you specify the --include-clustered argument, this will include instances which are part of a cluster as well.

restart

```
usage: trove restart <instance>
Restarts an instance.
Positional arguments:
  <instance>  ID or name of the instance.
```

Restarting the database server on an instance is required after some configuration changes. When such a change has been made, Trove will put the instance in the RESTART_REQUIRED state.

show

```
usage: trove show <instance>
Shows details of an instance.
Positional arguments:
  <instance>  ID or name of the instance.
```

The show subcommand shows details about an instance.

update

```
usage: trove update <instance>
                    [--name <name>] [--configuration <configuration>]
                    [--detach-replica-source] [--remove_configuration]
Updates an instance: Edits name, configuration, or replica source.
Positional arguments:
  <instance>                    ID or name of the instance.
Optional arguments:
  --name <name>                 Name of the instance.
  --configuration <configuration>
                                ID of the configuration reference to attach.
  --detach-replica-source       Detach the replica instance from its
                                replication source.
  --remove_configuration        Drops the current configuration reference.
```

The update subcommand is used to manipulate instances in one of four ways. These are to update the name (with the --name parameter), to associate a configuration group (with the --configuration parameter), to detach a configuration group associated with an instance (with the --remove_configuration parameter), and to detach a replica from its master (with the --detach-replica-source parameter). Specifying the --configuration parameter is equivalent to creating an instance and then executing the trove configuration-attach command.

Only one configuration group may be associated with an instance at any given time. Some configuration changes may require the instance to be restarted.

delete

```
usage: trove delete <instance>
Deletes an instance.
Positional arguments:
  <instance>  ID or name of the instance.
```

The delete subcommand deletes an instance and any Cinder volumes used for persistent storage associated with the instance.

Database Extensions Subcommands

database-create

```
usage: trove database-create <instance> <name>
                            [--character_set <character_set>]
                            [--collate <collate>]
Creates a database on an instance.
Positional arguments:
  <instance>                    ID or name of the instance.
  <name>                        Name of the database.
Optional arguments:
  --character_set <character_set>
                                Optional character set for database.
  --collate <collate>           Optional collation type for database.
```

For datastores that support the database extensions, this subcommand will create a database with the specified parameters.

database-delete

```
usage: trove database-delete <instance> <database>
Deletes a database from an instance.
Positional arguments:
  <instance>  ID or name of the instance.
  <database>  Name of the database.
```

For datastores that support the database extensions, this subcommand will delete a specified database.

database-list

```
usage: trove database-list <instance>
Lists available databases on an instance.
Positional arguments:
  <instance>  ID or name of the instance.
```

For datastores that support the database extensions, this subcommand will list databases on any given instance.

user-create

```
usage: trove user-create <instance> <name> <password>
                         [--host <host>]
                         [--databases <databases> [<databases> ...]]
Creates a user on an instance.
Positional arguments:
  <instance>                      ID or name of the instance.
  <name>                          Name of user.
  <password>                      Password of user.
Optional arguments:
  --host <host>                   Optional host of user.
  --databases <databases> [<databases> ...]
                                  Optional list of databases.
```

For datastores that support the user extension, this subcommand will create a user on an instance.

user-delete

```
usage: trove user-delete [--host <host>] <instance> <name>
Deletes a user from an instance.
Positional arguments:
  <instance>  ID or name of the instance.
  <name>      Name of user.
Optional arguments:
  --host <host>  Optional host of user.
```

For datastores that support the user extensions, this subcommand will delete a user on an instance. If a user was created with a --host specification, then the user will only be deleted if the --host is specified on the user-delete subcommand.

user-grant-access

```
usage: trove user-grant-access <instance> <name> <databases> [<databases> ...]
                               [--host <host>]
Grants access to a database(s) for a user.
Positional arguments:
  <instance>      ID or name of the instance.
  <name>          Name of user.
  <databases>     List of databases.
Optional arguments:
  --host <host>   Optional host of user.
```

For datastores that support the user and database extensions, this subcommand will grant the user access to the specified databases.

user-list

```
usage: trove user-list <instance>
Lists the users for an instance.
Positional arguments:
  <instance>  ID or name of the instance.
```

For datastores that support the user's extensions, this subcommand will list the registered users on the instance.

user-revoke-access

```
usage: trove user-revoke-access [--host <host>] <instance> <name> <database>
Revokes access to a database for a user.
Positional arguments:
  <instance>      ID or name of the instance.
  <name>          Name of user.
  <database>      A single database.
Optional arguments:
  --host <host>   Optional host of user.
```

For datastores that support the user and database extensions, this subcommand will revoke user access from the specified database.

user-show

```
usage: trove user-show [--host <host>] <instance> <name>
Shows details of a user of an instance.
Positional arguments:
  <instance>      ID or name of the instance.
  <name>          Name of user.
Optional arguments:
  --host <host>  Optional host of user.
```

For datastores that support the user extensions, this subcommand will show information about a specified user on an instance.

user-show-access

```
usage: trove user-show-access [--host <host>] <instance> <name>
Shows access details of a user of an instance.
Positional arguments:
  <instance>      ID or name of the instance.
  <name>          Name of user.
Optional arguments:
  --host <host>  Optional host of user.
```

For datastores that support the user and database extensions, this subcommand will display user access information.

user-update-attributes

```
usage: trove user-update-attributes <instance> <name>
                                    [--host <host>] [--new_name <new_name>]
                                    [--new_password <new_password>]
                                    [--new_host <new_host>]
Updates a user's attributes on an instance. At least one optional argument
must be provided.
Positional arguments:
  <instance>                       ID or name of the instance.
  <name>                           Name of user.
Optional arguments:
  --host <host>                    Optional host of user.
  --new_name <new_name>            Optional new name of user.
  --new_password <new_password>    Optional new password of user.
  --new_host <new_host>            Optional new host of user.
```

For datastores that support the user extensions, this subcommand can be used to manipulate the user's account and change the password, name, or host from where the user can connect to the system.

root-enable

```
usage: trove root-enable <instance>
Enables root for an instance and resets if already exists.
Positional arguments:
  <instance>  ID or name of the instance.
```

For datastores that support the user extensions, this subcommand will enable the database superuser account and return its credentials. There is no command to retrieve the superuser's credentials. If you misplace the credentials, you can execute this command again and get a new set of credentials that will invalidate the previous set.

root-show

```
usage: trove root-show <instance>
Gets status if root was ever enabled for an instance.
Positional arguments:
  <instance>  ID or name of the instance.
```

For datastores that support the user extensions, this subcommand will tell you whether or not the database superuser has ever been enabled.

Generating JSON Output from the trove Command

By default, the trove command generates a tabular output. This is not always the best option. Consider the situation where you would like to script a complex set of operations and use the Trove CLI to perform the individual operations. It is sometimes useful to be able to retrieve the output from a command in an easy to parse format.

This is easily accomplished using the --json command-line parameter to the trove command as shown next.

```
ubuntu@trove-book:~$ trove database-list m1
+--------------------+
| Name               |
+--------------------+
| performance:schema |
+--------------------+
ubuntu@trove-book:~$ trove --json database-list m1
[
  {
    "name": "performance:schema"
  }
]
```

Recall that --json is an optional argument to the trove command. It is therefore an error to add the --json at the end of the command line.

```
ubuntu@trove-book:~$ trove database-list m1 --json
[. . .]
error: unrecognized arguments: --json
Try 'trove help ' for more information.
```

Understanding What the trove Command Is Doing

The trove command is a Python encapsulation of the Trove API. To understand exactly what any given command is doing, you can use the --debug option.

```
ubuntu@trove-book:~$ trove --debug database-list m1 2>&1 | grep -v iso8601 | tail -n 11
DEBUG (session:195) REQ: curl -g -i --cacert "/opt/stack/data/CA/int-ca/ca-chain.pem" -X
GET http://192.168.117.5:8779/v1.0/70195ed77e594c63b33c5403f2e2885c/instances/0ccbd8ff-
a602-4a29-a02c-ea93acd79095/databases -H "User-Agent: python-keystoneclient" -H "Accept:
application/json" -H "X-Auth-Token: {SHA1}4a5e77a83afc22dd9b484e3b98eae9f708d6b254"
DEBUG (retry:155) Converted retries value: 0 -> Retry(total=0, connect=None, read=None,
redirect=0)
DEBUG (connectionpool:383) "GET /v1.0/70195ed77e594c63b33c5403f2e2885c/instances/0ccbd8ff-
a602-4a29-a02c-ea93acd79095/databases HTTP/1.1" 200 47
DEBUG (session:224) RESP: [200] date: Fri, 24 Apr 2015 12:04:40 GMT content-length: 47
content-type: application/json
RESP BODY: {"databases": [{"name": "performance:schema"}]}
+--------------------+
| Name               |
+--------------------+
| performance:schema |
+--------------------+
```

The preceding output has been abbreviated (we are showing the last 11 lines), and the last interaction with the Trove API service is shown here. The complete output of this command (unedited) shows the complete behavior of the command including getting a Keystone token and then querying the Trove API service to get a list of instances, and so on.

Environment Variables

The trove command uses a variety of environment variables to store tenant names, user names, and passwords and other information used by the client to authenticate with Keystone. Table B-2 lists these environment variables.

Table B-2. *trove Command Environment Variables*

Command Line Option	Environment Variable	Description
--os-auth-system	OS_AUTH_SYSTEM	One of these two options must be specified.
--os-auth-url	OS_AUTH_URL	Typically, OS_AUTH_URL (or --os-auth-url) point to the Keystone end point where the user can obtain a token.
--database-service-name	TROVE_DATABASE_SERVICE_NAME	By default, the Trove service is registered in Keystone as 'database'.
--os-database-api-version	OS_DATABASE_API_VERSIONS	Currently only v1.0 is supported.
--json, --os-json-output	OS_JSON_OUTPUT	Used to generate JSON output instead of tabular output.

(continued)

Table B-2. (*continued*)

Command Line Option	Environment Variable	Description
--profile	OS_PROFILE_HMACKEY	See the section on profiling for a detailed description of this parameter.
--os-tenant-name	OS_TENANT_NAME	The name of the tenant.
--os-auth-token	OS_AUTH_TOKEN	If an auth token was obtained and you wish to use that, specify it here.
--os-tenant-id	OS_TENANT_ID	Sometimes specified instead of the tenant name.
--os-region-name	OS_REGION_NAME	The region name in which to execute the subcommand.

Specifying environment variables makes it much easier to execute Trove commands. When the system is installed using devstack, you can set all the appropriate environment variables by executing the openrc script.

```
ubuntu@trove-book:~$ source devstack/openrc admin admin
```

The parameters you provide to the command are the OpenStack username and the OpenStack tenant name.

The trove-manage Command

Some low-level administration of a Trove installation requires the use of the trove-manage command. The functions provided by this command are not exposed via the RESTful API. These commands are only ever used by the operator, and they are used infrequently.

The trove-manage command supports the following subcommands, which are used in registering a new guest image and making the datastore available to users. Once you download an image, you need to register it with Glance.

```
ubuntu@trove-controller:~/downloaded-images$ glance image-create --name percona \
> --disk-format qcow2 \
> --container-format bare --is-public True < ./percona.qcow2
+------------------+--------------------------------------+
| Property         | Value                                |
+------------------+--------------------------------------+
| checksum         | 963677491f25a1ce448a6c11bee67066     |
| container_format | bare                                 |
| created_at       | 2015-03-18T13:19:18                  |
| deleted          | False                                |
| deleted_at       | None                                 |
| disk_format      | qcow2                                |
| id               | 80137e59-f2d6-4570-874c-4e9576624950 |
| is_public        | True                                 |
| min_disk         | 0                                    |
| min_ram          | 0                                    |
| name             | percona                              |
```

```
| owner          | 979bd3efad6f42448ffa55185a122f3b   |
| protected      | False                              |
| size           | 513343488                          |
| status         | active                             |
| updated_at     | 2015-03-18T13:19:30                |
| virtual_size   | None                               |
+----------------+------------------------------------+
```

Subcommand: datastore_update

```
usage: trove-manage datastore_update [-h] datastore_name default_version
Add or update a datastore. If the datastore already exists, the default
version will be updated.
positional arguments:
  datastore_name   Name of the datastore.
  default_version  Name or ID of an existing datastore version to set as the
                   default. When adding a new datastore, use an empty string.
optional arguments:
  -h, --help       show this help message and exit
```

You can use the datastore_update subcommand to add a new datastore (provide an empty string for the version). The command that follows creates a new datastore called percona.

```
ubuntu@trove-controller:$ trove-manage datastore_update percona ''
2015-03-18 09:23:24.469 INFO trove.db.sqlalchemy.session [-] Creating SQLAlchemy engine with
args: {'pool_recycle': 3600, 'echo': False}
Datastore 'percona' updated.
```

You can specify a default_version of a datastore by using the second positional argument. The command that follows sets version 5.5 to be the default version of the percona datastore:

```
ubuntu@trove-controller:$ trove-manage datastore_update percona 5.5
2015-03-18 09:26:12.875 INFO trove.db.sqlalchemy.session [-] Creating SQLAlchemy engine with
args: {'pool_recycle': 3600, 'echo': False}
Datastore 'percona' updated.
```

Subcommand: datastore_version_update

```
usage: trove-manage datastore_version_update [-h]
                                   datastore version_name manager
                                   image_id packages active
Add or update a datastore version. If the datastore version already exists,
all values except the datastore name and version will be updated.
positional arguments:
  datastore     Name of the datastore.
  version_name  Name of the datastore version.
  manager       Name of the manager that will administer the datastore
                version.
```

image_id	ID of the image used to create an instance of the datastore version.
packages	Packages required by the datastore version that are installed on first boot of the guest image.
active	Whether the datastore version is active or not. Accepted values are 0 and 1.

```
optional arguments:
  -h, --help    show this help message and exit
```

Once a Glance image ID is available, the datastore_version_update command can be used to register the guest image and map that image to a datastore and version.

Once registered, the datastore and the version are the keys and will not be changed. When the command is issued again, if a record with the same datastore and version is found, the other four parameters are used to update the information. If no match is found, a new record is created.

The following command registers the Glance ID (shown in the previous example) with the Percona datastore, version 5.5.

It sets the image as active (the active parameter is 1) indicating that users can launch instances with this image. Setting it to 0 would indicate that users cannot launch instances with that image.

```
ubuntu@trove-controller:~/downloaded-images$ trove-manage datastore_version_update percona 5.5 \
> percona 80137e59-f2d6-4570-874c-4e9576624950 \
> "percona-server-server-5.5" 1
2015-03-18 09:25:17.610 INFO trove.db.sqlalchemy.session [-] Creating SQLAlchemy engine with
args: {'pool_recycle': 3600, 'echo': False}
Datastore version '5.5' updated.
```

Subcommand: db_load_datastore_config_parameters

```
usage: trove-manage db_load_datastore_config_parameters [-h]
                                                        datastore
                                                        datastore_version
                                                        config_file_location
Loads configuration group parameter validation rules for a datastore version
into the database.
positional arguments:
  datastore              Name of the datastore.
  datastore_version      Name of the datastore version.
  config_file_location   Fully qualified file path to the configuration group
                         parameter validation rules.
optional arguments:
  -h, --help             show this help message and exit
```

The db_load_datastore_config_parameters command loads the validation rules to be used when managing configuration groups for the specified datastore and version. (For more details about configuration groups, refer to Chapter 5.

The datastore and version are used as keys in a lookup and if a datastore/version combination already has a set of validation rules, the rules are updated. If no match is found, a new record is created.

Summary

One can interact with a Trove installation in one of two ways. The first is through the Trove RESTful API and the second is through the Trove CLI. The Trove CLI consists of two commands, the `trove` command and the `trove-manage` command.

Each of these commands provides a number of subcommands that perform specific functions. The `trove` command is a wrapper around the Trove API and the `trove-manage` command makes changes directly to the Trove Infrastructure Database.

Environment variables can be used in the place of many commonly used parameters to the `trove` command. Specifying values that will be used for all `trove` subcommands makes `trove` commands shorter and easier to use.

APPENDIX C

■ ■ ■

The Trove API

This appendix describes the Trove API in detail, and documents the various interfaces that Trove provides. We use 'curl' and show how one can interact with Trove using its RESTful API.

The Trove API Service End Point

In the following examples, we interact with the Trove API service end point which is at http://192.168.117.5:8779. Port 8779 is, by default, the port that the Trove API service uses. This is configurable and if you so desire you could change the value of bind_port in trove-api.conf.

When operating Trove in a development environment, it is acceptable to leave the service end point listening on all interfaces on the machine (the default value of bind_host is 0.0.0.0). However, in a production environment, it is highly advisable that you bind the Trove API service to listen on a specific interface on your system.

The Trove API Service exposes a RESTful interface. All access to the interface must be authenticated and Trove relies on Keystone for this purpose. This means that in order to interact with Trove you need to obtain a Keystone token which you then provide to Trove as part of the API call. This sequence is illustrated as follows:

```
ubuntu@trove-book:~/api$ curl -s -d \
> '{"auth": {"tenantName": "admin", "passwordCredentials": \
> {"username" : "admin", "password": "882f520bd67212bf9670"}}}' \
> -H 'Content-Type: application/json' http://192.168.117.5:5000/v2.0/tokens \
> | python -m json.tool
{
[...]
        "token": {
            "audit_ids": [
                "T7s9WB8CQS6ntGSm3kH5-Q"
            ],
            "expires": "2015-04-24T13:52:46Z",
            "id": "60e360cdb7cf4abeb17f35e973809086",
            "issued_at": "2015-04-24T12:52:46.039378",
```

```
        "tenant": {
            "description": null,
            "enabled": true,
            "id": "70195ed77e594c63b33c5403f2e2885c",
            "name": "admin"
        }
    },
[...]
}
```

In order to make a request to Trove, the fields that you require in the response from keystone are the tenant id and the auth token (highlighted previously). In the simple request that follows you do not need the tenant ID.

```
ubuntu@trove-book:~/api$ curl -H "X-Auth-Token: 60e360cdb7cf4abeb17f35e973809086" \
> http://192.168.117.5:8779/ | python -m json.tool

{
    "versions": [
        {
            "id": "v1.0",
            "links": [
                {
                    "href": "http://192.168.117.5:8779/v1.0/",
                    "rel": "self"
                }
            ],
            "status": "CURRENT",
            "updated": "2012-08-01T00:00:00Z"
        }
    ]
}
```

API Conventions

We describe data parameters for each of the APIs as shown next. Some APIs accept additional data parameters as part of a request. The data parameter is a JSON (JavaScript Notation Object) object containing additional information about the request. Consider, for example, the two requests to resize an instance shown in Table C-1.

Table C-1. *Illustration of Data Parameters and Schema for Some Commands*

CLI Command	Data Parameter	Data Parameter Schema

`trove resize-volume m1 3`	`{`
	  `"resize": {`
	    `"volume": {`
	      `"size": 3`
	    `}`
	  `}`
	`}`
		`{`
		  `"resize": {`
		    `"volume": volume`
		  `}`
		`}`
		
		`volume = {`
		  `"type": "object",`
		  `"required": ["size"],`
		  `"properties": {`
		    `"size": volume_size,`
		    `"required": True`
		  `}`
		`}`

`trove resize-instance m1 3`	`{`
	  `"resize": {`
	    `"flavorRef": "3"`
	  `}`
	`}`
		`{`
		  `"resize": {`
		    `"flavorRef": flavorRef`
		  `}`
		`}`
		
		`flavorref = {`
		  `'oneOf': [`
		    `non_empty_string,`
		    `{`
		      `"type": "integer"`
		    `}]`
		`}`

The command-line invocation (first column) generates an API call with the data parameter shown in the second column. As the data parameter may provide several options and any given invocation may only supply some of them, we show the complete description of the data parameter, which is the data parameter schema, in the right-hand column.

Observe that to resize a flavor, you can specify the `flavorRef` in one of two ways, the first is as a `non_empty_string` and the second is as an `integer`. The sample invocation uses the integer form for the `flavorRef`. It is important to know that there is the other invocation where you could specify the `flavorRef` as a URI (uniform resource identifier) (`https://192.168.117.5:8779/flavors/3`) and for that reason in the following sections, we document not just the JSON object in a sample invocation but also the complete API schema of the request data that the Trove API service will accept.

247

List API Versions

Title	List all API versions known to the back end
URL	/
Method	GET
URL Parameters	None
Headers	Accept: application/json Content-Type: application/json
Data Parameters	None
Success Response	

```
{
    "versions": [
        {
            "id": "v1.0",
            "links": [
                {
                    "href": "http://127.0.0.1:8779/v1.0/",
                    "rel": "self"
                }
            ],
            "status": "CURRENT",
            "updated": "2012-08-01T00:00:00Z"
        }
    ]
}
```

Notes	The list API versions API call lists the currently supported API versions. At this time there is only one supported version and the code returns the response shown earlier.

Instance APIs

Table C-2 provides a description of the various instance-related APIs. These are all accessible at the end point(s) /v1.0/{tenant-id}/instances and /v1.0/{tenant-id}/instances/{id}.

Table C-2. *Instance-Related APIs*

Action	URI	Description
GET	/v1.0/{tenant-id}/instances	List instances
POST	/v1.0/{tenant-id}/instances	Create an instances
GET	/v1.0/{tenant_id}/instances/{id}	Show instance details
POST	/v1.0/{tenant_id}/instances/{id}/action	Perform an instance action
PATCH	/v1.0/{tenant_id}/instances/{id}	Patch instance-specific attributes
PUT	/v1.0/{tenant_id}/instances/{id}	Update some instance attributes
DELETE	/v1.0/{tenant_id}/instances/{id}	Destroy an instance
GET	/v1.0/{tenant_id}/instances/{id}/backups	List instance backups
GET	/v1.0/{tenant_id}/instances/{id}/configuration	List instance configuration information

List Instances

Title	List all running instances visible to the connected tenant
URL	/v1.0/{tenant-id}/instances
Method	GET
URL Parameters (Optional)	include_clustered = [Boolean]
Headers	X-Auth-Token: <token> Accept: application/json Content-Type: application/json
Data Parameters	None
Success Response	The response to a list instances API call is an instance dictionary. Code: 200

```
{
    "instances": [
        {
            "datastore": {"type": "mysql", "version": "5.6"},
            "flavor": {"id": "2", "links": [...]
            },
            "id": "0ccbd8ff-a602-4a29-a02c-ea93acd79095",
            "ip": ["10.0.0.2"],
            "links": [...],
            "name": "m1",
            "status": "ACTIVE",
            "volume": { "size": 2 }
        },
    ] ...
}
```

Notes	The List Instances API provides a list of the instances visible to the connected tenant. The response provides information that is datastore agnostic. The API takes one optional URL parameter, include_clustered, which defaults to False. When set to True, the output shows instances that are part of a cluster.

Create Instance

Title	Create a Trove instance
URL	/v1.0/{tenant_id}/instances
Method	POST
URL Parameters	None
Headers	X-Auth-Token: <token> Accept: application/json Content-Type: application/json

(continued)

Data Parameters	An instance object that describes all aspects of the instance to be created as shown below. The required attributes in the instance object are the name and the flavor reference. All other attributes are optional.
Success Response	The response to a Create Instance API call is an instance view dictionary like the one shown next.

Code: 202

```
{
    "instances": [
        {
            "datastore": {"type": "mysql", "version": "5.6"},
            "flavor": {"id": "2", "links": [...]
            },
            "id": "0ccbd8ff-a602-4a29-a02c-ea93acd79095",
            "ip": ["10.0.0.2"],
            "links": [...],
            "name": "m1",
            "status": "ACTIVE",
            "volume": { "size": 2 }
        },
    ] [...]
}
```

Notes	While the API does not require the specification of a volume size, if the datastore requires the creation of a persistent volume, a size must be specified. Failure to specify a volume size will result in an error being returned.

The data parameter for the Create Instance API call is shown next.

```
{
    "instance": {
        "type": "object",
        "required": ["name", "flavorRef"],
        "additionalProperties": True,
        "properties": {
            "name": non_empty_string,
            "configuration_id": configuration_id,
            "flavorRef": flavorref,
            "volume": volume,
            "databases": databases_def,
            "users": users_list,
            "restorePoint": {
                "type": "object",
                "required": ["backupRef"],
                "additionalProperties": True,
                "properties": {
                    "backupRef": uuid
                }
            },
```

```
                "availability_zone": non_empty_string,
                "datastore": {
                    "type": "object",
                    "additionalProperties": True,
                    "properties": {
                        "type": non_empty_string,
                        "version": non_empty_string
                    }
                },
                "nics": nics
            }
        }
    }
}

configuration_id = {
    'oneOf': [
        uuid
    ]
}

flavorref = {
    'oneOf': [
        non_empty_string,
        {
            "type": "integer"
        }]
}

volume = {
    "type": "object",
    "required": ["size"],
    "properties": {
        "size": volume_size,
        "required": True
    }
}

databases_def = {
    "type": "array",
    "minItems": 0,
    "items": {
        "type": "object",
```

```
        "required": ["name"],
        "additionalProperties": True,
        "properties": {
            "name": non_empty_string,
            "character_set": non_empty_string,
            "collate": non_empty_string
        }
    }
}

users_list = {
    "type": "array",
    "minItems": 0,
    "items": {
        "type": "object",
        "required": ["name", "password"],
        "additionalProperties": True,
        "properties": {
            "name": name_string,
            "password": non_empty_string,
            "host": host_string,
            "databases": databases_ref_list
        }
    }
}

nics = {
    "type": "array",
    "items": {
        "type": "object",
    }
}

host_string = {
    "type": "string",
    "minLength": 1,
    "pattern": "^[%]?[\w(-).]*[%]?$"
}
```

The create API can be used to create a singleton instance or a replica of an existing instance, as follows. Observe that the preceding schema supports additionalProperties.

Create a Singleton Instance

For the following request:

```
'{"instance": {"users": [{"password": "password1", "name": "user1", "databases":
[{"name": "db1"}]}], "flavorRef": "2", "replica_count": 1, "volume": {"size": 3},
"databases": [{"name": "db1"}], "name": "m5"}}'
```

The response is as follows:

```
{"instance": {"status": "BUILD", "updated": "2015-04-25T04:58:35", "name": "m5",
"links": [{"href": "https://192.168.117.5:8779/v1.0/70195ed77e594c63b33c5403f2e2885c/
instances/86652695-f51b-4c4e-815e-a4d102f334ad", "rel": "self"}, {"href":
"https://192.168.117.5:8779/instances/86652695-f51b-4c4e-815e-a4d102f334ad",
"rel": "bookmark"}], "created": "2015-04-25T04:58:35", "id": "86652695-f51b-4c4e-815e-
a4d102f334ad", "volume": {"size": 3}, "flavor": {"id": "2", "links": [{"href":
"https://192.168.117.5:8779/v1.0/70195ed77e594c63b33c5403f2e2885c/flavors/2", "rel": "self"},
{"href": "https://192.168.117.5:8779/flavors/2", "rel": "bookmark"}]}, "datastore":
{"version": "5.6", "type": "mysql"}}}
```

Create a Replica

For the following request:

```
'{"instance": {"volume": {"size": 3}, "flavorRef": "2", "name": "m5-prime", "replica_of":
"86652695-f51b-4c4e-815e-a4d102f334ad", "replica_count": 1}}'
```

The response is as follows:

```
{"instance": {"status": "BUILD", "updated": "2015-04-25T05:04:22", "name": "m5-prime",
"links": [{"href": "https://192.168.117.5:8779/v1.0/70195ed77e594c63b33c5403f2e2885c/instances/
c74833d9-7092-4a28-99a9-b637aa9c968c", "rel": "self"}, {"href": "https://192.168.117.5:8779/
instances/c74833d9-7092-4a28-99a9-b637aa9c968c", "rel": "bookmark"}], "created":
"2015-04-25T05:04:22", "id": "c74833d9-7092-4a28-99a9-b637aa9c968c", "volume": {"size": 3},
"flavor": {"id": "2", "links": [{"href": "https://192.168.117.5:8779/v1.0/70195ed77e594c63b33c5
403f2e2885c/flavors/2", "rel": "self"}, {"href": "https://192.168.117.5:8779/flavors/2",
"rel": "bookmark"}]}, "datastore": {"version": "5.6", "type": "mysql"}, "replica_of":
{"id": "86652695-f51b-4c4e-815e-a4d102f334ad", "links": [{"href": "https://192.168.117.5:8779/
v1.0/70195ed77e594c63b33c5403f2e2885c/instances/86652695-f51b-4c4e-815e-a4d102f334ad", "rel":
"self"}, {"href": "https://192.168.117.5:8779/instances/86652695-f51b-4c4e-815e-a4d102f334ad",
"rel": "bookmark"}]}}}
```

Show Instance

Title	Show details about a specified Trove instance
URL	/v1.0/{tenant_id}/instances/{id}
Method	GET
URL Parameters	None
Headers	X-Auth-Token: <token> Accept: application/json Content-Type: application/json
Data Parameters	None

(continued)

Success Response	The response to a Show Instance API call is an Instance Detail View dictionary like the one shown next.

Code: 200

```
{
  "status": "ACTIVE",
  "volume_used": 0.12,
  "updated": "2015-04-25T22:19:33",
  "datastore_version": "5.6",
  "name": "m3-prime",
  "created": "2015-04-25T22:19:03",
  "ip": "10.0.0.5",
  "datastore": "mysql",
  "volume": 2,
  "flavor": "2",
  "id": "62154bfe-b6bc-49c9-b783-89572b96162d",
  "replica_of": "c399c99a-ee17-4048-bf8b-0ea5c36bb1cb"
}
```

Notes	None

Instance Actions

Title	Perform instance actions
URL	/v1.0/{tenant_id}/instances/{id}/action
Method	POST
URL Parameters	None
Headers	X-Auth-Token: <token> Accept: application/json Content-Type: application/json
Data Parameters	Perform one of several instance actions. Actions can be one of the following: restart resize reset_password promote_to_replica_source eject_replica_source Only the resize action takes a data parameter. The data parameter is shown next.
Success Response	Code: 202
Notes	None

The data parameter to the resize action call can be one of the following:

```
{
    "resize": {
        "volume": volume
    }
}
```

or

```
{
    "resize": {
        "flavorRef": flavorRef
    }
}
```

```
flavorref = {
    'oneOf': [
        non_empty_string,
        {
            "type": "integer"
        }]
}
```

```
volume = {
    "type": "object",
    "required": ["size"],
    "properties": {
        "size": volume_size,
        "required": True
    }
}
```

Instance Action: Restart

The restart action will restart the database server on the guest instance (not the operating system on the guest instance).

```
ubuntu@trove-book:~/api$ cat ./restart.bash
curl -g -i -H 'Content-Type: application/json' \
-H 'X-Auth-Token: 772f29c631af4fa79edb8a970851ff8a' \
-H 'Accept: application/json' \
-X POST \
http://192.168.117.5:8779/v1.0/70195ed77e594c63b33c5403f2e2885c/instances/582b4c38-8c6b-
4025-9d1e-37b4aa50b25a/action  \
-d '{"restart": {}}'

ubuntu@trove-book:~/api$ . ./restart.bash
HTTP/1.1 202 Accepted
Content-Length: 0
Content-Type: application/json
Date: Fri, 24 Apr 2015 14:38:10 GMT
```

Instance Action: Resize Volume

The resize volume action will allow you to resize the Cinder volume used to store data on the instance.

```
ubuntu@trove-book:~/api$ trove show m3-prime
+-------------------+------------------------------------------+
| Property          | Value                                    |
+-------------------+------------------------------------------+
| created           | 2015-04-24T14:11:39                      |
| datastore         | mysql                                    |
| datastore_version | 5.6                                      |
| flavor            | 2                                        |
| id                | 62dc0129-abc2-44a2-8f16-de62c34e53d9     |
| ip                | 10.0.0.3                                 |
| name              | m3-prime                                 |
| replica_of        | 582b4c38-8c6b-4025-9d1e-37b4aa50b25a     |
| status            | ACTIVE                                   |
| updated           | 2015-04-24T14:31:51                      |
| volume            | 2                                        |
| volume_used       | 0.12                                     |
+-------------------+------------------------------------------+
ubuntu@trove-book:~/api$ cat ./resize-volume.bash
curl -g -i -H 'Content-Type: application/json' \
-H 'X-Auth-Token: 772f29c631af4fa79edb8a970851ff8a' \
-H 'Accept: application/json' \
-X POST \
http://192.168.117.5:8779/v1.0/70195ed77e594c63b33c5403f2e2885c/instances/62dc0129-abc2-
44a2-8f16-de62c34e53d9/action  \
-d '{"resize": {"volume": { "size": "3"}}}'
ubuntu@trove-book:~/api$ . ./resize-volume.bash
HTTP/1.1 202 Accepted
Content-Length: 0
Content-Type: application/json
Date: Fri, 24 Apr 2015 14:43:19 GMT
```

Instance Action: Eject Replica Source

The eject replica source API call is used to break a replication set in the event of a failed master. The eject replica source action is invoked by adding a data parameter as follows:

```
ubuntu@trove-book:~/api$ cat ./eject.bash
curl -g -i -H 'Content-Type: application/json' \
-H 'X-Auth-Token: 772f29c631af4fa79edb8a970851ff8a' \
-H 'Accept: application/json' \
-X POST \
http://192.168.117.5:8779/v1.0/70195ed77e594c63b33c5403f2e2885c/instances/582b4c38-8c6b-
4025-9d1e-37b4aa50b25a/action  \
-d '{"eject_replica_source": {}}'
```

```
ubuntu@trove-book:~/api$ . ./eject.bash
HTTP/1.1 202 Accepted
Content-Length: 0
Content-Type: application/json
Date: Fri, 24 Apr 2015 14:48:13 GMT
```

Instance Action: Promote to Replica Source

The promote to replica source API call makes a replica the new master of a replication set. The promote to replica source action is invoked by adding a data parameter as follows:

```
ubuntu@trove-book:~/api$ cat ./promote.bash
curl -g -i -H 'Content-Type: application/json' \
-H 'X-Auth-Token: 772f29c631af4fa79edb8a970851ff8a' \
-H 'Accept: application/json' \
-X POST \
http://192.168.117.5:8779/v1.0/70195ed77e594c63b33c5403f2e2885c/instances/62dc0129-abc2-
44a2-8f16-de62c34e53d9/action   \
-d '{"promote_to_replica_source": {}}'

ubuntu@trove-book:~/api$ . ./promote.bash
HTTP/1.1 202 Accepted
Content-Length: 0
Content-Type: application/json
Date: Fri, 24 Apr 2015 14:48:13 GMT
```

Patch Instance

Title	Update the attributes of an instance
URL	/v1.0/{tenant_id}/instances/{id}
Method	PATCH
URL Parameters	None
Headers	X-Auth-Token: <token> Accept: application/json Content-Type: application/json

(*continued*)

Data Parameters	

```
{
        "name": "instance_edit",
        "type": "object",
        "required": ["instance"],
        "properties": {
        "instance": {
            "type": "object",
            "required": [],
            "properties": {
                "slave_of": {},
                "name": non_empty_string,
                "configuration": configuration_id,
            }
        }
}
configuration_id = {
    'oneOf': [
        uuid
    ]
}
```

Success Response   Code: 202

Notes   You can specify more than one of the parameters, name, configuration_id, and slave_of in the same API call.

Specifying the name parameter causes the system to rename the instance. Provide the new name as the parameter.

Specifying the configuration is equivalent to the PUT request, it attempts to associate the configuration_id provided with the instance. A null value detaches the configuration.

Specifying the slave_of parameter on a replica will cause the system to attempt to detach the specified replica from its master.

Consider the following instance as the starting point of this example. Observe that it has no associated configuration group and is not part of any replication sets.

```
ubuntu@trove-book:~/api$ trove show m1
+-------------------+--------------------------------------+
| Property          | Value                                |
+-------------------+--------------------------------------+
| created           | 2015-04-24T11:04:34                  |
| datastore         | mysql                                |
| datastore_version | 5.6                                  |
| flavor            | 2                                    |
| id                | 0ccbd8ff-a602-4a29-a02c-ea93acd79095 |
| ip                | 10.0.0.2                             |
| name              | m1                                   |
| status            | ACTIVE                               |
| updated           | 2015-04-26T11:25:15                  |
| volume            | 3                                    |
| volume_used       | 0.11                                 |
+-------------------+--------------------------------------+
```

```
ubuntu@trove-book:~/api$ curl -g -i -H 'Content-Type: application/json' \
> -H 'X-Auth-Token: a25bc5e2893645b6b7bcd3e2604dc4da' \
> -H 'Accept: application/json' \
> http://192.168.117.5:8779/v1.0/70195ed77e594c63b33c5403f2e2885c/instances/0ccbd8ff-a602-
4a29-a02c-ea93acd79095 \
> -X PATCH -d '{ "instance": {"name": "new-m1" }}'
HTTP/1.1 202 Accepted
Content-Length: 0
Content-Type: application/json
Date: Sun, 26 Apr 2015 11:41:49 GMT

ubuntu@trove-book:~/api$ trove show 0ccbd8ff-a602-4a29-a02c-ea93acd79095
+-------------------+------------------------------------------+
| Property          | Value                                    |
+-------------------+------------------------------------------+
| created           | 2015-04-24T11:04:34                      |
| datastore         | mysql                                    |
| datastore_version | 5.6                                      |
| flavor            | 2                                        |
| id                | 0ccbd8ff-a602-4a29-a02c-ea93acd79095     |
| ip                | 10.0.0.2                                 |
| name              | new-m1                                   |
| status            | ACTIVE                                   |
| updated           | 2015-04-26T11:41:49                      |
| volume            | 3                                        |
| volume_used       | 0.11                                     |
+-------------------+------------------------------------------+
```

Now consider the following two instances that are part of a replicated pair of instances. The first instance, m3, is the master and the instance m3-prime is the replica.

```
ubuntu@trove-book:~/api$ trove show m3
+-------------------+------------------------------------------+
| Property          | Value                                    |
+-------------------+------------------------------------------+
| configuration     | 3226b8e6-fa38-4e23-a4e6-000b639a93d7     |
| created           | 2015-04-24T11:10:02                      |
| datastore         | mysql                                    |
| datastore_version | 5.6                                      |
| flavor            | 2                                        |
| id                | c399c99a-ee17-4048-bf8b-0ea5c36bb1cb     |
| ip                | 10.0.0.4                                 |
| name              | m3                                       |
| replicas          | 62154bfe-b6bc-49c9-b783-89572b96162d     |
| status            | ACTIVE                                   |
| updated           | 2015-04-24T11:27:40                      |
| volume            | 2                                        |
| volume_used       | 0.11                                     |
+-------------------+------------------------------------------+
ubuntu@trove-book:~/api$ trove show m3-prime
```

```
+-------------------+-------------------------------------+
| Property          | Value                               |
+-------------------+-------------------------------------+
| created           | 2015-04-25T22:19:03                 |
| datastore         | mysql                               |
| datastore_version | 5.6                                 |
| flavor            | 2                                   |
| id                | 62154bfe-b6bc-49c9-b783-89572b96162d |
| ip                | 10.0.0.5                            |
| name              | m3-prime                            |
| replica_of        | c399c99a-ee17-4048-bf8b-0ea5c36bb1cb |
| status            | ACTIVE                              |
| updated           | 2015-04-25T22:19:33                 |
| volume            | 2                                   |
| volume_used       | 0.12                                |
+-------------------+-------------------------------------+
ubuntu@trove-book:~/api$ cat ./detach.bash
curl -g -i -H 'Content-Type: application/json' \
-H 'X-Auth-Token: a25bc5e2893645b6b7bcd3e2604dc4da' \
-H 'Accept: application/json' \
http://192.168.117.5:8779/v1.0/70195ed77e594c63b33c5403f2e2885c/instances/62154bfe-b6bc-
49c9-b783-89572b96162d \
-X PATCH -d '{ "instance": {"slave_of": "" }}'
ubuntu@trove-book:~/api$ . ./detach.bash
HTTP/1.1 202 Accepted
Content-Length: 0
Content-Type: application/json
Date: Sun, 26 Apr 2015 11:49:23 GMT
```

This leaves us with the following. Note that the replication is now no longer in effect. The trove detach-replica command uses this API.

```
ubuntu@trove-book:~/api$ trove show m3
+-------------------+-------------------------------------+
| Property          | Value                               |
+-------------------+-------------------------------------+
| configuration     | 3226b8e6-fa38-4e23-a4e6-000b639a93d7 |
| created           | 2015-04-24T11:10:02                 |
| datastore         | mysql                               |
| datastore_version | 5.6                                 |
| flavor            | 2                                   |
| id                | c399c99a-ee17-4048-bf8b-0ea5c36bb1cb |
| ip                | 10.0.0.4                            |
| name              | m3                                  |
| status            | ACTIVE                              |
| updated           | 2015-04-24T11:27:40                 |
| volume            | 2                                   |
| volume_used       | 0.11                                |
+-------------------+-------------------------------------+
```

```
ubuntu@trove-book:~/api$ trove show m3-prime
+-------------------+----------------------------------------+
| Property          | Value                                  |
+-------------------+----------------------------------------+
| created           | 2015-04-25T22:19:03                    |
| datastore         | mysql                                  |
| datastore_version | 5.6                                    |
| flavor            | 2                                      |
| id                | 62154bfe-b6bc-49c9-b783-89572b96162d   |
| ip                | 10.0.0.5                               |
| name              | m3-prime                               |
| status            | ACTIVE                                 |
| updated           | 2015-04-26T11:49:39                    |
| volume            | 2                                      |
| volume_used       | 0.12                                   |
+-------------------+----------------------------------------+
```

The following example shows how to use this API to attach a configuration group to an instance:

```
ubuntu@trove-book:~/api$ trove configuration-show 3226b8e6-fa38-4e23-a4e6-000b639a93d7
+-------------------------+----------------------------------------------------+
| Property                | Value                                              |
+-------------------------+----------------------------------------------------+
| created                 | 2015-04-24T11:22:40                                |
| datastore_name          | mysql                                              |
| datastore_version_name  | 5.6                                                |
| description             | illustrate a special configuration group           |
| id                      | 3226b8e6-fa38-4e23-a4e6-000b639a93d7               |
| instance_count          | 2                                                  |
| name                    | special-configuration                              |
| updated                 | 2015-04-24T11:22:40                                |
| values                  | {"wait_timeout": 240, "max_connections": 200}      |
+-------------------------+----------------------------------------------------+
ubuntu@trove-book:~/api$ trove show new-m1
+-------------------+----------------------------------------+
| Property          | Value                                  |
+-------------------+----------------------------------------+
| created           | 2015-04-24T11:04:34                    |
| datastore         | mysql                                  |
| datastore_version | 5.6                                    |
| flavor            | 2                                      |
| id                | 0ccbd8ff-a602-4a29-a02c-ea93acd79095   |
| ip                | 10.0.0.2                               |
| name              | new-m1                                 |
| status            | ACTIVE                                 |
| updated           | 2015-04-26T11:41:49                    |
| volume            | 3                                      |
| volume_used       | 0.11                                   |
+-------------------+----------------------------------------+
```

```
ubuntu@trove-book:~/api$ cat attach.bash
curl -g -i -H 'Content-Type: application/json' \
-H 'X-Auth-Token: ece5078f2d124b1d85286d4b5ddcb999' \
-H 'Accept: application/json' \
http://192.168.117.5:8779/v1.0/70195ed77e594c63b33c5403f2e2885c/instances/0ccbd8ff-a602-
4a29-a02c-ea93acd79095 \
-X PATCH -d '{ "instance": {"configuration": "3226b8e6-fa38-4e23-a4e6-000b639a93d7" }}'

ubuntu@trove-book:~/api$ . ./attach.bash
HTTP/1.1 202 Accepted
Content-Length: 0
Content-Type: application/json
Date: Sun, 26 Apr 2015 12:51:38 GMT

ubuntu@trove-book:/opt/stack/trove$ trove show new-m1
```

+------------------+--------------------------------------+
| Property | Value |
+------------------+--------------------------------------+
configuration	**3226b8e6-fa38-4e23-a4e6-000b639a93d7**
created	2015-04-24T11:04:34
datastore	mysql
datastore_version	5.6
flavor	2
id	0ccbd8ff-a602-4a29-a02c-ea93acd79095
ip	10.0.0.2
name	new-m1
status	ACTIVE
updated	2015-04-26T13:25:13
volume	3
volume_used	0.11
+------------------+--------------------------------------+

The following example shows how to detach that configuration group using the same API call, by specifying a configuration_id of null:

```
ubuntu@trove-book:~/api$ cat ./detach-configuration.bash
curl -g -i -H 'Content-Type: application/json' \
-H 'X-Auth-Token: c0f6a0fc78604a50a1d23c19c4a0b1b0' \
-H 'Accept: application/json' \
http://192.168.117.5:8779/v1.0/70195ed77e594c63b33c5403f2e2885c/instances/0ccbd8ff-a602-
4a29-a02c-ea93acd79095  \
-X PATCH -d '{ "instance": {"configuration": null }}'
```

```
ubuntu@trove-book:~/api$ . ./detach-configuration.bash
HTTP/1.1 202 Accepted
Content-Length: 0
Content-Type: application/json
Date: Mon, 27 Apr 2015 17:07:28 GMT


ubuntu@trove-book:~/api$ trove show new-m1
+-------------------+------------------------------------+
| Property          | Value                              |
+-------------------+------------------------------------+
| created           | 2015-04-24T11:04:34                |
| datastore         | mysql                              |
| datastore_version | 5.6                                |
| flavor            | 2                                  |
| id                | 0ccbd8ff-a602-4a29-a02c-ea93acd79095 |
| ip                | 10.0.0.2                           |
| name              | new-m1                             |
| status            | RESTART_REQUIRED                   |
| updated           | 2015-04-27T17:07:28                |
| volume            | 3                                  |
| volume_used       | 0.11                               |
+-------------------+------------------------------------+
```

Note that the instance state is now set to RESTART_REQUIRED. You will need to restart the instance in order to bring it back to a state of ACTIVE.

Update Instance

Title	Update an instance's configuration group attribute
URL	/v1.0/{tenant_id}/instances/{id}
Method	PUT
URL Parameters	None
Headers	X-Auth-Token: <token> Accept: application/json Content-Type: application/json

(*continued*)

Data Parameters	The instance detail dictionary that is returned by a GET.

```
{
    "status": "ACTIVE",
    "volume_used": 0.12,
    "updated": "2015-04-25T22:19:33",
    "datastore_version": "5.6",
    "name": "m3-prime",
    "created": "2015-04-25T22:19:03",
    "ip": "10.0.0.5",
    "datastore": "mysql",
    "volume": 2,
    "flavor": "2",
    "id": "62154bfe-b6bc-49c9-b783-89572b96162d",
    "replica_of": "c399c99a-ee17-4048-bf8b-0ea5c36bb1cb",
    "configuration_id": "3226b8e6-fa38-4e23-a4e6-000b639a93d7"
}
```

Success Response	Code: 202
Notes	The PUT method only updates the configuration group attribute.
	If a `configuration_id` parameter is part of the data parameters, the system attempts to attach the configuration group specified to the instance.
	If the `configuration_id` parameter is not part of data parameter the API detaches the configuration group attached to the instance.
	The `trove update` command issues the PATCH request.

The following example demonstrates how to use this request. First, we perform a GET on an instance (m2) to obtain information about it.

```
ubuntu@trove-book:~/api$ cat ./get.bash
curl -g -i -H 'Content-Type: application/json' \
-H 'X-Auth-Token: ee9f1bece1294e07886517bd15c3a6d3' \
-H 'Accept: application/json' \
http://192.168.117.5:8779/v1.0/70195ed77e594c63b33c5403f2e2885c/instances/822777ab-5542-
4edb-aed6-73c83b0fdb8d -X GET
```

The system response to this request is as follows:

```
ubuntu@trove-book:~/api$ . ./get.bash
HTTP/1.1 200 OK
Content-Type: application/json
Content-Length: 1097
Date: Mon, 27 Apr 2015 17:14:38 GMT

{"instance": {"status": "ACTIVE", "updated": "2015-04-24T11:27:24", "name": "m2",
"links": [{"href": "https://192.168.117.5:8779/v1.0/70195ed77e594c63b33c5403f2e
2885c/instances/822777ab-5542-4edb-aed6-73c83b0fdb8d", "rel": "self"}, {"href":
"https://192.168.117.5:8779/instances/822777ab-5542-4edb-aed6-73c83b0fdb8d", "rel":
"bookmark"}], "created": "2015-04-24T11:07:40", "ip": ["10.0.0.3"], "id":
```

```
"822777ab-5542-4edb-aed6-73c83b0fdb8d", "volume": {"used": 0.11, "size": 2}, "flavor":
{"id": "2", "links": [{"href": "https://192.168.117.5:8779/v1.0/70195ed77e594c63b33c540
3f2e2885c/flavors/2", "rel": "self"}, {"href": "https://192.168.117.5:8779/flavors/2",
"rel": "bookmark"}]}, "configuration": {"id": "3226b8e6-fa38-4e23-a4e6-000b639a93d7",
"links": [{"href": "https://192.168.117.5:8779/v1.0/70195ed77e594c63b33c5403f2e288
5c/configurations/3226b8e6-fa38-4e23-a4e6-000b639a93d7", "rel": "self"}, {"href":
"https://192.168.117.5:8779/configurations/3226b8e6-fa38-4e23-a4e6-000b639a93d7",
"rel": "bookmark"}], "name": "special-configuration"}, "datastore": {"version": "5.6",
"type": "mysql"}}}
```

In the preceding code, we have highlighted the configuration. We detach the configuration by sending the same information back with a `configuration` value of `null`.

```
ubuntu@trove-book:~/api$ cat ./put.bash
curl -g -i -H 'Content-Type: application/json' \
-H 'X-Auth-Token: ee9f1bece1294e07886517bd15c3a6d3' \
-H 'Accept: application/json' \
http://192.168.117.5:8779/v1.0/70195ed77e594c63b33c5403f2e2885c/instances/822777ab-5542-
4edb-aed6-73c83b0fdb8d \
-X PUT -d '{"instance": {"status": "ACTIVE", "updated": "2015-04-24T11:27:24", "name":
"m2", "links": [{"href": "https://192.168.117.5:8779/v1.0/70195ed77e594c63b33c5403
f2e2885c/instances/822777ab-5542-4edb-aed6-73c83b0fdb8d", "rel": "self"}, {"href":
"https://192.168.117.5:8779/instances/822777ab-5542-4edb-aed6-73c83b0fdb8d", "rel":
"bookmark"}], "created": "2015-04-24T11:07:40", "ip": ["10.0.0.3"], "id": "822777ab-5542-
4edb-aed6-73c83b0fdb8d", "volume": {"used": 0.11, "size": 2}, "flavor": {"id": "2", "links":
[{"href": "https://192.168.117.5:8779/v1.0/70195ed77e594c63b33c5403f2e2885c/flavors/2",
"rel": "self"}, {"href": "https://192.168.117.5:8779/flavors/2", "rel": "bookmark"}]},
"configuration": null, "datastore": {"version": "5.6", "type": "mysql"}}}'

ubuntu@trove-book:~/api$ . ./put.bash
HTTP/1.1 202 Accepted
Content-Length: 0
Content-Type: application/json
Date: Mon, 27 Apr 2015 17:17:16 GMT

ubuntu@trove-book:~/api$ trove show m2
+-------------------+-------------------------------------+
| Property          | Value                               |
+-------------------+-------------------------------------+
| created           | 2015-04-24T11:07:40                 |
| datastore         | mysql                               |
| datastore_version | 5.6                                 |
| flavor            | 2                                   |
| id                | 822777ab-5542-4edb-aed6-73c83b0fdb8d|
| ip                | 10.0.0.3                            |
| name              | m2                                  |
| status            | RESTART_REQUIRED                    |
| updated           | 2015-04-27T17:17:16                 |
| volume            | 2                                   |
| volume_used       | 0.11                                |
+-------------------+-------------------------------------+
```

The code for the PUT API call only looks to see whether we have provided the configuration parameter; it does not validate the rest of the data. Therefore, you can simplify the API call and achieve the same thing by merely passing a data parameter that reads as follows:

```
'{"instance": {"configuration": null}}'
```

As with the PATCH call, note that this leaves the instance in a state of RESTART_REQUIRED.

Delete Instance

Title	Delete an instance
URL	/v1.0/{tenant_id}/instances/{id}
Method	DELETE
URL Parameters	None
Headers	X-Auth-Token: <token> Accept: application/json Content-Type: application/json
Data Parameters	None
Success Response	Code: 202
Notes	The DELETE request will begin the process of instance deletion.

```
ubuntu@trove-book:~/api$ trove show m3-prime
+-------------------+--------------------------------------+
| Property          | Value                                |
+-------------------+--------------------------------------+
| configuration     | 3226b8e6-fa38-4e23-a4e6-000b639a93d7 |
| created           | 2015-04-25T22:19:03                  |
| datastore         | mysql                                |
| datastore_version | 5.6                                  |
| flavor            | 2                                    |
| id                | 62154bfe-b6bc-49c9-b783-89572b96162d |
| ip                | 10.0.0.5                             |
| name              | m3-prime                             |
| status            | ACTIVE                               |
| updated           | 2015-04-26T13:34:41                  |
| volume            | 2                                    |
| volume_used       | 0.12                                 |
+-------------------+--------------------------------------+
ubuntu@trove-book:~/api$ cat ./delete.bash
curl -g -i -H 'Content-Type: application/json' \
-H 'X-Auth-Token: ee9f1bece1294e07886517bd15c3a6d3' \
-H 'Accept: application/json' \
http://192.168.117.5:8779/v1.0/70195ed77e594c63b33c5403f2e2885c/instances/62154bfe-b6bc-
49c9-b783-89572b96162d \
-X DELETE
```

```
ubuntu@trove-book:~/api$ . ./delete.bash
HTTP/1.1 202 Accepted
Content-Length: 0
Content-Type: application/json
Date: Mon, 27 Apr 2015 17:25:27 GMT
```

The deletion process has begun and in a short while, the instance will be gone.

```
ubuntu@trove-book:~/api$ trove show m3-prime
+-------------------+------------------------------------------+
| Property          | Value                                    |
+-------------------+------------------------------------------+
| created           | 2015-04-25T22:19:03                      |
| datastore         | mysql                                    |
| datastore_version | 5.6                                      |
| flavor            | 2                                        |
| id                | 62154bfe-b6bc-49c9-b783-89572b96162d     |
| ip                | 10.0.0.5                                 |
| name              | m3-prime                                 |
| status            | SHUTDOWN                                 |
| updated           | 2015-04-27T17:25:27                      |
| volume            | 2                                        |
+-------------------+------------------------------------------+
ubuntu@trove-book:~/api$ trove show m3-prime
ERROR: No instance with a name or ID of 'm3-prime' exists.
```

List Backups

Title	List instance backups
URL	/v1.0/{tenant_id}/instances/{id}/backups
Method	GET
URL Parameters	None
Headers	X-Auth-Token: <token> Accept: application/json Content-Type: application/json
Data Parameters	None
Success Response	Code: 200
Notes	Get a list of all backups of an instance.

The following example demonstrates the use of the API call to list backups:

```
ubuntu@trove-book:~/api$ cat ./get-backups.bash
curl -g -i -H 'Content-Type: application/json' \
-H 'X-Auth-Token: 179d38408bca417080b29249f845a1d1' -H 'Accept: application/json' \
http://192.168.117.5:8779/v1.0/70195ed77e594c63b33c5403f2e2885c/instances/822777ab-5542-
4edb-aed6-73c83b0fdb8d/backups -X GET
```

```
ubuntu@trove-book:~/api$ . ./get-backups.bash
HTTP/1.1 200 OK
Content-Type: application/json
Content-Length: 1704
Date: Mon, 27 Apr 2015 17:46:28 GMT
[...]
```

The returned JSON object is shown next after formatting with json.tool. The instance has three backups, a full backup called 'backup 1' an incremental backup called 'backup 1 incr', which is an incremental backup from 'backup 1', and a third backup called 'backup 2'.

```
{
    "backups": [
        {
            "created": "2015-04-27T17:45:18",
            "datastore": {
                "type": "mysql",
                "version": "5.6",
                "version_id": "b39198b7-6791-4ed2-ab27-e2b9bac3f7b1"
            },
            "description": "second full backup of m2",
            "id": "867878a8-e228-4722-b310-61bc0559e708",
            "instance_id": "822777ab-5542-4edb-aed6-73c83b0fdb8d",
            "locationRef": "http://192.168.117.5:8080/v1/AUTH_70195ed77e594c63b33c5403f2e288
5c/database_backups/867878a8-e228-4722-b310-61bc0559e708.xbstream.gz.enc",
            "name": "backup 2",
            "parent_id": null,
            "size": 0.11,
            "status": "COMPLETED",
            "updated": "2015-04-27T17:45:23"
        },
        {
            "created": "2015-04-27T17:44:43",
            "datastore": {
                "type": "mysql",
                "version": "5.6",
                "version_id": "b39198b7-6791-4ed2-ab27-e2b9bac3f7b1"
            },
            "description": "first incremental backup of m2",
            "id": "3498140e-5f0c-4b43-8368-80568b6d6e5d",
            "instance_id": "822777ab-5542-4edb-aed6-73c83b0fdb8d",
            "locationRef": "http://192.168.117.5:8080/v1/AUTH_70195ed77e594c63b33c5403f2e288
5c/database_backups/3498140e-5f0c-4b43-8368-80568b6d6e5d.xbstream.gz.enc",
            "name": "backup 1 incr",
            "parent_id": "deb78f09-e4f5-4ebb-b0e7-4625c4f136f5",
            "size": 0.11,
            "status": "COMPLETED",
            "updated": "2015-04-27T17:44:50"
        },
```

```
{
        "created": "2015-04-27T17:43:19",
        "datastore": {
            "type": "mysql",
            "version": "5.6",
            "version_id": "b39198b7-6791-4ed2-ab27-e2b9bac3f7b1"
        },
        "description": "first full backup of m2",
        "id": "deb78f09-e4f5-4ebb-b0e7-4625c4f136f5",
        "instance_id": "822777ab-5542-4edb-aed6-73c83b0fdb8d",
        "locationRef": "http://192.168.117.5:8080/v1/AUTH_70195ed77e594c63b33c5403
        f2e2885c/database_backups/deb78f09-e4f5-4ebb-b0e7-4625c4f136f5.xbstream.gz.enc",
        "name": "backup 1",
        "parent_id": null,
        "size": 0.11,
        "status": "COMPLETED",
        "updated": "2015-04-27T17:43:30"
    }
  ]
}
```

List Instance Configuration

Title	List instance configuration
URL	/v1.0/{tenant_id}/instances/{id}/configuration
Method	GET
URL Parameters	None
Headers	X-Auth-Token: <token> Accept: application/json Content-Type: application/json
Data Parameters	None
Success Response	Code: 200
Notes	Get the complete configuration information for an instance.

The following example demonstrates the use of the API call to list instance configurations:

```
ubuntu@trove-book:~/api$ cat get-configuration.bash
curl -g -H 'Content-Type: application/json' \
-H 'X-Auth-Token: 179d38408bca417080b29249f845a1d1' \
-H 'Accept: application/json' \
http://192.168.117.5:8779/v1.0/70195ed77e594c63b33c5403f2e2885c/instances/822777ab-5542-
4edb-aed6-73c83b0fdb8d/configuration -X GET
```

The response to this API call is shown next with formatting by `json.tool`.

```
ubuntu@trove-book:~/api$ . ./get-configuration.bash | python -m json.tool
{
    "instance": {
        "configuration": {
            "basedir": "/usr",
            "connect_timeout": "15",
            "datadir": "/var/lib/mysql",
            "default_storage_engine": "innodb",
            "innodb_buffer_pool_size": "600M",
            "innodb_data_file_path": "ibdata1:10M:autoextend",
            "innodb_file_per_table": "1",
            "innodb_log_buffer_size": "25M",
            "innodb_log_file_size": "50M",
            "innodb_log_files_in_group": "2",
            "join_buffer_size": "1M",
            "key_buffer_size": "200M",
            "local-infile": "0",
            "max_allowed_packet": "4096K",
            "max_connections": "400",
            "max_heap_table_size": "64M",
            "max_user_connections": "400",
            "myisam-recover": "BACKUP",
            "open_files_limit": "2048",
            "pid_file": "/var/run/mysqld/mysqld.pid",
            "port": "3306",
            "query_cache_limit": "1M",
            "query_cache_size": "32M",
            "query_cache_type": "1",
            "read_buffer_size": "512K",
            "read_rnd_buffer_size": "512K",
            "server_id": "334596",
            "skip-external-locking": "1",
            "sort_buffer_size": "1M",
            "table_definition_cache": "1024",
            "table_open_cache": "1024",
            "thread_cache_size": "16",
            "thread_stack": "192K",
            "tmp_table_size": "64M",
            "tmpdir": "/var/tmp",
            "user": "mysql",
            "wait_timeout": "120"
        }
    }
}
```

Datastores API

In this section we provide a description of the various datastore-related APIs. These are all accessible at the end point(s) /v1.0/{tenant-id}/datastores.

Table C-3. *Datastore-Related APIs*

Action	URI	Description
GET	/v1.0/{tenant-id}/datastores	List datastores
GET	/v1.0/{tenant_id}/datastores/{id}/versions	List datastore versions
GET	/v1.0/{tenant_id}/datastores/{did}/versions/{vid}	Show datastore version by datastore ID and version ID
GET	/v1.0/{tenant_id}/datastores/versions/{uuid}	Show datastore version by UUID
GET	/v1.0/{tenant_id}/datastores/versions/{version}/parameters	List datastore version configuration options
GET	/v1.0/{tenant_id}/datastores/versions/{version}/parameters/{name}	Show datastore version configuration options
GET	/v1.0/{tenant_id}/datastores/{datastore}/versions/{id}/parameters	List datastore version configuration options
GET	/v1.0/{tenant_id}/datastores/{datastore}/versions/{id}/parameters/{name}	Show datastore version configuration options

The datastores API provides a way to get information about the various datastores, their versions, and their parameters registered in Trove.

■ **Note**   The API calls in rows 2 and 4, 5 and 7, and 6 and 8 produce the same information. The difference is that API calls in row 4, 5, and 6 omit the datastore ID in the URI and it is implied based on the version ID.

List Datastores

Title	List datastores
URL	/v1.0/{tenant-id}/datastores
Method	GET
URL Parameters	None
Headers	X-Auth-Token: <token> Accept: application/json Content-Type: application/json
Data Parameters	None
Success Response	Code: 200
Notes	List all the datastores available to the tenant.

The following example demonstrates the use of the API call to list datastores:

```
ubuntu@trove-book:~/api$ cat ./get-datastores.bash
curl -g -i -H 'Content-Type: application/json' \
-H 'X-Auth-Token: cfc0afcccb1242709062c4f25b25060f' \
-H 'Accept: application/json' \
http://192.168.117.5:8779/v1.0/70195ed77e594c63b33c5403f2e2885c/datastores  \
-X GET
ubuntu@trove-book:~/api$ . ./get-datastores.bash
HTTP/1.1 200 OK
Content-Type: application/json
Content-Length: 2515
Date: Fri, 24 Apr 2015 11:29:52 GMT

[...]
```

The output has been annotated as follows:

```
{
    "datastores": [
        {
            "default_version": "15b7d828-49a5-4d05-af65-e974e0aca7eb",
            "id": "648d260d-c346-4145-8a2d-bbd4d78aedf6",
            "links": [...],
            "name": "mongodb",
            "versions": [
                {
                    "active": 1,
                    "id": "15b7d828-49a5-4d05-af65-e974e0aca7eb",
                    "image": "af347500-b62b-46df-8d44-6e40fd2a45c0",
                    "links": [...],
                    "name": "2.4.9",
                    "packages": "mongodb"
                }
            ]
        },
        {
            "default_version": "d51d3c44-846c-4cfe-838c-b3339e53746e",
            "id": "7f8dbd88-6b9a-4fc6-99aa-b3691d33cbac",
            "links": [...],
            "name": "percona",
            "versions": [
                {
                    "active": 1,
                    "id": "d51d3c44-846c-4cfe-838c-b3339e53746e",
                    "image": "036715fd-b140-4290-b502-1dde622e3784",
                    "links": [...],
                    "name": "5.5",
                    "packages": "percona-server-server-5.5"
                }
            ]
        },
```

```
{
    "default_version": "b39198b7-6791-4ed2-ab27-e2b9bac3f7b1",
    "id": "a2a3b211-7b71-4a3e-b373-65b951f2587a",
    "links": [...],
    "name": "mysql",
    "versions": [
        {
            "active": 1,
            "id": "b39198b7-6791-4ed2-ab27-e2b9bac3f7b1",
            "image": "3844de61-f5a6-4fb2-b0cb-2bb2004454e4",
            "links": [...],
            "name": "5.6",
            "packages": "mysql-server-5.6"
        }
    ]
}
]
}
```

Observe that the system has three datastores configured, one for MySQL, one for Percona, and one for MongoDB.

List Datastore Versions

Title	List datastore versions
URL	/v1.0/{tenant-id}/datastores/{id}/versions
Method	GET
URL Parameters	None
Headers	X-Auth-Token: \<token\> Accept: application/json Content-Type: application/json
Data Parameters	None
Success Response	Code: 200
Notes	None

The following example demonstrates the use of the API call to list datastore versions:

```
ubuntu@trove-book:~/api$ cat ./get-datastore-versions.bash
curl -g -H 'Content-Type: application/json' \
-H 'X-Auth-Token: cfc0afcccb1242709062c4f25b25060f' \
-H 'Accept: application/json' \
http://192.168.117.5:8779/v1.0/70195ed77e594c63b33c5403f2e2885c/datastores/648d260d-c346-
4145-8a2d-bbd4d78aedf6/versions -X GET
```

```
ubuntu@trove-book:~/api$ . ./get-datastore-versions.bash | python -m json.tool
{
    "versions": [
        {
            "active": 1,
            "datastore": "648d260d-c346-4145-8a2d-bbd4d78aedf6",
            "id": "15b7d828-49a5-4d05-af65-e974e0aca7eb",
            "image": "af347500-b62b-46df-8d44-6e40fd2a45c0",
            "links": [...],
            "name": "2.4.9",
            "packages": "mongodb"
        }
    ]
}
```

Show Datastore Version (by Datastore and Version)

Title	Show datastore
URL	/v1.0/{tenant-id}/datastores/{id}/versions/{version-id}
Method	GET
URL Parameters	None
Headers	X-Auth-Token: <token> Accept: application/json Content-Type: application/json
Data Parameters	None
Success Response	Code: 200
Notes	Shows a specific datastore. The data produced by this API is identical to the one shown by List Datastore Versions. The only difference is that since this API call is producing only information about a single version, the dictionary produces a single "version" but the List Database Versions API returns "versions" which is a list.

The following example demonstrates the use of the API call to datastore versions:

```
ubuntu@trove-book:~/api$ cat ./show-datastore-versions.bash
curl -g -H 'Content-Type: application/json' \
-H 'X-Auth-Token: cfc0afcccb1242709062c4f25b25060f' \
-H 'Accept: application/json' \
http://192.168.117.5:8779/v1.0/70195ed77e594c63b33c5403f2e2885c/datastores/648d260d-c346-
4145-8a2d-bbd4d78aedf6/versions/15b7d828-49a5-4d05-af65-e974e0aca7eb -X GET

ubuntu@trove-book:~/api$ . ./show-datastore-versions.bash | python -m json.tool
{
    "version": {
        "active": true,
        "datastore": "648d260d-c346-4145-8a2d-bbd4d78aedf6",
        "id": "15b7d828-49a5-4d05-af65-e974e0aca7eb",
        "image": "af347500-b62b-46df-8d44-6e40fd2a45c0",
```

```
        "links": [...],
        "name": "2.4.9",
        "packages": "mongodb"
    }
}
```

Show Datastore Version (by UUID)

Title	Show datastore
URL	/v1.0/{tenant_id}/datastores/versions/{uuid}
Method	GET
URL Parameters	None
Headers	X-Auth-Token: <token> Accept: application/json Content-Type: application/json
Data Parameters	None
Success Response	Code: 200
Notes	Shows a specific datastore providing only the datastore UUID. The information provided is identical to the previous Show Datastore API call except that the URI does not provide the datastore id, just the UUID of the datastore version.

The following example demonstrates the use of the API call to show a database version:

```
ubuntu@trove-book:~/api$ cat ./show-datastore-versions-uuid.bash
curl -g -H 'Content-Type: application/json' \
-H 'X-Auth-Token: cfc0afcccb1242709062c4f25b25060f' \
-H 'Accept: application/json' \
http://192.168.117.5:8779/v1.0/70195ed77e594c63b33c5403f2e2885c/datastores/
versions/15b7d828-49a5-4d05-af65-e974e0aca7eb -X GET

ubuntu@trove-book:~/api$ . ./show-datastore-versions-uuid.bash | python -m json.tool
{
    "version": {
        "active": true,
        "datastore": "648d260d-c346-4145-8a2d-bbd4d78aedf6",
        "id": "15b7d828-49a5-4d05-af65-e974e0aca7eb",
        "image": "af347500-b62b-46df-8d44-6e40fd2a45c0",
        "links": [...],
        "name": "2.4.9",
        "packages": "mongodb"
    }
}
```

List Datastore Version Configuration Options

Title	List datastore version configuration options
URL	/v1.0/{tenant-id}/datastores/versions/{vid}/parameters
Method	GET
URL Parameters	None
Headers	X-Auth-Token: <token> Accept: application/json Content-Type: application/json
Data Parameters	None
Success Response	Code: 200
Notes	List all parameters that can be configured for this datastore version using the configuration groups features of Trove. This information comes from the validation-rules.json file that is configured along with a datastore. If configuration groups are not supported for a datastore, an empty list is returned. This API only provides the datastore version ID in the URI. The datastore ID is implied.

The following example demonstrates the use of the API call to list datastore version configuration options:

```
ubuntu@trove-book:~/api$ cat show-datastore-versions-parameters.bash
curl -g -H 'Content-Type: application/json' \
-H 'X-Auth-Token: cfc0afcccb1242709062c4f25b25060f' \
-H 'Accept: application/json' \
http://192.168.117.5:8779/v1.0/70195ed77e594c63b33c5403f2e2885c/datastores/versions/
d51d3c44-846c-4cfe-838c-b3339e53746e/parameters -X GET

ubuntu@trove-book:~/api$ . ./show-datastore-versions-parameters.bash | python -m json.tool
{
    "configuration-parameters": [
        {
            "datastore_version_id": "d51d3c44-846c-4cfe-838c-b3339e53746e",
            "max": 1,
            "min": 0,
            "name": "autocommit",
            "restart_required": false,
            "type": "integer"
        },
        {
            "datastore_version_id": "d51d3c44-846c-4cfe-838c-b3339e53746e",
            "max": 65535,
            "min": 1,
            "name": "auto_increment_increment",
            "restart_required": false,
            "type": "integer"
        },
```

```
    {
        "datastore_version_id": "d51d3c44-846c-4cfe-838c-b3339e53746e",
        "max": 65535,
        "min": 1,
        "name": "auto_increment_offset",
        "restart_required": false,
        "type": "integer"
    }, ...   ]
}
```

The output has been truncated, and in the preceding code we show only the first three configuration parameters.

Show Datastore Version Configuration Option

Title	Show a specific configuration option for a datastore version
URL	/v1.0/{tenant-id}/datastores/versions/{vid}/parameters/{name}
Method	GET
URL Parameters	None
Headers	X-Auth-Token: <token> Accept: application/json Content-Type: application/json
Data Parameters	None
Success Response	Code: 200
Notes	This information comes from the validation-rules.json file that is configured along with a datastore.
	This API only provides the datastore version ID in the URI. The datastore ID is implied.

The following example lists the configuration parameter auto_increment_offset on a Percona datastore.

```
ubuntu@trove-book:~/api$ cat ./show-datastore-versions-parameter.bash
curl -g -H 'Content-Type: application/json' \
-H 'X-Auth-Token: cfc0afcccb1242709062c4f25b25060f' \
-H 'Accept: application/json' \
http://192.168.117.5:8779/v1.0/70195ed77e594c63b33c5403f2e2885c/datastores/7f8dbd88-6b9a-
4fc6-99aa-b3691d33cbac/versions/d51d3c44-846c-4cfe-838c-b3339e53746e/parameters/auto_
increment_offset -X GET
ubuntu@trove-book:~/api$ . ./show-datastore-versions-parameter.bash | python -m json.tool
{
    "datastore_version_id": "d51d3c44-846c-4cfe-838c-b3339e53746e",
    "max": 65535,
    "min": 1,
    "name": "auto_increment_offset",
    "restart_required": false,
    "type": "integer"
}
```

List Datastore Version Configuration Options

Title	List datastore version configuration options
URL	/v1.0/{tenant-id}/datastores/{id}/versions/{vid}/parameters
Method	GET
URL Parameters	None
Headers	X-Auth-Token: <token> Accept: application/json Content-Type: application/json
Data Parameters	None
Success Response	Code: 200
Notes	List all parameters that can be configured for this datastore version using the configuration groups features of Trove. This information comes from the validation-rules.json file that is configured along with a datastore. If configuration groups are not supported for a datastore, an empty list is returned.

The following example demonstrates the use of the API call to list datastore version configuration options:

```
ubuntu@trove-book:~/api$ cat show-datastore-versions-parameters.bash
curl -g -H 'Content-Type: application/json' \
-H 'X-Auth-Token: cfc0afcccb1242709062c4f25b25060f' \
-H 'Accept: application/json' \
http://192.168.117.5:8779/v1.0/70195ed77e594c63b33c5403f2e2885c/datastores/7f8dbd88-6b9a-
4fc6-99aa-b3691d33cbac/versions/d51d3c44-846c-4cfe-838c-b3339e53746e/parameters -X GET

ubuntu@trove-book:~/api$ . show-datastore-versions-parameters.bash | python -m json.tool
{
    "configuration-parameters": [
        {
            "datastore_version_id": "d51d3c44-846c-4cfe-838c-b3339e53746e",
            "max": 1,
            "min": 0,
            "name": "autocommit",
            "restart_required": false,
            "type": "integer"
        }, ...
    ]
}
```

The configuration parameter shown previously is autocommit, the setting controlling transaction commits in the Percona 5.5 datastore.

Show Datastore Version Configuration Option

Title	Show a specific configuration option for a datastore version
URL	/v1.0/{tenant-id}/datastores/{id}/versions/{vid}/parameters/{name}
Method	GET
URL Parameters	None
Headers	X-Auth-Token: <token> Accept: application/json Content-Type: application/json
Data Parameters	None
Success Response	Code: 200
Notes	This information comes from the validation-rules.json file that is configured along with a datastore.

The following example demonstrates the use of the API call to show a datastore version configuration option:

```
ubuntu@trove-book:~/api$ cat ./show-datastore-versions-parameter.bash
curl -g -H 'Content-Type: application/json' \
-H 'X-Auth-Token: cfc0afcccb1242709062c4f25b25060f' \
-H 'Accept: application/json' \
http://192.168.117.5:8779/v1.0/70195ed77e594c63b33c5403f2e2885c/datastores/7f8dbd88-6b9a-
4fc6-99aa-b3691d33cbac/versions/d51d3c44-846c-4cfe-838c-b3339e53746e/parameters/max_user_
connections -X GET

ubuntu@trove-book:~/api$ . ./show-datastore-versions-parameter.bash | python -m json.tool
{
    "datastore_version_id": "d51d3c44-846c-4cfe-838c-b3339e53746e",
    "max": 100000,
    "min": 1,
    "name": "max_user_connections",
    "restart_required": false,
    "type": "integer"
}
```

The preceding example lists the configuration parameter max_user_connections on a Percona datastore.

Flavors API

In this section we provide a description of the flavor-related APIs. These are all accessible at the end point(s) /v1.0/{tenant-id}/flavors and /v1.0/{tenant-id}/flavors/{id}.

Table C-4. *Flavor-related APIs*

Action	URI	Description
GET	/v1.0/{tenant-id}/flavors	List flavors
GET	/v1.0/{tenant-id}/flavors/{id}	Show flavor

List Flavors

Title	List Flavors
URL	/v1.0/{tenant-id}/flavors
Method	GET
URL Parameters	None
Headers	X-Auth-Token: <token> Accept: application/json Content-Type: application/json
Data Parameters	None
Success Response	Code: 200
Notes	None

The following example demonstrates the use of the API call to list flavors:

```
ubuntu@trove-book:~/api$ cat ./get-flavors.bash
curl -g -i -H 'Content-Type: application/json' \
-H 'X-Auth-Token: 5c63994f772940a28c6b6418eaa2db3b' \
-H 'Accept: application/json' \
-X GET \
http://192.168.117.5:8779/v1.0/70195ed77e594c63b33c5403f2e2885c/flavors

ubuntu@trove-book:~/api$ . ./get-flavors.bash
HTTP/1.1 200 OK
Content-Type: application/json
Content-Length: 1712
Date: Fri, 24 Apr 2015 13:32:35 GMT
```

{"flavors": [{"str_id": "1", "ram": 512, "id": 1, "links": [{"href": "https://192.168.117.5:
8779/v1.0/70195ed77e594c63b33c5403f2e2885c/flavors/1", "rel": "self"}, {"href":
"https://192.168.117.5:8779/flavors/1", "rel": "bookmark"}], "name": "m1.tiny"}, {"str_id":
"2", "ram": 2048, "id": 2, "links": [{"href": "https://192.168.117.5:8779/v1.0/70195ed77e
594c63b33c5403f2e2885c/flavors/2", "rel": "self"}, {"href": "https://192.168.117.5:8779/
flavors/2", "rel": "bookmark"}], "name": "m1.small"}, {"str_id": "3", "ram": 4096, "id":
3, "links": [{"href": "https://192.168.117.5:8779/v1.0/70195ed77e594c63b33c5403f2e288

5c/flavors/3", "rel": "self"}, {"href": "https://192.168.117.5:8779/flavors/3", "rel": "bookmark"}], "name": "m1.medium"}, {"str_id": "4", "ram": 8192, "id": 4, "links": [{"href": "https://192.168.117.5:8779/v1.0/70195ed77e594c63b33c5403f2e2885c/flavors/4", "rel": "self"}, {"href": "https://192.168.117.5:8779/flavors/4", "rel": "bookmark"}], "name": "m1.large"}, {"str_id": "42", "ram": 64, "id": 42, "links": [{"href": "https://192.168.117.5:8779/v1.0/70195ed77e594c63b33c5403f2e2885c/flavors/42", "rel": "self"}, {"href": "https://192.168.117.5:8779/flavors/42", "rel": "bookmark"}], "name": "m1.nano"}, {"str_id": "5", "ram": 16384, "id": 5, "links": [{"href": "https://192.168.117.5:8779/v1.0/70195ed77e594c63b33c5403f2e2885c/flavors/5", "rel": "self"}, {"href": "https://192.168.117.5:8779/flavors/5", "rel": "bookmark"}], "name": "m1.xlarge"}, {"str_id": "84", "ram": 128, "id": 84, "links": [{"href": "https://192.168.117.5:8779/v1.0/70195ed77e594c63b33c5403f2e2885c/flavors/84", "rel": "self"}, {"href": "https://192.168.117.5:8779/flavors/84", "rel": "bookmark"}], "name": "m1.micro"}]}

This information is shown by the Trove CLI command trove flavor-list.

```
ubuntu@trove-book:~/api$ trove flavor-list
+----+-----------+-------+
| ID | Name      |  RAM  |
+----+-----------+-------+
|  1 | m1.tiny   |   512 |
|  2 | m1.small  |  2048 |
|  3 | m1.medium |  4096 |
|  4 | m1.large  |  8192 |
|  5 | m1.xlarge | 16384 |
| 42 | m1.nano   |    64 |
| 84 | m1.micro  |   128 |
+----+-----------+-------+
```

Show Flavor

Title	Show flavor details
URL	/v1.0/{tenant-id}/flavors/{id}
Method	GET
URL Parameters	None
Headers	X-Auth-Token: <token> Accept: application/json Content-Type: application/json
Data Parameters	None
Success Response	Code: 200
Notes	None

The following example demonstrates the use of the API call to show details about a flavor:

```
ubuntu@trove-book:~/api$ cat ./show-flavors.bash
curl -g -i -H 'Content-Type: application/json' \
-H 'X-Auth-Token: 5c63994f772940a28c6b6418eaa2db3b' \
-H 'Accept: application/json' \
-X GET \
http://192.168.117.5:8779/v1.0/70195ed77e594c63b33c5403f2e2885c/flavors/84
```

```
ubuntu@trove-book:~/api$ . ./show-flavors.bash
HTTP/1.1 200 OK
Content-Type: application/json
Content-Length: 255
Date: Fri, 24 Apr 2015 13:35:19 GMT

{"flavor": {"str_id": "84", "ram": 128, "id": 84, "links": [{"href": "https://192.168.117.5:
8779/v1.0/70195ed77e594c63b33c5403f2e2885c/flavors/84", "rel": "self"}, {"href":
"https://192.168.117.5:8779/flavors/84", "rel": "bookmark"}], "name": "m1.micro"}}
```

Limits API

In this section we provide a description of the limits-related API. This API provides information about the limits assigned to the current tenant and is accessible at the end point(s) /v1.0/{tenant-id}/limits.

Table C-5. Limits-Related API

Action	URI	Description
GET	/v1.0/{tenant-id}/limits	List limits

List Limits

Title	Get limits information for the current tenant
URL	/v1.0/{tenant-id}/limits
Method	GET
URL Parameters	None
Headers	X-Auth-Token: <token> Accept: application/json Content-Type: application/json
Data Parameters	None
Success Response	Code: 200
Notes	This call gets both the absolute limits (quota) as well as the rate limits for Trove API calls

The following example demonstrates the use of the API call to list limits:

```
ubuntu@trove-book:~/api$ cat get-limits.bash
curl -g -i -H 'Content-Type: application/json' \
-H 'X-Auth-Token: 675ca8e416514704a6e6319322bf7a05' \
-H 'Accept: application/json' \
-X GET \
http://192.168.117.5:8779/v1.0/70195ed77e594c63b33c5403f2e2885c/limits
ubuntu@trove-book:~/api$ . ./get-limits.bash
HTTP/1.1 200 OK
```

```
Content-Type: application/json
Content-Length: 781
Date: Fri, 24 Apr 2015 13:45:58 GMT
```

```
{"limits": [{"max_backups": 50, "verb": "ABSOLUTE", "max_volumes": 20, "max_instances": 5},
{"regex": ".*", "nextAvailable": "2015-04-24T13:45:58Z", "uri": "*", "value": 200,
"verb": "POST", "remaining": 200, "unit": "MINUTE"}, {"regex": ".*", "nextAvailable":
"2015-04-24T13:45:58Z", "uri": "*", "value": 200, "verb": "PUT", "remaining": 200, "unit":
"MINUTE"}, {"regex": ".*", "nextAvailable": "2015-04-24T11:06:10Z", "uri": "*", "value":
200, "verb": "DELETE", "remaining": 199, "unit": "MINUTE"}, {"regex": ".*", "nextAvailable":
"2015-04-24T13:45:58Z", "uri": "*", "value": 200, "verb": "GET", "remaining": 199, "unit":
"MINUTE"}, {"regex": "^/mgmt", "nextAvailable": "2015-04-24T13:45:58Z", "uri": "*/mgmt",
"value": 200, "verb": "POST", "remaining": 200, "unit": "MINUTE"}]}
```

Backups API

In this section we provide a description of the backup-related APIs. These are all accessible at the end point(s) /v1.0/{tenant-id}/backups.

Table C-6. *Backup-Related APIs*

Action	URI	Description
GET	/v1.0/{tenant-id}/backups	List backups
GET	/v1.0/{tenant-id}/backups/{id}	Show details about a specific backup
POST	/v1.0/{tenant-id}/backups	Create backup
DELETE	/v1.0/{tenant-id}/backups/{id}	Delete backup

List Backups

Title	List backups visible to tenant
URL	/v1.0/{tenant-id}/backups
Method	GET
URL Parameters	None
Headers	X-Auth-Token: <token> Accept: application/json Content-Type: application/json
Data Parameters	None
Success Response	Code: 200
Notes	None

The following example demonstrates the use of the API call to list backups visible to a tenant:

```
ubuntu@trove-book:~/api$ cat ./backup-list.bash
curl -g -i -H 'Content-Type: application/json' \
-H 'X-Auth-Token: 9e63fe4c76b6430190c4567f51420fd7' \
-H 'Accept: application/json' \
-X GET \
http://192.168.117.5:8779/v1.0/70195ed77e594c63b33c5403f2e2885c/backups

ubuntu@trove-book:~/api$ . ./backup-list.bash
HTTP/1.1 200 OK
Content-Type: application/json
Content-Length: 540
Date: Fri, 24 Apr 2015 13:48:57 GMT
```

```
{"backups": [{"status": "COMPLETED", "updated": "2015-04-24T13:47:44", "description":
"backup 1", "datastore": {"version": "5.6", "type": "mysql", "version_id": "b39198b7-6791-
4ed2-ab27-e2b9bac3f7b1"}, "id": "8b2c43ce-9e12-40ee-b277-05a77917404e", "size": 0.11,
"name": "b1", "created": "2015-04-24T13:47:35", "instance_id": "582b4c38-8c6b-4025-9d1e-
37b4aa50b25a", "parent_id": null, "locationRef": "http://192.168.117.5:8080/v1/AUTH_70195ed7
7e594c63b33c5403f2e2885c/database_backups/8b2c43ce-9e12-40ee-b277-05a77917404e.xbstream
.gz.enc"}]}
```

Show Backup

Title	Show details about a backup
URL	/v1.0/{tenant-id}/backups/{id}
Method	GET
URL Parameters	None
Headers	X-Auth-Token: <token>
	Accept: application/json
	Content-Type: application/json
Data Parameters	None
Success Response	Code: 200
Notes	None

The following example demonstrates the use of the API call to show details about a backup:

```
ubuntu@trove-book:~/api$ cat ./backup-show.bash
curl -g -i -H 'Content-Type: application/json' \
-H 'X-Auth-Token: 9e63fe4c76b6430190c4567f51420fd7' \
-H 'Accept: application/json' \
-X GET \
http://192.168.117.5:8779/v1.0/70195ed77e594c63b33c5403f2e2885c/backups/8b2c43ce-9e12-40ee-
b277-05a77917404e
```

```
ubuntu@trove-book:~/api$ . ./backup-show.bash
HTTP/1.1 200 OK
Content-Type: application/json
Content-Length: 537
Date: Fri, 24 Apr 2015 13:51:02 GMT
```

{"backup": {"status": "COMPLETED", "updated": "2015-04-24T13:47:44", "description": "backup 1", "datastore": {"version": "5.6", "type": "mysql", "version_id": "b39198b7-6791-4ed2-ab27-e2b9bac3f7b1"}, "id": "8b2c43ce-9e12-40ee-b277-05a77917404e", "size": 0.11, "name": "b1", "created": "2015-04-24T13:47:35", "instance_id": "582b4c38-8c6b-4025-9d1e-37b4aa50b25a", "parent_id": null, "locationRef": "http://192.168.117.5:8080/v1/AUTH_70195ed77e594c63b33c5403f2e2885c/database_backups/8b2c43ce-9e12-40ee-b277-05a77917404e.xbstream.gz.enc"}}

Create Backup

Title	Creates a backup
URL	/v1.0/{tenant-id}/backups
Method	POST
URL Parameters	None
Headers	X-Auth-Token: <token> Accept: application/json Content-Type: application/json

Data Parameters	<pre>{
	    "backup": {
	        "type": "object",
	        "required": ["instance", "name"],
	        "properties": {
	            "description": non_empty_string,
	            "instance": uuid,
	            "name": non_empty_string,
	            "parent_id": uuid
	        }
	    }
	}</pre>

Success Response	Code: 202
Notes	The parent_id parameter is the ID of an existing backup. If specified, it indicates that an incremental backup is being requested. A backup is generated of the instance identified by the data parameter instance.

The following example demonstrates the use of the API call to create a backup:

```
ubuntu@trove-book:~/api$ trove show m3
+-------------------+---------------------------------------+
| Property          | Value                                 |
+-------------------+---------------------------------------+
| created           | 2015-04-24T13:43:02                   |
| datastore         | mysql                                 |
| datastore_version | 5.6                                   |
| flavor            | 2                                     |
| id                | 582b4c38-8c6b-4025-9d1e-37b4aa50b25a  |
| ip                | 10.0.0.2                              |
| name              | m3                                    |
| status            | ACTIVE                                |
| updated           | 2015-04-24T13:43:08                   |
| volume            | 2                                     |
| volume_used       | 0.11                                  |
+-------------------+---------------------------------------+
ubuntu@trove-book:~/api$ cat ./backup-create.bash
curl -g -i -H 'Content-Type: application/json' \
-H 'X-Auth-Token: 9e63fe4c76b6430190c4567f51420fd7' \
-H 'Accept: application/json' \
-X POST \
http://192.168.117.5:8779/v1.0/70195ed77e594c63b33c5403f2e2885c/backups \
-d '{ "backup": { "description": "third backup", "instance": "582b4c38-8c6b-4025-9d1e-
37b4aa50b25a", "name": "b3", "parent_id": "abdf7b3c-f974-4669-a1fc-db0852fd4b4b" }}'

ubuntu@trove-book:~/api$ . ./backup-create.bash
HTTP/1.1 202 Accepted
Content-Type: application/json
Content-Length: 435
Date: Fri, 24 Apr 2015 14:03:46 GMT

{"backup": {"status": "NEW", "updated": "2015-04-24T14:03:46", "description": "third
backup", "datastore": {"version": "5.6", "type": "mysql", "version_id": "b39198b7-6791-
4ed2-ab27-e2b9bac3f7b1"}, "id": "57dc5726-75c6-400b-b8d0-3a5e54219db4", "size": null,
"name": "b3", "created": "2015-04-24T14:03:46", "instance_id": "582b4c38-8c6b-4025-9d1e-
37b4aa50b25a", "parent_id": "abdf7b3c-f974-4669-a1fc-db0852fd4b4b", "locationRef": null}}
```

After a brief period you can confirm that the incremental backup requested here (note the setting of the parent_id parameter) is complete.

Delete Backup

Title	Delete a backup
URL	/v1.0/{tenant-id}/backups/{id}
Method	POST
URL Parameters	None
Headers	X-Auth-Token: <token>
	Accept: application/json
	Content-Type: application/json
Data Parameters	None
Success Response	Code: 202
Notes	If you delete a backup that is the parent of another backup, the system deletes the backup and all of its children.

The following example demonstrates the use of the API call to delete a backup:

```
ubuntu@trove-book:~/api$ cat ./backup-delete.bash
curl -g -i -H 'Content-Type: application/json' \
-H 'X-Auth-Token: 9e63fe4c76b6430190c4567f51420fd7' \
-H 'Accept: application/json' \
-X DELETE \
http://192.168.117.5:8779/v1.0/70195ed77e594c63b33c5403f2e2885c/backups/8b2c43ce-9e12-40ee-
b277-05a77917404e

ubuntu@trove-book:~/api$ . ./backup-delete.bash
HTTP/1.1 202 Accepted
Content-Length: 0
Content-Type: application/json
Date: Fri, 24 Apr 2015 14:08:41 GMT
```

Database Extensions API

Trove provides an extensions API that supports some capabilities like the creation of databases and users. The extensions API is also used to control access to the database superuser on a database.

Table C-7. *Extensions-Related APIs*

Action	URI	Description
GET	/v1.0/{tenant-id}/instance/{id}/root	Get root-enabled status
POST	/v1.0/{tenant-id}/instance/{id}/root	Enable database superuser
GET	/v1.0/{tenant-id}/instance/{id}/databases	Get database list
POST	/v1.0/{tenant-id}/instance/{id}/databases	Create a database
DELETE	/v1.0/{tenant-id}/instance/{id}/databases/{name}	Delete a database
GET	/v1.0/{tenant-id}/instance/{id}/users	Get user list
POST	/v1.0/{tenant-id}/instance/{id}/users	Create a user
DELETE	/v1.0/{tenant-id}/instance/{id}/users/{name}	Delete a user
GET	/v1.0/{tenant-id}/instance/{id}/users/{name}	Show user information
GET	/v1.0/{tenant-id}/instance/{id}/users/{name}/databases	Get user database access
POST	/v1.0/{tenant-id}/instance/{id}/users/{name}/databases	Grant user database access
DELETE	/v1.0/{tenant-id}/instance/{id}/users/{name}/databases	Revoke user database access

Get Root-enabled Status

Title	Get status of database superuser on instance.
URL	/v1.0/{tenant-id}/instances/{instance}/root
Method	GET
URL Parameters	None
Headers	X-Auth-Token: <token> Accept: application/json Content-Type: application/json
Data Parameters	None
Success Response	Code: 200 {"rootEnabled": boolean}
Notes	The response indicates whether the superuser was enabled at any point during the lifetime of the instance.

The following example demonstrates the use of the API call to get root-enabled status:

```
ubuntu@trove-book:~/api$ cat ./get-root.bash
curl -g -i -H 'Content-Type: application/json' \
-H "X-Auth-Token: $(./get-token.py)" \
-H 'Accept: application/json' \
```

```
-X GET \
http://192.168.117.5:8779/v1.0/$(./get-tenant.py)/instances/2bb174c4-1272-42dc-b86e-
bd4370dcc85a/root
ubuntu@trove-book:~/api$ . ./get-root.bash
HTTP/1.1 200 OK
Content-Type: application/json
Content-Length: 22
Date: Sat, 25 Apr 2015 00:40:27 GMT

{"rootEnabled": false}
```

Enable Root

Title	Enable the database superuser on an instance
URL	/v1.0/{tenant-id}/instances/{instance}/root
Method	POST
URL Parameters	None
Headers	X-Auth-Token: <token> Accept: application/json Content-Type: application/json
Data Parameters	None

Success Response	Code: 200
	
	{
	    "user": {
	        "password": non-empty-string,
	        "name": non-empty-string
	    }
	}

Notes	None

The following example demonstrates the use of the API call to enable root on a guest instance:

```
ubuntu@trove-book:~/api$ cat ./enable-root.bash
curl -g -i -H 'Content-Type: application/json' \
-H "X-Auth-Token: $(./get-token.py)" \
-H 'Accept: application/json' \
-X POST \
http://192.168.117.5:8779/v1.0/$(./get-tenant.py)/instances/2bb174c4-1272-42dc-b86e-
bd4370dcc85a/root

ubuntu@trove-book:~/api$ . ./enable-root.bash
HTTP/1.1 200 OK
Content-Type: application/json
Content-Length: 78
Date: Sat, 25 Apr 2015 00:43:20 GMT

{"user": {"password": "TGv4k2hah9UTyRwsWEuuPaF4FsJvccsxxcbu", "name": "root"}}
```

Database List

Title	Get a list of databases on an instance
URL	/v1.0/{tenant-id}/instances/{instance}/databases
Method	GET
URL Parameters	None
Headers	X-Auth-Token: \<token\> Accept: application/json Content-Type: application/json
Data Parameters	None

Success Response	Code: 200
	{
	    "databases": [
	        {
	            "name": non-empty-string
	        }, ...
	    ]
	}

Notes	None

The following example demonstrates the use of the API call to list databases on an instance:

```
ubuntu@trove-book:~/api$ cat ./get-databases.bash
curl -g -i -H 'Content-Type: application/json' \
-H "X-Auth-Token: $(./get-token.py)" \
-H 'Accept: application/json' \
-X GET \
http://192.168.117.5:8779/v1.0/$(./get-tenant.py)/instances/2bb174c4-1272-42dc-b86e-
bd4370dcc85a/databases

ubuntu@trove-book:~/api$ . ./get-databases.bash
HTTP/1.1 200 OK
Content-Type: application/json
Content-Length: 47
Date: Sat, 25 Apr 2015 00:47:07 GMT

{"databases": [{"name": "performance:schema"}]}
```

Database Create

Title	Create databases on an instance
URL	/v1.0/{tenant-id}/instances/{instance}/databases
Method	POST
URL Parameters	None
Headers	X-Auth-Token: \<token\> Accept: application/json Content-Type: application/json

Data Parameters	```{```
	 ``` "databases": [```
	 ``` {```
	 ``` "name": non-empty-string,```
	 ``` "character_set": non-empty-string,```
	 ``` "collate": non-empty-string```
	 ``` }, ...```
	 ```]```
	 ```}```

Success Response	Code: 202
Notes	None

The following example demonstrates the use of the API call to create a database on an instance:

```
ubuntu@trove-book:~/api$ cat ./create-database.bash
curl -g -i -H 'Content-Type: application/json' \
-H "X-Auth-Token: $(./get-token.py)" \
-H 'Accept: application/json' \
-X POST \
http://192.168.117.5:8779/v1.0/$(./get-tenant.py)/instances/2bb174c4-1272-42dc-b86e-
bd4370dcc85a/databases \
-d '{"databases": [{ "name": "db1"}, {"name": "db2", "character_set": "utf8", "collate":
"utf8_general_ci"}]}'

ubuntu@trove-book:~/api$ . ./create-database.bash
HTTP/1.1 202 Accepted
Content-Length: 0
Content-Type: application/json
Date: Sat, 25 Apr 2015 01:00:56 GMT
```

Database Delete

Title	Delete databases on an instance
URL	/v1.0/{tenant-id}/instances/{instance}/databases/{name}
Method	DELETE
URL Parameters	None
Headers	X-Auth-Token: <token> Accept: application/json Content-Type: application/json
Data Parameters	None
Success Response	Code: 202
Notes	None

The following example demonstrates the use of the API call to delete a database on an instance:

```
ubuntu@trove-book:~/api$ cat ./delete-database.bash
curl -g -i -H 'Content-Type: application/json' \
-H "X-Auth-Token: $(./get-token.py)" \
-H 'Accept: application/json' \
-X DELETE \
http://192.168.117.5:8779/v1.0/$(./get-tenant.py)/instances/2bb174c4-1272-42dc-b86e-
bd4370dcc85a/databases/db1

curl -g -i -H 'Content-Type: application/json' \
-H "X-Auth-Token: $(./get-token.py)" \
-H 'Accept: application/json' \
-X DELETE \
http://192.168.117.5:8779/v1.0/$(./get-tenant.py)/instances/2bb174c4-1272-42dc-b86e-
bd4370dcc85a/databases/db2

ubuntu@trove-book:~/api$ . ./delete-database.bash
HTTP/1.1 202 Accepted
Content-Length: 0
Content-Type: application/json
Date: Sat, 25 Apr 2015 01:02:33 GMT

HTTP/1.1 202 Accepted
Content-Length: 0
Content-Type: application/json
Date: Sat, 25 Apr 2015 01:02:34 GMT
```

User Create

Title	Create database users and optionally grant access to databases
URL	/v1.0/{tenant-id}/instances/{instance}/users
Method	POST
URL Parameters	None
Headers	X-Auth-Token: <token> Accept: application/json Content-Type: application/json

Data Parameters

```
users_list = {
    "type": "array",
    "minItems": 0,
    "items": {
        "type": "object",
        "required": ["name", "password"],
        "additionalProperties": True,
        "properties": {
            "name": name_string,
            "password": non_empty_string,
            "host": host_string,
            "databases": databases_ref_list
        }
    }
}

host_string = {
    "type": "string",
    "minLength": 1,
    "pattern": "^[%]?[\w(-).]*[%]?$"
}
name_string = {
    "type": "string",
    "minLength": 1,
    "maxLength": 16,
    "pattern": "^.*[0-9a-zA-Z]+.*$"
}

databases_ref_list = {
    "type": "array",
    "minItems": 0,
    "uniqueItems": True,
    "items": {
        "type": "object",
        "required": ["name"],
        "additionalProperties": True,
        "properties": {
            "name": non_empty_string
        }
    }
}
```

Success Response	Code: 202
Notes	None

The following example demonstrates the use of the API call to create a user on an instance:

```
ubuntu@trove-book:~/api$ cat ./user-create.bash
curl -g -i -H 'Content-Type: application/json' \
-H "X-Auth-Token: $(./get-token.py)" \
-H 'Accept: application/json' \
-X POST \
http://192.168.117.5:8779/v1.0/$(./get-tenant.py)/instances/e0242146-ee25-4e3d-ac41-
01e0742fa066/users \
-d '{"users": [{"name": "user1", "password": "password", "host": "%", "databases":
[ {"name": "db1"}, {"name": "db2"}]}]}'

ubuntu@trove-book:~/api$ . ./user-create.bash
HTTP/1.1 202 Accepted
Content-Length: 0
Content-Type: application/json
Date: Sat, 25 Apr 2015 03:54:30 GMT

ubuntu@trove-book:~/api$ trove user-list m4
+-------+------+-----------+
| Name  | Host | Databases |
+-------+------+-----------+
| user1 | %    | db1, db2  |
+-------+------+-----------+
```

User List

Title	List users registered on an instance and show database and host permissions
URL	/v1.0/{tenant-id}/instances/{instance}/users
Method	GET
URL Parameters	None
Headers	X-Auth-Token: <token> Accept: application/json Content-Type: application/json
Data Parameters	None
Success Response	Code: 200
Notes	None

The following example demonstrates the use of the API call to list users on an instance:

```
ubuntu@trove-book:~/api$ more user-list.bash
curl -g -i -H 'Content-Type: application/json' \
-H "X-Auth-Token: $(./get-token.py)" \
-H 'Accept: application/json' \
-X GET \
http://192.168.117.5:8779/v1.0/$(./get-tenant.py)/instances/e0242146-ee25-4e3d-ac41-
01e0742fa06
6/users
```

```
ubuntu@trove-book:~/api$ . ./user-list.bash
HTTP/1.1 200 OK
Content-Type: application/json
Content-Length: 92
Date: Sat, 25 Apr 2015 04:06:44 GMT

{"users": [{"host": "%", "name": "user1", "databases": [{"name": "db1"}, {"name": "db2"}]}]}
```

User Show Access

Title	Show information about a specific user and show database and host permissions
URL	/v1.0/{tenant-id}/instances/{instance}/users/{name}
Method	GET
URL Parameters	None
Headers	X-Auth-Token: <token> Accept: application/json Content-Type: application/json
Data Parameters	None
Success Response	Code: 200
Notes	None

The following example demonstrates the use of the API call show details about a specific user on an instance:

```
ubuntu@trove-book:~/api$ cat ./user-show.bash
curl -g -i -H 'Content-Type: application/json' \
-H "X-Auth-Token: $(./get-token.py)" \
-H 'Accept: application/json' \
-X GET \
http://192.168.117.5:8779/v1.0/$(./get-tenant.py)/instances/e0242146-ee25-4e3d-ac41-
01e0742fa066/users/user1

ubuntu@trove-book:~/api$ . ./user-show.bash
HTTP/1.1 200 OK
Content-Type: application/json
Content-Length: 89
Date: Sat, 25 Apr 2015 04:08:35 GMT

{"user": {"host": "%", "name": "user1", "databases": [{"name": "db1"}, {"name": "db2"}]}}
```

User Delete

Title	Delete a database user
URL	/v1.0/{tenant-id}/instances/{instance}/users/{name}
Method	DELETE
URL Parameters	None
Headers	X-Auth-Token: <token> Accept: application/json Content-Type: application/json
Data Parameters	None
Success Response	Code: 202
Notes	None

The following example demonstrates the use of the API call to delete a user:

```
ubuntu@trove-book:~/api$ cat ./user-delete.bash
curl -g -i -H 'Content-Type: application/json' \
-H "X-Auth-Token: $(./get-token.py)" \
-H 'Accept: application/json' \
-X DELETE \
http://192.168.117.5:8779/v1.0/$(./get-tenant.py)/instances/e0242146-ee25-4e3d-ac41-
01e0742fa066/users/user1

ubuntu@trove-book:~/api$ . ./user-delete.bash
HTTP/1.1 202 Accepted
Content-Length: 0
Content-Type: application/json
Date: Sat, 25 Apr 2015 04:12:51 GMT
```

User Grant Access

Title	Grant a user access to a specified database
URL	/v1.0/{tenant-id}/instances/{instance}/users/{name}/databases
Method	PUT
URL Parameters	None
Headers	X-Auth-Token: <token> Accept: application/json Content-Type: application/json

(continued)

296

Data Parameters	```
	{
	    "databases": databases_ref_list
	}
	
	databases_ref_list = {
	    "type": "array",
	    "minItems": 0,
	    "uniqueItems": True,
	    "items": {
	        "type": "object",
	        "required": ["name"],
	        "additionalProperties": True,
	        "properties": {
	            "name": non_empty_string
	        }
	    }
	}
	``

Success Response	Code: 202
Notes	None

The following example demonstrates the use of the API call to grant database access to a user:

```
ubuntu@trove-book:~/api$ cat ./user-grant-access.bash
curl -g -i -H 'Content-Type: application/json' \
-H "X-Auth-Token: $(./get-token.py)" \
-H 'Accept: application/json' \
-X PUT \
http://192.168.117.5:8779/v1.0/$(./get-tenant.py)/instances/e0242146-ee25-4e3d-ac41-
01e0742fa066/users/user1/databases \
-d '{"databases": [ {"name": "db3"}]}'

ubuntu@trove-book:~/api$ trove user-list m4
+-------+------+-----------+
| Name  | Host | Databases |
+-------+------+-----------+
| user1 | %    | db1, db2  |
+-------+------+-----------+
ubuntu@trove-book:~/api$ . ./user-grant-access.bash
HTTP/1.1 202 Accepted
Content-Length: 0
Content-Type: application/json
Date: Sat, 25 Apr 2015 04:29:19 GMT

ubuntu@trove-book:~/api$ trove user-list m4
+-------+------+---------------+
| Name  | Host | Databases     |
+-------+------+---------------+
| user1 | %    | db1, db2, db3 |
+-------+------+---------------+
```

User Show Access

Title	Show user database access
URL	/v1.0/{tenant-id}/instances/{instance}/users/{name}/databases
Method	GET
URL Parameters	None
Headers	X-Auth-Token: <token> Accept: application/json Content-Type: application/json
Data Parameters	None
Success Response	Code: 200
Notes	None

The following example demonstrates the use of the API call to show a user's access:

```
ubuntu@trove-book:~/api$ cat ./user-show-access.bash
curl -g -i -H 'Content-Type: application/json' \
-H "X-Auth-Token: $(./get-token.py)" \
-H 'Accept: application/json' \
-X GET \
http://192.168.117.5:8779/v1.0/$(./get-tenant.py)/instances/e0242146-ee25-4e3d-ac41-
01e0742fa066/users/user1/databases
ubuntu@trove-book:~/api$ . ./user-show-access.bash
HTTP/1.1 200 OK
Content-Type: application/json
Content-Length: 66
Date: Sat, 25 Apr 2015 04:32:07 GMT

{"databases": [{"name": "db1"}, {"name": "db2"}, {"name": "db3"}]}
```

User Revoke Access

Title	Revoke a user's access to a database
URL	/v1.0/{tenant-id}/instances/{instance}/users/{user-name}/ databases/{db-name}
Method	DELETE
URL Parameters	None
Headers	X-Auth-Token: <token> Accept: application/json Content-Type: application/json
Data Parameters	None
Success Response	Code: 202
Notes	None

The following example demonstrates the use of the API call to revoke a user's access:

```
ubuntu@trove-book:~/api$ cat ./user-delete-access.bash
curl -g -i -H 'Content-Type: application/json' \
-H "X-Auth-Token: $(./get-token.py)" \
-H 'Accept: application/json' \
-X DELETE \
http://192.168.117.5:8779/v1.0/$(./get-tenant.py)/instances/e0242146-ee25-4e3d-ac41-
01e0742fa066/users/user1/databases/db2

ubuntu@trove-book:~/api$ trove user-list m4
+-------+------+---------------+
| Name  | Host | Databases     |
+-------+------+---------------+
| user1 | %    | db1, db2, db3 |
+-------+------+---------------+
ubuntu@trove-book:~/api$ . ./user-delete-access.bash
HTTP/1.1 202 Accepted
Content-Length: 0
Content-Type: application/json
Date: Sat, 25 Apr 2015 04:34:28 GMT

ubuntu@trove-book:~/api$ trove user-list m4
+-------+------+-----------+
| Name  | Host | Databases |
+-------+------+-----------+
| user1 | %    | db1, db3  |
+-------+------+-----------+
```

Clusters API

This section describes the Trove Clusters API. Trove provides this API to manage clusters of database instances. Database clustering is a technique that is used to improve resiliency and performance of databases and Trove currently supports clustering with MongoDB and Vertica.

Table C-8. *Cluster-Related APIs*

Action	URI	Description
GET	/{tenant-id}/clusters	List clusters
GET	/{tenant-id}/clusters/{id}	Show cluster details
POST	/{tenant-id}/clusters	Create a cluster
DELETE	/{tenant-id}/clusters/{id}	Delete a cluster

List Cluster

Title	List database clusters
URL	/{tenant-id}/clusters
Method	GET
URL Parameters	None
Headers	X-Auth-Token: <token> Accept: application/json Content-Type: application/json
Data Parameters	None
Success Response	Code: 202
Notes	None

The following example demonstrates the use of the API call to list a cluster:

```
GET /v1.0/70195ed77e594c63b33c5403f2e2885c/cluster

{
    "cluster": {
        "created": "2015-04-24T11:36:11",
        "datastore": {
            "type": "mongodb",
            "version": "2.4.9"
        },
        "id": "b06473c0-7509-4e6a-a15f-4456cb817104",
        "instances": [
            {
                "id": "6eead1b5-3801-4d47-802e-fea7e9be6639",
                "links": [...],
                "name": "mongo1-rs1-2",
                "shard_id": "c1bea1ee-d510-4d70-b0e4-815f5a682f34",
                "type": "member"
            },
            {
                "id": "86d7f7f8-fdd0-4f85-86a7-1fe4abd704cd",
                "links": [...],
                "name": "mongo1-rs1-3",
                "shard_id": "c1bea1ee-d510-4d70-b0e4-815f5a682f34",
                "type": "member"
            },
            {
                "id": "c5cbff7f-c306-4ba5-9bf0-a6ad49a1b4d0",
                "links": [...],
                "name": "mongo1-rs1-1",
                "shard_id": "c1bea1ee-d510-4d70-b0e4-815f5a682f34",
                "type": "member"
            }
```

```
        ],
        "links": [...],
        "name": "mongo1",
        "task": {
            "description": "Building the initial cluster.",
            "id": 2,
            "name": "BUILDING"
        },
        "updated": "2015-04-24T11:36:11"
    }
}
```

Show Cluster

Title	Show cluster details
URL	/{tenant-id}/clusters/{id}
Method	GET
URL Parameters	None
Headers	X-Auth-Token: \<token\> Accept: application/json Content-Type: application/json
Data Parameters	None
Success Response	Code: 202
Notes	None

The following example demonstrates the use of the API call to show cluster details:

```
GET /v1.0/70195ed77e594c63b33c5403f2e2885c/clusters/b06473c0-7509-4e6a-a15f-4456cb817104

{
    "cluster": {
        "created": "2015-04-24T11:36:11",
        "datastore": {
            "type": "mongodb",
            "version": "2.4.9"
        },
        "id": "b06473c0-7509-4e6a-a15f-4456cb817104",
        "instances": [
            {
                "flavor": {
                    "id": "10",
                    "links": [...]
                },
                "id": "6eead1b5-3801-4d47-802e-fea7e9be6639",
                "ip": [
                    "10.0.0.5"
                ],
```

```
                    "links": [...],
                    "name": "mongo1-rs1-2",
                    "shard_id": "c1bea1ee-d510-4d70-b0e4-815f5a682f34",
                    "status": "BUILD",
                    "type": "member",
                    "volume": {
                        "size": 2
                    }
                },
                {
                    "flavor": {
                        "id": "10",
                        "links": [...],
                    "links": [...],
                    "name": "mongo1-rs1-3",
                    "shard_id": "c1bea1ee-d510-4d70-b0e4-815f5a682f34",
                    "status": "BUILD",
                    "type": "member",
                    "volume": {
                        "size": 2
                    }
                },
                {
                    "flavor": {
                        "id": "10",
                        "links": [...]
                    },
                    "id": "c5cbff7f-c306-4ba5-9bf0-a6ad49a1b4d0",
                    "ip": [
                        "10.0.0.2"
                    ],
                    "links": [...],
                    "name": "mongo1-rs1-1",
                    "shard_id": "c1bea1ee-d510-4d70-b0e4-815f5a682f34",
                    "status": "BUILD",
                    "type": "member",
                    "volume": {
                        "size": 2
                    }
                }
            ],
            "ip": [
                "10.0.0.6"
            ],
            "links": [...],
            "name": "mongo1",
            "task": {
                "description": "Building the initial cluster.",
                "id": 2,
                "name": "BUILDING"
            },
            "updated": "2015-04-24T11:36:11"
    }
}
```

Create a Cluster

Title	Create a cluster
URL	/{tenant-id}/clusters
Method	POST
URL Parameters	None
Headers	X-Auth-Token: <token> Accept: application/json Content-Type: application/json
Data Parameters	

```
{
        "type": "object",
        "required": ["cluster"],
        "additionalProperties": True,
        "properties": {
            "cluster": {
                "type": "object",
                "required": ["name", "datastore", "instances"],
                "additionalProperties": True,
                "properties": {
                    "name": non_empty_string,
                    "datastore": {
                        "type": "object",
                        "required": ["type", "version"],
                        "additionalProperties": True,
                        "properties": {
                            "type": non_empty_string,
                            "version": non_empty_string
                        }
                    },
                    "instances": {
                        "type": "array",
                        "items": {
                            "type": "object",
                            "required": ["flavorRef"],
                            "additionalProperties": True,
                            "properties": {
                                "flavorRef": flavorref,
                                "volume": volume
                            }
                        }
                    }
                }
            }
        }
}
```

Success Response	Code: 202
Notes	None

The cluster create API is used to create a clustered database instance as shown next.

With MongoDB, the API assumes the creation of a single shard and the instances specified are used as members of the replica set for that shard. The data parameter below creates a three-member replica set of flavor 10 with each instance having a 2 GB data volume. The cluster is called "mongo1"

```
'{"cluster": {"instances": [{"volume": {"size": "2"}, "flavorRef": "10"}, {"volume":
{"size": "2"}, "flavorRef": "10"}, {"volume": {"size": "2"}, "flavorRef": "10"}],
"datastore": {"version": "2.4.9", "type": "mongodb"}, "name": "mongo1"}}'
```

The system response to this request is as follows:

```
{
    "cluster": {
        "created": "2015-04-24T11:36:11",
        "datastore": {
            "type": "mongodb",
            "version": "2.4.9"
        },
        "id": "b06473c0-7509-4e6a-a15f-4456cb817104",
        "instances": [
            {
                "id": "6eead1b5-3801-4d47-802e-fea7e9be6639",
                "links": [...],
                "name": "mongo1-rs1-2",
                "shard_id": "c1bea1ee-d510-4d70-b0e4-815f5a682f34",
                "type": "member"
            },
            {
                "id": "86d7f7f8-fdd0-4f85-86a7-1fe4abd704cd",
                "links": [...],
                "name": "mongo1-rs1-3",
                "shard_id": "c1bea1ee-d510-4d70-b0e4-815f5a682f34",
                "type": "member"
            },
            {
                "id": "c5cbff7f-c306-4ba5-9bf0-a6ad49a1b4d0",
                "links": [...],
                "name": "mongo1-rs1-1",
                "shard_id": "c1bea1ee-d510-4d70-b0e4-815f5a682f34",
                "type": "member"
            }
        ],
        "links": [...],
        "name": "mongo1",
        "task": {
            "description": "Building the initial cluster.",
            "id": 2,
            "name": "BUILDING"
        },
        "updated": "2015-04-24T11:36:11"
    }
}
```

Perform Cluster Action to Add Instances

Title	Add a cluster instance
URL	/{tenant-id}/clusters/{id}/action
Method	POST
URL Parameters	None
Headers	X-Auth-Token: <token> Accept: application/json Content-Type: application/json

Data Parameters	{
	    "add_shard": {}
	}

Success Response	Code: 202
Notes	Add a shard to an existing cluster. This is currently only implemented by the MongoDB guest agent.

The cluster actions API provides the ability to add a shard to an existing cluster. The implementation will add a new shard that is identical to the current shard.

```
curl -g -i -H 'Content-Type: application/json' -H 'X-Auth-Token:
1f2419810dd54fd6974bca4407fca50a' -H 'Accept: application/json' http://192.168.117.5:8779/
v1.0/70195ed77e594c63b33c5403f2e2885c/clusters/b06473c0-7509-4e6a-a15f-4456cb817104 -X POST
-d '{ "add_shard": {} }'
```

```
HTTP/1.1 202 Accepted
Content-Length: 0
Content-Type: application/json
Date: Fri, 24 Apr 2015 23:48:46 GMT
```

Delete a Cluster

Title	Delete a database cluster
URL	/{tenant-id}/clusters/{id}
Method	DELETE
URL Parameters	None
Headers	X-Auth-Token: <token> Accept: application/json Content-Type: application/json
Data Parameters	None
Success Response	Code: 202
Notes	None

The following example demonstrates the use of the API call to delete a cluster:

```
ubuntu@trove-book:~/api$ curl -g -i -H 'Content-Type: application/json' -H 'X-Auth-Token:
1f2419810dd54fd6974bca4407fca50a' -H 'Accept: application/json' http://192.168.117.5:8779/
v1.0/70195ed77e594c63b33c5403f2e2885c/clusters/b06473c0-7509-4e6a-a15f-4456cb817104 -X
DELETE

HTTP/1.1 202 Accepted
Content-Length: 0
Content-Type: application/json
Date: Fri, 24 Apr 2015 23:59:35 GMT
```

Summary

The Trove API service provides a RESTful API that exposes the complete capabilities of Trove. This appendix provided a detailed description of the Trove API.

In order to interact with the API, a request or must provide a Keystone authentication token. This token is obtained by the client directly from Keystone by making a request on its public API.

Once authenticated, the client can make requests to Trove. The Trove API can be roughly divided into the following groups.

- Instance API

- Datastores API

- Flavors API

- Limits API

- Backups API

- Database Extensions API

- Clusters API

With the exception of the versions list API, all other API calls are found under the /v1.0/ URI. Most APIs also require the specification of the tenant-id and are therefore found under /v1.0/{tenant-id}/.

Many APIs return a 200 code on success. These are the APIs that are handled synchronously by the Trove API service. Other APIs that require processing by the Trove task manager return a 202 code on success and are processed asynchronously.

Index

Get the eBook for only $5!

Why limit yourself?

Now you can take the weightless companion with you wherever you go and access your content on your PC, phone, tablet, or reader.

Since you've purchased this print book, we're happy to offer you the eBook in all 3 formats for just $5.

Convenient and fully searchable, the PDF version enables you to easily find and copy code—or perform examples by quickly toggling between instructions and applications. The MOBI format is ideal for your Kindle, while the ePUB can be utilized on a variety of mobile devices.

To learn more, go to www.apress.com/companion or contact support@apress.com.

Printed in the United States
By Bookmasters